JAMES JOYCE'S
PORTRAIT:
A NEW READING

The musical Joyce. Photograph taken by Ottocaro Weiss in Zurich in 1915.

JAMES JOYCE'S *PORTRAIT:* A NEW READING

David Pierce

EER

Edward Everett Root, Publishers, Brighton, 2019.

EER

Edward Everett Root, Publishers, Co. Ltd.,
30 New Road, Brighton, Sussex, BN1 IBN, England.

Full details of our overseas agents are given on our website.

www.eerpublishing.com

edwardeverettroot@yahoo.co.uk

David Pierce, *James Joyce's* Portrait: *A New Reading*

First published in Great Britain in 2019.
© David Pierce 2019.

This edition © Edward Everett Root 2019

ISBN 9781912224661 Hardback
ISBN 9781912224654 Paperback
ISBN 9781912224678 eBook

Cover illustration, painting of *Magenta Evening, Dublin*, courtesy of the artist John Nolan.

Cover design and typesetting by Head & Heart Book Design.

To family and friends, at home and abroad

Also by David Pierce

Attitudes to Class in the English Novel (with Mary Eagleton) (London: Thames and Hudson, 1979).

W. B. Yeats: A Guide Through the Critical Maze (Bristol: Bristol Classical Press, 1989).

James Joyce's Ireland (London and New Haven: Yale University Press, 1992).

James Joyces Irland (trans. Jörg Rademacher and Cristoforo Sweeger) (Köln and Basel: Bruckner and Thünker, 1996).

Yeats's Worlds: Ireland, England and the Poetic Imagination (London and New Haven: Yale University Press, 1995).

Sterne in Modernism/Postmodernism (co-editor with Peter de Voogd) (Amsterdam: Rodopi, 1996).

W.B. Yeats: Critical Assessments 4 Vols. (Robertsbridge: Helm Information, 2000).

The House of Music and the Cupboard Under the Stairs (Privately Printed, 2000).

Irish Writing in the Twentieth Century: A Reader (Cork: Cork University Press, 2001).

Light, Freedom and Song: A Cultural History of Modern Irish Writing (London and New Haven: Yale University Press, 2005).

Joyce and Company (London: Continuum, 2006).

Reading Joyce (Harlow: Pearson Longman, 2007).

The Long Apprenticeship: A Writer's Memoir (Knebworth: Troubador, 2012).

The Joyce Country: Literary Scholarship and Irish Culture (Brighton: Edward Everett Root, 2018).

CONTENTS

LIST OF ILLUSTRATIONS

ACKNOWLEDGEMENTS

As ever, I am grateful to my constant companion, Mary Eagleton, for all her careful oversight of this book, which would be much poorer without her. This is also the place to thank our son and daughter-in-law, Matthew Eagleton-Pierce and Ammara Maqsood, for their cheerful companionship and understanding during this period. The book has taken me the best part of 2018 to write and longer than I had anticipated. When John Spiers asked me to consider such a book I responded immediately, thinking it would be a project of manageable size. The organisation of the material took time to get right, for I wanted something that was readable for a younger generation of students in particular without being overbearing or another guide book to Joyce's novel. Finally, let me also thank the people at Edward Everett Root, including Lucy Llewellyn and her production team at Head & Heart Book Design, for all their courtesy and enthusiasm shown to me during the writing of this book.

ABBREVIATIONS

CW James Joyce, *The Critical Writings of James Joyce* (eds. Ellsworth Mason and Richard Ellmann) (1959; New York: Viking, 1966).

D James Joyce, *'Dubliners': Text, Criticism, and Notes*, (eds. Robert Scholes and A. Walton Litz) (New York: Viking, 1979).

FW James Joyce, *Finnegans Wake* (1939; London: Faber and Faber, 1964). Page number is given first, followed by line number.

JJ Richard, Ellmann, *James Joyce,* revised edition (Oxford and New York: Oxford University Press, 1982).

Letters I Letters of James Joyce Volume I (ed. Richard Ellmann) (New York: Viking, 1966).

Letters II Letters of James Joyce Volume II (ed. Richard Ellmann) (New York: Viking, 1966).

MBK Stanislaus Joyce, *My Brother's Keeper* (ed. Richard Ellmann) (London: Faber and Faber, 1958).

P James Joyce, *'A Portrait of the Artist as a Young Man': Text, Criticism, and Notes* (ed. Chester Anderson) (New York: Viking, 1968).

SH James Joyce, *Stephen Hero* (eds. John J. Slocum and Herbert Cahoon) (1944; New York: New Directions, 1963).

SL Selected Letters of James Joyce (ed. Richard Ellmann) (New York: Viking Press, 1975).

U James Joyce, *Ulysses: The Corrected Text* (ed. Hans Walter Gabler with Wolfhard Steppe and Claus Melchior) (London: The Bodley Head, 1986). Chapter number is followed by line number.

Photograph of Joyce taken in 1904 by his friend Constantine Curran.
Asked what he was thinking at the time, Joyce wondered if the
photographer might lend him five shillings.

CHAPTER 1: INTRODUCTION

THE ONLY ADVICE

In 'How Should One Read a Book?' (1926) Virginia Woolf signals her alignment with the common reader against the professional critic or reviewer: 'The only advice…that one person can give another about reading is to take no advice, to follow your own instincts, to use your own reason, to come to your own conclusions.'[1] It is good advice but, as she goes on to admit, it is not the only advice: 'Do not dictate to your author; try to become him. Be his fellow-worker and accomplice.' (259) Cautionary advice such as this is always valuable, even with a difficult writer such as James Joyce. I tend to agree with Woolf that we should trust our own responses when taking down a novel from the shelf, but that is not so easy for many readers, especially when confronted with *A Portrait of the Artist as a Young Man*.[2] And sometimes there is nothing wrong either with being an accomplice or with relying on others.

Guide books serve a useful purpose, as do reliable notes, but we ought never to forget that *A Portrait* is a work of fiction not a documentary account. It is for this reason I begin this study with a discussion focussed on writing and leave the life and times of James Joyce to the following chapter. At the same time, we cannot straighten out the warping that went into Joyce's imagination. We need, therefore, to be aware, even as we use them, of certain limitations with annotated

---

1 Virginia Woolf, *The Common Reader: Second Series* (1932; London: Hogarth Press, 1986), 258.
2 Throughout the book that follows I use the abbreviated form *A Portrait*.

1

editions. The recommended or standard edition of *A Portrait*, which was first published in 1968 by the Viking Press and edited by Chester Anderson and which is the one I use here, contains some 70 pages of notes to accompany 254 pages of text.[3] This is over a quarter of notes to enhance or disrupt the reading experience. The attractively produced Alma Press edition contains nearly 100 pages of notes compared with just over 200 pages of text.[4] Nearly a third, that is. And future editions might see readers facing half the book devoted to notes and half to text. The 2007 Norton Critical edition has an up-to-date authoritative text with a full range of relevant background material and well-chosen critical essays. It is deliberately restrained in the notes it provides, and these are inserted not at the end of the volume but at the bottom of the page. However, many readers will baulk at reading a novel that requires constant recourse to notes wherever they are positioned. Ezra Pound famously declared that literature is news that stays news, but with annotated editions such as these we find ourselves at times thinking otherwise.

The difficulty reading a novel such as Henry James's *The Spoils of Poynton* (1897) lies not in our ignorance of external or contextual information but in how, for example, we interpret the character of Fleda Vetch.[5] Ford Madox Ford's *The Good Soldier* (1915), which was published a year before *A Portrait*, has its own unique set of difficulties largely on account of its complex plot and an unreliable narrator, but, again, the novel requires few footnotes.[6] *A Portrait* is different, and, perhaps inevitably, a century and more after its publication, we are obliged, as fellow-workers, to rely on notes and commentary. For those not familiar with late-nineteenth-century Irish history, this particular context will need supplying. Equally, the novel is steeped in all kinds of material from Joyce's past, including his family and friends at school and university, the Dublin intellectual milieu at the turn of the twentieth century, his Irish Catholic upbringing, his reading, his rebellion. Indeed, with only brief acquaintance, we might well

---

3 *A Portrait of the Artist: Text, Criticism and Notes* (ed. Chester Anderson) (New York: Viking, 1968).

4 *A Portrait of the Artist as a Young Man* (eds. Marc A. Mamigonian and John Turner) (Richmond, Surrey: Alma, 2012). See also 'Notes for *Stephen Hero*' by the same authors in *James Joyce Quarterly*, Vol. 40, No. 3 (Spring, 2003).

5 Henry James, *The Spoils of Poynton* (intro. David Lodge) (1897; London: Penguin, 1987).

6 Ford Madox Ford, *The Good Soldier* (second edition) (ed. Martin Stannard) (1915; New York: Norton Critical Edition, 2012).

conclude that there is precious little in his life as a child, adolescent, and young man which does not find its way into the novel. So we are confronted not only with his biography but also with how he shaped and fictionalised his life story. *Stephen Hero*, his first attempt at writing a semi-autobiographical novel, gives us one version, *A Portrait* another, but, although it can help, placing the two novels side by side tends to complicate the picture. This brings us to Joyce's contribution to a new way of writing, particularly as it affects narrative theory, the role of the reader, and how stories are told from inside the consciousness of the individual. So both the external world we associate with history and the internal world that rightly belongs to the private world of consciousness are redrawn by Joyce in a manner that is both original and at times dependent on sources outside the novel.

FIRST ENCOUNTERS WITH CHAPTER 1 OF *A PORTRAIT*

Looking back on my first encounters with *A Portrait* has reminded me of the initial difficulties with this novel. These issues were not so much about references to the world outside the novel as to tracking the course of the narrative. What is going on I would ask myself. Out of hearing of anyone around, I would mutter Help! Is there something wrong with me that I am struggling so badly? This is especially true of encounters with the long and disjointed first chapter. So, it might help if I summarise how I went about tackling the novel, beginning with comments on primary aspects to be found in the opening chapter. With the divisions as set out by the asterisks in the text, I am going to focus on four main areas: early impressions (7-8), Clongowes Wood College (8-27), Christmas Dinner scene (27-39), and Clongowes Wood College again (40-59). The page references here and throughout this study are keyed to the Viking 1968 edition.

The opening two pages of the novel contain a series of seemingly uncoordinated impressions, which may or may not turn out to be uncoordinated. I use the term 'impressions' but perhaps we should follow the philosophers and say 'sensations'. The reader has impressions but the boy has sensations, and these come at him so fast that, constantly, we as readers are forced to pause for breath. Five senses are activated, and we might recall that, according to Aristotle, senses mark the beginning of knowledge, for nothing is in the intellect which was not first in the senses. Eyes are singled out in the opening, and we wonder if sight will become a theme. Seeing, that is, as a metaphor, but here also the actual eyes of a person under threat. Fairy tales and modern narrative – how do they belong together as an opening to a story? Then, too, there is the shame associated with childhood, which is exacerbated by adults. So psychology is important, but then I wanted to know if we are dealing with cognitive psychology or individual psychology and psychoanalysis? Are we dealing with the artist as a type or an individual?

Other questions then spring to mind. What has the boy done to merit such a punishment? 'Apologise!' is nearly always intimidating, especially when it appears out of nowhere on the first page. As a person 'Dante' is troubling, as is her name, and I wondered if she had any connection with the medieval Italian poet, Dante Alighieri. Naming must constitute another theme in the novel I thought. Her brushes are named after Michael Davitt and Charles Stewart Parnell, who were Irish leaders in the early 1880s on the same side in their struggles against landlordism and British rule in Ireland. Their presence seems to cast a shadow over what will happen, or why else would they be included? As for the boy's mother and father, we can note how the novel begins with his father telling an unnamed boy a story. The family appear to be happy. There is music and dancing and singing. The words of the song, such as the 'wild rose' and the 'green place', might have symbolic meaning or refer to Ireland and, for some readers, to Oscar Wilde. The boy's rendering of words from a ballad as 'green wothe botheth' seems to register the gap between language and experience, something the novel will perhaps go on to explore. Some things the boy can understand, some things will have to wait until he is older. In the Norton corrected edition of the novel 'green' is spelt 'geen'.

In the second section of the novel, we move on, with the boy at boarding school, Clongowes Wood College. The playground now acts as a focus for Stephen's sensations. His vocabulary has advanced considerably, with the future artist referring to a football in flight as a 'greasy leather orb'. The world is changing. One minute words get stuck in the boy's mouth, the next he has acquired the use of poetic imagery. It is worth noting that we become acquainted with his name through dialogue. 'What kind of name is that?' he is asked in a threatening manner. As readers, and, as fellow-workers, we are invited to recall the classical Greek myth of Daedalus and Icarus. Stephen's classical heritage is not disclosed to him either by the author or by the narrator. He is equally ignorant that his first name is the same as St Stephen, the first Christian martyr. The boys are inquisitive and insist on knowing if his father is a 'gentleman', and we infer that Stephen's social class is not as posh as that of his contemporaries.

Stephen's resolve not to answer leads to an example on page 9 of incomplete dialogue, or perhaps we should reverse this and say that the incomplete dialogue implies something about Stephen's resolve. *A Portrait* is about implicature or the theory of implication, about how we interpret such forms of indirect communication or, if we think of syllogisms, of the excluded middle.[7] It's beginning to look as if a rudimentary account is straying into something more advanced. Some guide books convey the impression that an outline can be imposed on the novel and the matter settled. But, when approaching Joyce, there is value in staying close to the experience of reading. Keep noticing the lie of land and jotting down what comes into mind with associations, not all of which will prove relevant.

Let me insert at this point a relevant piece of external information which might help with a first reading of the novel. Clongowes Wood College was the Eton of Catholic Ireland. It was a school founded in 1813 and run by the Jesuits for the gentry and upper middle class in Ireland. Joyce attended this school in County Kildare as a boarder from the ages of six to nine. After a break in his schooling and for a short time attending a Christian Brothers school, he then entered Belvedere College in Dublin as a day pupil and remained there until he went to the Jesuit-run Royal University (now University College Dublin) in Stephen's Green. *A Portrait* adheres closely to the story of Joyce's experience of the Irish education system under the Jesuits, and perhaps it is not really surprising that he considered himself a Jesuit rather than a Catholic.

When we return to the text, we can notice how mention of the word 'belt' unsettles Stephen, as does the general sense of intimidation around him. His switch to thoughts of home and his mother is unannounced by the narrator. The impression created is that dealing with the rough and tumble of life away from home will become important for the boy, for *A Portrait* is, after all, in the tradition of Victorian fiction about schooldays. Stephen at this point recalls his father telling him not to 'peach' on a fellow. He is brought back to the present when he hears the boys being called in from the playground with the shout of 'All in!'. These switches or transitions can be confusing, especially when they occur in the middle of a paragraph. We are doing well if we remember which world we are in - the mind of

---

7 Implicature is a term in pragmatics associated with the work of H.P.Grice.

Stephen or the 'orb' circling around him. As also occurs in Joyce's later fiction, sounds and voices play a powerful role throughout *A Portrait*.

The novel is full of interruption and disruption, juxtaposed in these early pages with passages of continuous prose full of non-sequiturs. Thus on page 11 there is a sentence where conjunctions resemble disjunctions: 'Father Arnall knew more than Dante because he was a priest but both his father and uncle Charles said that Dante was a clever woman and a wellread woman.' 'Because', 'but', 'and' – such a sequence, which an adult rarely gets wrong, is part of the learning process for a child. This is equally the case for comparisons involving 'more than'. As for 'both', this, again, can present difficulties for a child, who must bring together things s/he has learned as separate. 'Wellread' is not a typo, but as we will see later, Joyce's preferred way of rendering hyphenated words in English.

This can raise interesting issues or conundrums for us. For Joyce does not say 'This is how Stephen began to categorise the world'. On the other hand, in another sense this is what he does say. In the interests of keeping close to his subject, Joyce exploits the gap between fictional and discursive prose, for he is writing an inside story rather than an outsider's account. Equally, as Dorrit Cohn insightfully suggests in *Transparent Minds* (1978), 'The narrator's knowledge of Stephen's psyche seems to coincide with Stephen's self-knowledge.'[8] Moreover, Joyce's narration of Stephen's consciousness 'cannot be grasped as a separate entity' (30). We do well to reflect on the presence or absence of the authorial voice in *A Portrait* and also on how the third-person narration is working. Cohn's general term 'psycho-narration' is useful in this regard, but there may be other less theoretical but equally valid accounts which place less emphasis on consciousness. Joyce's friend and one-time assistant, Samuel Beckett, famously declared that the language of *Finnegans Wake* is 'not about something: it is that something itself'.[9] So, we might want to say of *A Portrait* that it is frequently not so much about something but aspires to be the thing itself.

Other activities of the school day follow. In Fr Arnall's class the boys are divided into two groups, York versus Lancaster, and we might be reminded of the English civil war in an Irish classroom and what that means or implies. We accompany Stephen from the refectory, to

---

8 Dorrit Cohn, *Transparent Minds: Narrative Modes for Presenting Consciousness in Fiction* (Princeton, NJ: Princeton University Press, 1978), 31.

9 See Samuel Beckett *et al.*, *Our Exagmination Round His Factification for Incamination of Work in Progress* (1929; New York: New Directions, 1972), 14.

the playroom, to the study hall. Then come night prayers in the chapel and sleep in the dormitory. All the time Stephen's head is trying to absorb what is happening to him, and this is interspersed with thoughts of home. In the morning he is sick after, the previous day, being thrown into a ditch, and he finds himself in the infirmary with the kind-hearted Brother Michael. There is a touching scene where the six-year-old imagines writing home to tell his mother to come and collect him. I say six-year-old because this was the age Joyce started at Clongowes Wood. The section ends with reflections on his father's social standing and Parnell's body being returned to Ireland, which provides a cue for what is to come in the next scene.

The third aspect of Chapter 1 of *A Portrait* that I want to focus on is the Christmas Dinner scene. This is one of the great set pieces in the novel. Stephen, home from Clongowes and dressed in his Eton jacket, is essentially an onlooker, but we are there with him in this drama, as we witness a turbulent passage of history through the eyes of a child who forgot nothing. We might want to contrast the way memory functions here with the previous two sections, and I leave that to the reader to explore further. The scene, then, is set, with the fire banked high, the servants in attendance, the turkey on the table, his brothers and sisters in the nursery, and in attendance other family members as well as John Casey, a friend of Stephen's father. What should have been a pleasant occasion in a middle-class Catholic family turns into a shouting match about Parnell's reputation after his relationship with the wife of one of his M.P.s at Westminster was made public in a divorce case in 1890. We notice how Dante begins the novel in the 1880s siding with Parnell and honouring him with a specially marked brush, but now she has turned against him for his adultery. Matched against her are the Fenian Casey and Stephen's father, Simon, with his mother in the middle pleading for peace on this one day in the year.

The adults are centre stage in this section with Stephen in the wings. And yet, throughout, we are conscious of seeing the events as they happen through his eyes. Occasionally he is addressed by his father and at one point Dante declares, 'O, he'll remember all this when he grows up' (*P* 33). Children should be seen and not heard is a familiar adage, but Dante insists on something else, that children should not hear certain things said by adults. Normally such a comment is unexceptional but we are not certain how to respond when the character is not particularly attractive. What we do know is that Stephen is recording everything and that he may be ignored or assumed not to be listening, but, as *A Portrait* confirms, in time he will transpose the whole episode into fiction. And if we wanted to dwell further on this, 'in time' is a phrase we might consider, for this is the boy who becomes an adult writing about a boy half-aware of what the future might hold when he looks back.

Little touches in the narrative also deserve our attention, even if we are unsure of their implication. When his father, Simon, 'winks' at Stephen after holding up the 'pope's nose' (*P* 32-3), a number of interpretations come to mind. He is head of the household performing his patriarchal duties; he is reminding Stephen that, as father and son, they belong together in a man's world; he is deliberately mocking the Church and continuing his dispute with Dante. Or it could be the narrator is reminding us that Stephen is still watching from the wings, but he is on his way to becoming centre stage and focaliser of the narrative, that is the person through whom a scene or episode is told. As is often the case in real life, the 'wink' is a tiny non-verbal gesture but full of meaning.

In the remaining pages of this first chapter we return to Clongowes Wood College. *A Portrait* is a study in the relationship between narrative and discourse, how a story is told and what we as readers make of such a story. It is a study in what was happening then and what it perhaps means to us now. Themes such as religion or home or sexuality belong to discourse, as do symbols such as those associated with flight. With regard to the narrative, so many different experiences are on display and nearly all of them engross us, especially the classroom scene with Fr Dolan beating Stephen for not doing his work. Linking them together, whether in terms of narrative or of discourse, involves us as readers. It is worth remembering that at a boarding school the outside, such as the playing fields or playground or outside toilets, is like an open space where rules no longer apply in the same way as inside the school where order can be more easily controlled by the masters. Cricket has a raised profile in this section, which ends with Stephen's triumph after his encounter inside with the Rector and the sounds of 'pick, pack, pock, puck' from the cricket pitch. To my mind, such sounds have a symbolic quality, and they perhaps invite us to reflect on the passage of time and also on a past now being consigned to history, a past which possibly includes the colonial encounter between Britain and Ireland, cricket being the coloniser's game.

It is also in the grounds outside that Stephen learns of boys being expelled for 'smugging' (*P* 42), a word he has difficulty understanding.

As an innocent young boy and away from home, Stephen discovers language is running ahead of experience, or perhaps we should say the opposite, that this is experience running in advance of language. I write more about 'smugging' in my final chapter, but here we can notice the general point about the relationship between narrative and discourse and the specific point about the observance or otherwise of school rules in the school grounds. Stephen's glasses are broken on the cinder path after a collision with a boy running. The consequences are felt inside when he is unfairly punished by Fr Dolan, the Director of Studies, and, as suggested, his moment of triumph takes place in the school grounds outside. So we can begin to recognise how narrative and discourse are pieced together as we read further in this novel. Of course nothing can take away the menace from Fr Dolan's entry into the classroom 'The door opened quietly and closed' (*P* 48). And for ten pages and more the narrative holds us spellbound.

I trust that my discursive comments above help the reader to orientate her/himself in their initial encounters with the opening chapter of *A Portrait*. Some passages repay considerable attention, and here in this study I find myself returning to them from different angles. The novel at times resembles a piece of sculpture in a gallery, in turn requiring us to change positions to get a full perspective. I now want to provide a series of brief comments on some intriguing aspects and themes that struck me when reading the remaining chapters.

BRIEF ENCOUNTERS WITH CHAPTERS 2-5 OF *A PORTRAIT*

We can begin with two general observations. Firstly, because we will see Joyce referring back to moments or episodes already mentioned in Chapter 1, it is worth considering how Joyce achieves narrative cohesion. In part this arises from the simple repetition of details such as Eileen, or Parnell, or the names of Clongowes Wood pupils already mentioned, or the Fr Dolan incident. Throughout his major work, Joyce relied on repetition, so this always deserves attention. *A Portrait* also stresses the idea of stages in Stephen's development, and how as he grows so does his vocabulary. The novel constantly reminds us not so much of the unitary or integrated self as the sequential self. At the same time Joyce skilfully manages to weave together the overall narrative and make it of a piece. In spite of all its extraordinary variety in terms of information, the novel flows. His schooling by the Jesuits helps in this respect, for their influence gave him a perspective on life that never left him. Thus as a small example we might notice the initials A.M.D.G. *Ad Majorem Dei Gloriam* (for the greater glory of God) which were inscribed at the top of every piece of writing in traditional Catholic schools and seminaries, especially those run by the Jesuits. Even when he is home between schools, as he was before entering Belvedere College, Stephen continues the practice, only in this case there is nothing religious about what follows, for Stephen begins writing romantic verses to E---C--- (that is Emma Clery). (70) This in turn reminds us of something wider, how *A Portrait* contains a study in the relationship between religion, sexuality and writing.

Secondly, I am interested in the role of history. In Chapter 1 of *A Portrait* history is afforded a significant focus, so in approaching Chapter 2 I am alert to how such a theme develops. For some reason Bob Dylan's *Chronicles* comes into my mind, and how, when he was a boy, he had no idea which stage of history he was living through, whether that was an early archaic period or some classical period or a 'slacking off period where decadence makes things fall apart'.[10] Dylan never managed to settle on an answer. By contrast, Joyce is keen to show us history at work from the start, and it is a history from the ground up, subject to turbulence and change, and accompanied by a sense that the future is moving against Stephen. Dylan's awakening to his fate came through music, and, unlike Stephen/Joyce, when it arrived, he never imagined leaving his country. This, too, allows for a contrast to be noticed, for we begin to realise that *A Portrait* is not only a story about time and consciousness but it also has for its trajectory the exile's departure from Ireland.

Three more specific points are also notable, beginning with the significance of Stephen's schooling. The first mention of Belvedere College, the day school run by the Jesuits in Dublin, where Stephen will complete his secondary education, appears on page 71. To most readers, classes have odd-sounding names such as Elements, Higher Line, and Third Line. These are not explained in the novel, though anyone attending such a school would have known the meaning. The value of guide books lies in supplying information no longer available to readers today. From his experience at Clongowes Wood College, Stephen is familiar with this world and becomes an active member of his new College. At the Whitsuntide play (75ff) he performs in front of an adult audience, but it becomes increasingly clear to the reader that Stephen's mind is now taking centre stage.

---

10 Bob Dylan, *Chronicles* Volume 1 (London: Simon and Schuster, 2004), 35.

In the cut-and-thrust of school life, Stephen, who in the first chapter is thrown into a ditch, is shown in this chapter confronting his classmates, especially Heron. With his bird-like name, Heron is a rival who taunts Stephen, the 'hawklike man' (69), about his feelings for a girl. When he challenges Stephen to 'Admit' (78) we recall the 'Apologise' on the first page; the command also anticipates the confession he will have to make for his sins in Chapter 3. *A Portrait* can be read as a study in how conscience can overwhelm the individual raised in a strongly religious culture and community. 'Apologise', 'admit', 'confess' conveys something of the suffering Stephen repeatedly endures in the novel. Later, he responds with the simple defiance contained in the triplet 'silence, exile, and cunning' (*P* 247).

Secondly, we witness the making of Stephen as an artist. We learn, for example, on page 73 that Stephen has a reputation for essay writing. He is also judging the writing of others. The reference to Newman (John Henry Newman) on page 80 reminds us of the Victorian context to the novel. It is difficult to decide what to make of the claim that Newman was the greatest writer of prose or Byron of poetry. Joyce might be allowing either for his own youthful enthusiasm or for Stephen's. Of course, Joyce was always alert to rivals and the need to break free of English models. His own writing also begins to come under scrutiny, as when we learn that quarrelsome comradeship 'had not seduced Stephen from his habits of quiet obedience' (83). The style here sounds a little precious, reminding us of a boy trying to write and at the same time constructing an image of himself to hide behind. The word that stands out is 'seduce', for he writes not 'distract', which is a more neutral, descriptive word, but a word which is closer to a moral (and sexual) universe. *A Portrait* is a novel about language and style, and one of its delights lies in discovering the person behind the writing. Or, as I spend time discussing in Chapter 5, the person who wrote the novel, Stephen or Joyce?

The phrase 'horse piss' (86) is a sharp reminder for Stephen of the world around him. He has flights of fancy but the real world constantly intervenes. ' - That is horse piss and rotted straw, he thought.' The addition of 'he thought', coming after the speech mark, deserves our attention, especially in connection with Cohn's suggestion concerning the difficulty of distinguishing the third-person comment from Stephen's psyche and vice-versa. In other words, who is telling us 'he thought'? And this we might agree is different from the free indirect discourse in, say, Jane Austen's fiction. According to Cohn, '[O]ne of the most important advantages of psycho-narration over the other modes of rendering consciousness lies in its verbal independence from self-articulation.'[11] In the context of 'horse piss' there is little to merit the phrase 'he thought', and there is also little a conventional artist can do with 'horse piss'. Unless it is here designed to recall Stephen wetting the bed and linked to the theme of bodily emission. If we were to collect all the earthy words in the novel, we would be surprised the artist ever managed to take off.

Thirdly, we might reflect on the trip to Cork to sell off his father's property. This is another memorable episode, and, intermittently, throughout this study I explore its various aspects. The trip includes the long train journey through the night, as well as his father singing a sentimental come-all-ye about youth and folly and love fading away like the morning dew. As he watches his father with his old cronies, he feels older than them. What greets him on visiting the college where his father was a student is the word 'foetus' etched into one of the desks. With his father falling further in his estimation, life begins to lose its shine for Stephen, and he becomes increasingly alienated from the world around him. As he battles the surrounding squalor, he takes to wandering the maze of narrow streets in Dublin, and eventually finds relief in the arms of a prostitute in the red-light area, at which stage he becomes conscious of nothing but 'her softly parting lips' (*P* 101).

CHAPTER 3

This chapter is dominated by the sermons given during the days of retreat at Belvedere. A retreat was a period of heightened religious activity over several days with Mass, devotions, and a series of sermons delivered by the retreat priest in the chapel. Silence would have been observed, and it would have culminated in the boys going to confession and saying sorry for their past sins. The intimidation Stephen has endured in the first two chapters is as nothing compared with what he experiences listening to the priest. And the sermons have the effect of blocking out Stephen's voice entirely.

The sermons force Stephen to reflect on the 'salvation of one's soul'. Soul is a word I explore in my final Chapter. The four last things are defined in the catechism as death, judgement, heaven, and hell. When a person dies, they are judged by God, and sent either to heaven as a reward for a good life or, if not, dispatched to purgatory or hell. The retreat priest spends a long time on hell and on the last moment of

---

11 *Transparent Minds*, 46.

consciousness. For the righteous, death is a blessed moment. Stephen feels every word of the sermon 'as if it was for him'. There follows a period of shame and 'foul memories' (116). Later in the novel, Stephen will harness the words to his own rebellion, but here Lucifer's declaration *non serviam* (I will not serve) reminds us of Stephen's abasement. Stephen feels all his senses are being 'tortured' in turn, and we might recall how the novel begins with the five senses.

The movement from now until the end of the Chapter is towards the confessional, but even here not everything points in the one direction. Stephen's conscience now plagues him, and he prays for forgiveness. His imagination is at the mercy of outside forces, as, too, is his language. We see this for example in the graphic phrase 'evil seed of lust' (106) to describe sin and sexuality. Mention of 'grace', a theological concept open to interpretation, recalls an important moral disposition for Catholics to aim at, a state of grace that is. The reference to the sodality of the Blessed Virgin Mary on page 104 needs perhaps glossing. This is an organisation with a long history in Jesuit-run schools. It fostered an attitude of piety and devotion among pupils, and Joyce/Stephen were active members at Belvedere College. At one point we read of a 'dark peace' being established between body and soul. (103) It comes in an odd sentence, for, when we think about narrative voice or psycho-narration, this might carry a judgment on the part of a narrator who might be unrelated to Stephen: 'no part of body or soul had been maimed but a dark peace had been established between them'. The tension in the Chapter finally breaks. Thomas Aquinas believed the soul tends towards God, but Stephen on his way to confession, his adolescent sensibility still intact, is distracted by girls and thoughts of bodily temptation. In the confessional the Capuchin priest wants to know his age and details surrounding his experiences with prostitutes and masturbation. And then on his way home Stephen notices the 'muddy streets were gay' (145).

CHAPTER 4

Chapter 4 of *A Portrait* is dominated by Stephen's religious phase, one he has to endure. Or at least that is what many readers feel. Joyce allows his protagonist the freedom to pursue a course that might have issued in him becoming a Jesuit, but then he tells us he obeyed a 'wayward instinct' (165) and pulled back. Stephen realises his destiny is away from religion and society. The religious life, one suspects, would not have suited Joyce. In his religious phase, in a slightly mocking tone, Stephen wonders why he should continue to live since he has entered the holy life. He undergoes the mortification of the senses, never consciously changes his position in bed, and then his religious scruples begin. He recalls being 'pandied' twice, but he admires the Jesuits even if they had made him 'diffident of himself' and aware of his 'equivocal' position at Belvedere. (*P* 156)

Stephen or the narrator tells us, and we already sense this is the case, that he is passing out of his 'accustomed world'. When the family's belongings are loaded onto the removal van because of their increasing inability to pay the rent, we have yet another image of Stephen's own gathering sense of dispossession. It is put to him that he might consider a vocation to the priesthood, and Stephen is excited by the idea. He imagines listening to the sins of others in the confessional and how, by contrast, there would linger no touch of sin on his own hands. Incident and theme are here uneasily allied, for throughout the novel, as with his encounters with Cranly, we are repeatedly reminded of 'hands' and what part they play especially in sexual encounters with others.

The idea of university arrives, and his father is positive but not so his mother. 'The university!' is how Stephen greets the moment, the sentries of his boyhood and the ordeal of childhood now behind him. His reflections on words for example (166) now have a greater sense of maturity, and the issue of his name is revisited amid talk of the 'hawklike man' and the figure of Daedalus (167-9). 'His soul had arisen from the grave of boyhood' (170) is a striking sentence that could have been written by Stephen the mature artist or by the narrator telling us about the artist Stephen. The chapter closes on a high when, walking barefoot along by the shore by Dublin Bay, he sees an attractive girl midstream, a beautiful 'seabird', and he imagines her eyes calling to him. 'His soul was swooning into some new world.' (172)

CHAPTER 5

The focus of the final chapter of *A Portrait* is the university and in particular Stephen's contact with other students and teachers. His intellectual development takes place in a context where he is keen to establish himself as a leading player of his generation. On page 176, which begins with Stephen walking through the 'sloblands of Fairvew', a marshy district on the outskirts of Dublin where his family were then living, we encounter the names of Gerhart Hauptmann, a contemporary German dramatist, the dark humour of Guido Cavalcanti, the spirit of

Henrik Ibsen, Ben Jonson and Elizabethan lyrics, as well as Aristotle and Thomas Aquinas. For a fictional account of life as an undergraduate there are few better places to start than with the picture on display in Joyce's *A Portrait*. The closely-observed portrait of his fellow students is impressive and allows Stephen to emerge against a realistic background where his ideas are given a sharper definition. When we reflect on Stephen leaving Ireland we remember his close friend, the down-to-earth Cranly, who tries to persuade Stephen against his course of action, Davin the 'peasant student' who is the only one to call Stephen 'Stevie', MacCann, the political student with the goatee beard, the supercilious and argumentative Temple, Heron, his interrogator and rival, and Lynch the salty cynic, who in real life, according to Herbert Gorman, was Joyce's 'constant companion'.[12] As can be seen in my next chapter, 'The Life and Times of James Joyce', all these figures, and others, had counterparts in real life.

The set-piece with the Dean of Studies in the lecture theatre is one that readers of *A Portrait* often consult for Joyce's theory of beauty and aesthetics. Stephen's encounter with the Dean is about to start with a discussion of Aquinas and beauty when he is distracted by the Dean's reference to a 'funnel' for pouring oil into a lamp. In Ireland, according to Stephen, the proper word is 'tundish' (188). This prompts Stephen's hackles to rise when he thinks about the English background of the Dean and the language he speaks. When the discussion is resumed, Stephen explains the three aspects of beauty, namely '*wholeness, harmony and radiance*' (212). How the reader is supposed to respond to this excursion in neo-scholastic philosophy is not very clear, but some might be tempted to apply Stephen's theory to the novel s/he is reading. As suggested above, at times, we are unsure if we are reading a novel written by Stephen or Joyce.

There is then a long section on the Villanelle sequence, which begins with Lynch whispering to Stephen 'Your beloved is here'. For a more in-depth discussion of this episode see 'Writing Poetry' in Chapter 5 below. The remainder of Joyce's Chapter 5 sees a return to contemporary politics, as evidenced by the petition against Yeats's play *The Countess Cathleen* for blasphemy. Like Joyce, Stephen refuses to sign. Perhaps the most engaging and painful moment in this final section occurs when Cranly quizzes Stephen on his mother and a mother's love. It is a moment which anticipates the scene where his mother packs his 'secondhand clothes' ready for departure and prays

---

12 Herbert Gorman, *James Joyce* (New York: Rinehart, 1948), 58.

that he may learn in his own way and away from home and friends 'what the heart is and what it feels' (252). This is painful to read, made more so by the coldness of Stephen's response 'Amen'. By positioning this passage at the opening to *Stephen D.* (1964) and then starting the play with a voice singing a sailor's hornpipe 'Tralala lala', Hugh Leonard manages to drain the scene of its cynicism.[13] As it stands, however, there is something lacking in Stephen's emotional response.

When considering the diary entries at the end of *A Portrait*, again it is not easy to arrive at a settled position on how to read these. The diary format is yet another form of writing to complement all the other forms in the novel including sermons, poetry, songs, reflective prose, graffiti, conversation and dialogue of all sorts. The diary format is without a third-person-narrator present, but here, in this ending to the novel, we might be reminded of an impersonal narrator, self-absorbed, detached, resisting the influence of others. It is as if the long-suffering author wanted to put to bed a project that had taken him ten long years to write. There is no time for reflections on the novel we have just finished reading or a final embrace between author and protagonist. So when we encounter the final words 'Dublin 1904 Trieste 1914', we are more than a little surprised.

The novel ends therefore not with the artist Stephen boarding a boat at the North Wall in Dublin to begin his journey abroad but with the author advertising how long it had taken him to write the novel. If we were cruel we might conclude that the two deserve each other, but I think that would be unkind. Stephen leaves the stage with a slightly overdone hymn to life, where he calls on his father, the old artificer, Daedalus, not now to help him fly but to 'stand me now and ever in good stead' (*P* 253). Stephen's stress on standing, with Daedalus's warning to Icarus perhaps ringing in our ears, in part absolves him from being only interested in flight. The next time we see him is at the beginning of *Ulysses* when his wings have been clipped and he has fallen back to earth in the city he had once fled.

'I WRITE'

If *A Portrait* is primarily about anything, it is writing, and this is a cue to the study that follows. In the 1930s Maria Jolas accompanied Joyce to a reception held at the British Institute in Paris for Sir James Frazer

---

13 Hugh Leonard, *Stephen D.: A Play in Two Acts* (London and New York: Evans Brothers, 1964), 11. This play makes good use of the set pieces in the novel and they remind us of the essentially dramatic quality of *A Portrait*.

to honour the author of *The Golden Bough* (1890). After waiting in line to be introduced, Joyce was asked by the leading anthropologist of his day, 'What name?' Joyce replied, 'Joyce, James Joyce'. 'And what do you do?' 'I write,' was his answer.[14] It is not recorded how Frazer responded, but Joyce, like his protagonist in *A Portrait*, was characteristically reluctant to give too much away. He might have replied 'I am a writer', but he did not and the distinction is worth dwelling on. Joyce wrote poetry, plays, criticism, newspaper articles, short stories, novels, and a final text that refuses easy categorization. But Joyce is not drawing attention to his expertise in different genres. He is stressing the importance of writing as an end in itself. Not for nothing did he call his closest fictional persona in *Finnegans Wake* 'Shem the Penman'.

Frazer might have wondered to himself: what kind of writer is Joyce? Does his writing include myth and ritual? Does he write copy for newspapers? Is he involved in writing what today we call op.eds? Is he in advertising? What precisely is his field? Is he the author of potboilers or popular romances? Does he supplement his income by writing or does he write for a living? How much time did he devote to editing his work or was he, like me, a compulsive reviser? And this might have been followed by a series of supplementary questions such as where he wrote, or the hours of the day or night when he wrote, or even why he wrote. We could go on. Millions of people around the world write, some in long hand, some by an old-fashioned typewriter, most today in front of a screen or electronic device, and some of these might have replied in similar fashion to Frazer's question with 'I write'. Tear away, then, all the images and stereotypes associated with 'writer' - or with Thoth, Hermes or Mercury, the writing deities of the classical world - and what are we left with? The lonely figure of the artist whom Stephen compared to 'the God of creation…within or behind or beyond or above his handiwork, invisible, refined out of existence, indifferent, paring his fingernails' (*P* 215).

By retreating behind the protection of an intransitive verb, nothing crossed over from the subject 'I' to what lay on the other side of the verb 'write'. Indeed, the content that constitutes the 'I' is more opaque than transparent, and we are reminded of the intriguing common ground that both unites the protagonist of *A Portrait* with his author

---

14 Jacques Aubert and Maria Jolas, *Joyce and Paris 1902….1920 – 1940….1975* (Paris: Éditions du CNRS, 1979), 9.

and separates him. In her late diaries Virginia Woolf, who understood as much about writing as Joyce, tells us something we might consider surprising from someone who is so in control of her writing: 'I think writing, my writing, is a species of mediumship. I become the person.'[15] This was written in 1937 as she was composing *Three Guineas*. In the same diary entry she speaks of being 'in the middle of my magic bubble'. The two images of 'mediumship' and 'magic bubble' evoke for us the feeling of immersion which overcomes many authors in sitting down to write, and Joyce is no exception. In turn the reference to becoming a person reminds us of William Butler Yeats and how in revising his poetry he insisted that 'It is myself that I remake'.[16] Part of the fascination I explore in the pages of the book which follows lies in the way Joyce is also involved in these preoccupations of mediumship and forms of remaking not so much as a person but as a writer. At the same time, while consciously hiding behind a fictional persona, he forces us as readers to look not only at himself writing but also, and perhaps more importantly, at writing itself.

Joyce did court publicity but only on his own terms. For the last issue in 1929 of *The Little Review*, the magazine which had printed thirteen excerpts from *Ulysses* before it was published in 1922, the editors, Margaret Anderson and Jane Heap, asked some sixty and more writers and artists to complete a questionnaire on a variety of topics including fears for the future, happiest moment, weakest characteristic, attitude toward art today, world view, and reasons for going on living. The cohort who responded included T.S.Eliot, William Carlos Williams, Ernest Hemingway, H.D., Gertrude Stein, Aldous Huxley, and Marianne Moore. Joyce initially gave the impression to the editors that he would respond but then telephoned 'for he really could find nothing to say'.[17] Instead, he sent a draft page of what became *Finnegans Wake*, complete with his precise, scrawling, black, intrusive lines and corrections by hand. The editors included Berenice Abbott's photo of Joyce with an eye patch over his left eye. It was the last issue of the little magazine that had done so much to promote him, but Joyce declines to participate in its signing-off celebration.

---

15 Virginia Woolf, *A Writer's Diary* (ed. Leonard Woolf) (1953; San Diego, New York, and London: Harcourt, 1983), 274. Diary entry 11 July 1937.

16 W.B.Yeats, *Selected Poetry* (ed. Timothy Webb) (London: Penguin, 1991), 62. The lines were written as a preliminary poem to the second volume of his *Collected Works* (1908).

17 *The Little Review* May 1929, 50.

For someone who was determined to conceal so much of himself from the world, it is surprising how much he achieved. A novel such as *A Portrait* has been in print since its first publication in 1916, and in recent years, with the end of copyright, the flow of editions and critical books on the novel has been overwhelming. A critic today contemplating a monograph on Joyce's *A Portrait* will almost certainly underestimate the task at hand. There is a certain irony in Joyce claiming 'he really could find nothing to say' when he said it all by claiming such. At the same time, and again the irony is worth reflecting on, Joyce may have sought invisibility for his narrator, but in many ways he has cornered the market for himself.

The Little Review sought to bring writers and artists together under a banner we would now describe as modernist. Long before modernism took off as a movement, the editors understood or anticipated that 'I write' should perhaps be better rendered as 'We wrote'. In *The Anti-Modernism of Joyce's A Portrait of the Artist as a Young Man* (1994) the well-respected critic, Thornton Weldon, sought to counter the view that Joyce was a modernist. It was a book at variance with conventional wisdom and prompted a response that is worth quoting at length, not least because it reminds us just how much there remains to be said about Joyce's links with a movement that continues to fascinate us today. According to Wheldon *A Portrait* is not a modernist text or is not a text that upholds the basic thrust of modernism. Instead, Joyce's purpose in writing the novel is not to celebrate a self-contained and self-determining individualism but to 'show how superficial and insufficient this understanding of the psyche is'.[18] And, by way of illustration, Weldon suggests that while Stephen is under the influence of the 'Modernist Syndrome', as he calls it, Joyce 'reveals to us the shallowness and insufficiency of Stephen's views' (38).

Weldon overplays the difference between Stephen and Joyce, for, as I emphasise throughout the study which follows and particularly in Chapter 5, we always need to keep that relationship in play. Bernard Benstock understands what is at stake here, and in his enthusiastic reply, complete with a litany of the novel's qualities, he celebrates Joyce's achievement in a movement Joyce almost certainly would never have wanted to join:

---

18 Thornton Weldon, *The Anti-Modernism of Joyce's A Portrait of the Artist as a Young Man* (Syracuse, NY: Syracuse University Press, 1994), 2.

Every modernist artist was both an apostate and a heretic, in rebellion against tradition and orthodoxy, while unable or unwilling to join any other modernist for very long under any particular artistic code.... The only determining characteristic of Modernism may be stylistic – the tendency toward innovation and finding one's individual voice – in which case *A Portrait* qualifies as a modernist text, given the stripping away from the narrative process of all developmental material that does not inherently contribute to the possibility of the artist, the *Bildungsroman* superstructure a facade for the symbolic base structure, the linguistic affinity with the language facility of the growing protagonist, the undulating rhythms of triumphal resolutions followed by new debasements, the fading away of all participating characters as the protagonist moves beyond them into new realms, the poetic qualities of sound patterns and repetitions and ambiguities that confuse the genres, and the uniqueness of its governing aesthetics.[19]

Writing for Joyce possessed immense fascination. From his late teens to his death within a few months of his 59th birthday he wrote. His reply to Frazer captures his youthful ambition to become a writer. But when he had come into his own as a writer, the task he set himself was to some extent the same, for what he faced was the blank page or a page waiting for additions or corrections. Joyce might well have replied to Frazer, 'I revise'. It was something he valued at the very start of his career. In his 1902 essay on the 1840s Irish poet James Clarence Mangan, he regrets that he 'could not often revise what he wrote' (*CW* 78).

The manuscripts of *Ulysses*, which are for the most part extant and now available, show a compulsive reviser at work. *A Portrait* is slightly different in this regard because, although we have the remains of an earlier draft in *Stephen Hero*, we do not have a running account of the surviving process of composition, only a fair copy in Joyce's handwriting, as well as the revisions he suggested to texts already

---

19 Bernard Benstock, 'Review of Thornton Weldon's *The Anti-Modernism of Joyce's A Portrait of the Artist as a Young Man*'. In *English Literature in Transition 1880-1920* 38: 2, 1995, 260.

published.[20] After the novel was published by Benjamin Huebsch in New York in 1916, Joyce, along with his patron Harriet Shaw Weaver, spotted some 400 errors, which were later corrected.[21] Today, modern standard editions make use of Joyce's fair copy in the National Library of Ireland, as well as the Egoist Press second edition of 1918, and the Jonathan Cape third edition of 1924.[22] The fair copy has not become the copy-text, for it is not itself error-free and it is but part of the process in establishing a copy-text. With the exception of ensuring dashes were inserted before dialogue and not inverted commas, most of the corrections to the various editions are fairly small but consistent. For example, Joyce preferred lower case to upper case in words such as 'catholic church' and 'jewish', and joining up compound words or words with hyphens, so not 'long-drawn' but 'longdrawn', not 'breast-pocket' but 'breastpocket'.

By way of illustrative purposes here, we can notice a couple of changes which look as though they are authorial, and in both cases they involve changes to his fair copy. One concerns the deletion near the beginning of the novel on page 10 of two sentences: 'He shivered and longed to cry. It would be so nice to be at home'. In the fair copy these sentences were inserted between 'A fellow had once seen a big rat jump into the scum' and 'Mother was sitting at the fire'. This particular deletion serves several purposes: it ensures the transition in Stephen's consciousness from the external world to what is inside his mind is made more abrupt. It also reduces the sentimental danger of an author intruding too much into the scene. Keep pulling back from too much involvement in what a character thinks or feels, Joyce must have told himself.

The second example comes at the beginning of Chapter 2. It is not his 'outspoken nephew' who suggests Uncle Charles enjoy his

---

20 For a detailed analysis of Joyce's revisions, see Hans Walter Gabler 'Towards a Critical Text of James Joyce's *A Portrait of the Artist As a Young Man*' in *Studies in Bibliography* 27 (1974), 1-54.

21 For a list of selected variants, see James Joyce, *A Portrait of The Artist as a Young Man* (ed. Jeri Johnson) (Oxford: Oxford University Press, 2008), 215-221. See also Peter Spielberg, 'James Joyce's Errata for the American Edition of *A Portrait*' in Thomas Connolly (ed,), *Joyce's Portrait: Criticisms and Critiques* (London: Peter Owen, 1967).

22 For an up-to-date assessment of the text of *A Portrait*, see Hans Walter Gabler, 'A Note on the Text' in James Joyce, *A Portrait of the Artist as a Young Man* (eds. Hans Walter Gabler and Walter Hettche) (London: Vintage, 2012), 247-9). The Vintage edition is very close to the edition published by the Viking Press in 1964, which is the one used by Joyce scholars around the world.

morning smoke in the outhouse but simply 'his nephew'. Again, we know that Simon Dedalus would keep nothing to himself so there is no need for 'outspoken'. Again, the author seems to be saying, 'Let the reader do some work filling in.' And we are reminded of Woolf's view of the reader as a fellow-worker. In comparison with corrections to *Ulysses*, the alterations to *A Portrait* are on a limited scale, but, as always with Joyce, not without interest.

When he was at work on *Ulysses* in Zurich in 1918-9, he became friends with the English artist, Frank Budgen. In the course of their conversations Budgen wanted to learn how it was progressing:

> 'I have been working hard on it all day,' said Joyce.
>
> 'Does that mean you have written a great deal?' I said.
>
> 'Two sentences,' said Joyce.
>
> I looked sideways, but Joyce was not smiling. I thought of Flaubert.
>
> 'You have been seeking the *mot juste*?' I said.
>
> 'No,' said Joyce. 'I have the words already. What I am seeking is the perfect order of words in every way appropriate. I think I have it.'[23]

Two sentences in a day would make most writers conclude that they had embarked on a wrong career, defeated in whatever they were attempting. A retreat to a Tuscan villa might serve to unblock things, but on the other hand the absence of black marks on a white page might still remain. If he struggled with his material, Joyce never gave up. The episode in Trieste in February 1911 when he threw a draft of the manuscript of *A Portrait* into the stove was perhaps the only example when he was almost completely overcome with frustration (fortunately it was retrieved by his sister, Eileen, and his wife, Nora). Unlike the English novelist, Arnold Bennett, who wrote a hundred books in thirty-three years and between 300,000 and 400,000 words a year, Joyce was a patient writer, who, like his French predecessor, Gustave Flaubert, understood the slow process of writing and getting the words in the right order, and he expected an appropriately patient response from his reader.

Joyce, then, was a struggler, but few writers have been so determined to succeed in their chosen profession. In spite of the early

---

23 Frank Budgen, *James Joyce and the Making of Ulysses and Other Writings* (intro. Clive Hart) (London: Oxford University Press, 1972), 20.

promise in his teenage years, winning national prizes for his essays and someone who stood out among his contemporaries at university, when it came to fiction, nothing was accomplished with ease. The manuscript of *Stephen Hero*, which he probably started in January 1904, ran to some 150,000 words and 914 hand-written pages.[24] For whatever reason, presumably because the novel didn't sufficiently represent a new departure for fiction, the first 476 pages are no longer extant, and the remaining fragment was never published in his lifetime. *Stephen Hero* itself grew out of some 70 plus epiphanies composed between 1900 and 1903. Another attempt at writing was his essay-story, 'A Portrait of the Artist', which was submitted in 1904 to the free-thinking magazine, *Dana*, only to be rejected by the editors. *A Portrait* is a medium-size novel of some 84,971 words, which took ten years to write between 1904 and 1914.[25] To complete the picture, the stories of *Dubliners* were composed for the most part over a three-year period between 1904 and 1907, *Ulysses* took seven years from 1914 to 1921, and *Finnegans Wake* the best part of two decades from 1923 to 1938. Joyce, therefore, had form when he replied to Frazer, 'I write'.

In an early review of *A Portrait*, which appeared in *The Egoist* in February 1917, Pound emphasised Joyce's writing style:

> Mr. Joyce's novel appears in book form, and intelligent readers gathering few by few will read it, and it will remain a permanent part of English literature - written by an Irishman in Trieste and first published in New York City. I doubt if a comparison of Mr. Joyce to other English writers or Irish writers would much help to define him. One can only say that he is rather unlike them. *The Portrait* is very different from *L'Education Sentimentale*, but it would be easier to compare it with that novel of Flaubert's than with anything else. Flaubert pointed out that if France had studied his work they might have been saved a good deal in 1870. If more people had read *The Portrait* and

---

24 See Joyce's letter to Grant Richards on 13 March 1906 in *LII*, 131-2.

25 For these and other figures regarding word count, I have made effective use of Leslie Hancock's *Word Index to James Joyce's Portrait of the Artist* (Carbondale, IL: Southern Illinois Press, 1967). As for the 1904 date, this is Joyce's, so he must have been signaling that the whole process of writing *A Portrait* included *Stephen Hero*.

A PORTRAIT OF THE ARTIST AS A YOUNG MAN

By JAMES JOYCE

THE first edition of this masterpiece among works of modern fiction (for which not only was no British publisher to be found willing to publish, but *no British printer willing to print*) is now nearly exhausted. Copies of the first edition, "Printed in America," will be very valued possessions when *The Portrait* becomes more widely recognized—as it certainly will—as an outstanding feature in the permanent literature of the present period. Readers of THE EGOIST who have not already secured a copy should *order at once*.

EXTRACTS FROM FIRST PRESS NOTICES

MR. H. G. WELLS in **The Nation** : Its claim to be literature is as good as the claim of the last book of *Gulliver's Travels*. . . . The writing is great writing. . . . The technique is startling but upon the whole it succeeds. . . . One conversation in the book is a superb success. I write with all due deliberation that Sterne himself could not have done it better. . . . Like some of the best novels in the world it is the story of an upbringing ; it is by far the most living and convincing picture that exists of an Irish-Catholic upbringing. . . . The interest of the book depends entirely upon its quintessential and unfailing reality. One believes in Stephen Dedalus as one believes in few characters in fiction. . . . A second thing of immense importance to the English reader is the fact that every one in this story accepts as a matter of course, as a thing like nature or the sea, that the English are to be hated. . . . That is the political atmosphere in which Stephen Dedalus grows up. . . . I am afraid it is only too true an account of the atmosphere in which a number of brilliant young Irishmen have grown up. . . . No single book has ever shown how different they [the English and Irish] are as completely as this most memorable novel.

The Times Literary Supplement : We should like the book to have as many readers as possible. . . . As one reads one remembers oneself in it. . . . Like all good fiction, it is as particular as it is universal. . . . Mr. Joyce can present the external world excellently. . . . No living writer is better at conversations. . . . The talk is more real than real talk. . . . His hero is one of the many Irishmen who cannot reconcile themselves to things ; above all he cannot reconcile himself to himself. . . . His mind is a mirror in which beauty and ugliness are intensified. . . . His experience is so intense, such a conflict of beauty and disgust, that for a time it drives him into an immoral life, in which also there is beauty and disgust. . . . But for all that he is not futile, because of the drifting passion and the flushing and fading beauty of his mind. . . . It is wild youth, and wild as Hamlet's, and full of music.

Manchester Guardian : When one recognizes genius in a book one had perhaps best leave criticism alone. Genius is so rare that humility must needs mingle with the gratitude it inspires. . . . There are many pages, and not a few whole scenes, in Mr. Joyce's book which are undoubtedly the work of a man of genius. . . . A subtle sense of art has worked amidst the chaos, making this hither-and-thither record of a young mind and soul. . . . a complete and ordered thing. . . . Among the new-fangled heroes of the newest fiction devoted to the psychology of youth he is almost unique in having known at least once a genuine sense of sin and undergone a genuine struggle. There is drama in Stephen.

Scotsman : To readers who knew Mr. Joyce's former book, *Dubliners*, his new story may be at once described and recommended as a more elaborate work in the same vein. . . . It has the same accomplished literary craftsmanship in the realistic characterization of the young Irishmen of to-day. . . . Written with a rare skill in charging simple forcible language with an uncommon weight of original feeling.

Glasgow Herald : James Joyce is a remarkable writer. As a pure stylist he is equalled by few and surpassed by none. . . . His thought is crystallized out in clear sentences with many facets, transparent, full of meaning, free from unessentials. . . . His economy of words is wonderful . . . a ruthless excision of all that is irrelevant to the theme in hand. . . . The reader instead of moving across a laboriously bridged gulf . . . leaps confidently from one peak to another in the clear radiance emanating from the summits themselves. . . . We have acknowledged fully his greatness as an artist in form, and as fully acknowledge his sincerity of purpose, but we quarrel with him on æsthetic values.

Birmingham Post : *Dubliners* showed the author to be a relentless realist whose craftsmanship was undeniable. The qualities which won praise for that volume are emphasized in this novel, but its realism will displease many.

Liverpool Daily Post : A remarkable book, as original in style as it is abrupt. . . . A book which flashes its truth upon one like a searchlight and a moment later leaves the dazzled reader in darkness. The family quarrel over Parnell is the vividest piece of writing of modern times. The Roman Catholic school, the fear of hell, the wild sinning and the melodramatic repentance pass in swift succession through a boy's imaginative brain . . . dizzy in a body thrilling with life.

Eastern Morning News : There is power in "A Portrait" and an originality that is almost overwhelming. . . . The book is immensely clever ; whether it is pleasant or not we leave our readers to decide for themselves. Of its literary value there can be no doubt.

MR. ERNEST A. BOYD : With a frankness and veracity as appalling as they are impressive, Mr. Joyce sets forth the relentless chronicle of a soul stifled by material and intellectual squalor. . . . The pages of the book are redolent of the ooze of our shabby respectability, with its intolerable tolerance of most shameful barbarism. . . . A truly amazing piece of spiritual and moral dissection.

Southport Guardian : A ruthless, relentless essay in realism ; a conscious, candid effort at perfection in portraiture, with no reticences and no reserves—almost brutally frank.

Cambridge Review : His vivid chapters on life in a Catholic school place him at once amongst the few great masters of analytic reminiscence.

Literary World : Rather a study of a temperament than a story in the ordinary way. . . . It has the intimate veracity, or appearance of veracity, of the great writers of confessions. . . . At times the analysis reminds one of Andreyed . . . at others the writing is pure lyrical beauty.

Everyman : Garbage. . . . We feel that Mr. Joyce would be at his best in a treatise on drains.

Published Price 6s. (5s. net, postage 4d.)

THE EGOIST LIMITED
OAKLEY HOUSE, BLOOMSBURY STREET, LONDON, W.C.

Extracts from first reviews of *A Portrait* which appeared in *The Egoist* in 1917. It is worth comparing these responses with how we read the novel today.

certain stories in Mr. Joyce's *Dubliners* there might
have been less recent trouble in Ireland. A clear
diagnosis is never without its value.

Apart from Mr. Joyce's realism - the school-life, the
life in the University, the family dinner with the
discussion of Parnell depicted in his novel - apart
from, or of a piece with, all this is the style, the
actual writing: hard, clear-cut, with no waste of
words, no bundling up of useless phrases, no filling
in with pages of slosh.[26]

Pound's provocative comments command assent, even if he does
misname the title and indulge in shifting registers. They help us to
position Joyce against the background of European fiction and the
novels of Flaubert. That is certainly one line of inquiry, but in this
book, in the chapters which follow, I emphasise the wider aesthetic
movement Joyce inherited as well as his place among Irish writers such
as Yeats and George Moore.

The single-mindedness of Joyce is often commented on by readers
and critics, but, to repeat, we can also learn as much from placing
him against the background of other writers and movements. In this
regard I have sought to highlight the ground he shares both with his
contemporaries and with the cultural contexts he inherited. Equally,
Joyce is involved in a continuous process of reassessment, and he never
stops answering back or anticipating those who were determined to
place him. To this extent we keep being reminded of his response to
Frazer, 'I write'.

DAEDALUS AND ICARUS

Pound could also have quoted a sentence from the novel which
contains a reference to the god of writers:

A sense of fear of the unknown moved in the heart
of his weariness, a fear of symbols and portents, of
the hawklike man whose name he bore soaring out
of his captivity on osier-woven wings, of Thoth, the

---

26 *The Egoist* IV, 2 (February 1917), 21-22. Printed in *Pound/Joyce: The Letters
of Ezra Pound to James Joyce* (New: New Directions, 1984), 89. The first extracts
of *A Portrait* were published in *The Egoist* in 1914, a magazine edited by Dora
Marsden and Harriet Shaw Weaver.

god of writers, writing with a reed upon a tablet and
bearing on his narrow ibis head the cusped moon.
(*P* 225)

Joyce enjoyed a classical education, as well as a religious one. Like a
good Victorian, whenever he addressed a question, he went back to
origins or basics. Hence his interest in etymology. He noticed how
writing, with its reeds and tablets, embraces nearly every civilisation,
and it was honoured by the Egyptians, Greeks, and Romans with
godly status. Greek myths in particular not only accompany Joyce's
writings they also inform them. In *A Portrait* they are there at the
outset. In Stephen's family name, the myth of Daedalus is invoked,
and it is revived periodically throughout the novel especially in the
rich imagery of birds in flight. Indeed, *A Portrait* reminds us of a story
that takes up into it the pre-Socratic four elements of earth, fire, air,
and water and turns them into vital symbols for use again in the
modern world.

I am reminded of the artist Michael Ayrton's beautiful account of
the Greek myth in *The Testament of Daedalus* (1962), which is worth
quoting at length:

> I do know that we live by myth, inventing it when
> necessary, returning to it with satisfaction when it
> seems useful. Who is Icarus?.... Is Icarus the perpetual
> hero who, given more, dares more than normal men
> and therefore seems a little childish? And who is
> Daedalus, the *polytechnos,* 'maker of things', greatest
> mythical progenitor, after Prometheus, of what the
> artist is? He is also the cunning man, creator and
> trickster, thinking faster and better than others,
> yet a man whose sensitivity runs counter to his
> intelligence and who is intelligently aware of his
> failure in sensitivity. Is not he, too, perpetual?
>
> All these things revolved in my brain around the
> axis of a simple tale in which a man made wings
> to get himself out of a difficult situation and took
> his son with him from Crete towards Cumae by
> air, in prehistoric times. The son ignored his father's
> warning, flew too near the sun and the wings his
> father had made for him melted and came apart.

> Icarus fell into the sea and was drowned. That is all
> there is in mythology about Icarus....
>
> In the course of writing this narrative...I realised that
> I must explain for myself the relationship between
> Daedalus and his son and the passion Icarus had for
> Apollo. Those images in which I came to portray
> Icarus at the climax of his flight, in suicidal contact
> with the sun itself, are the result of the narrative. The
> narrative, on the other hand, is the result of many
> previous images, the reliefs, bronzes, drawings and
> paintings out of which it grew.[27]

Joyce's fascination with the myth was that it allowed him scope to drive forward a narrative concerned with freedom. Every reference to flight reminds us, whether overtly or in passing, of the myth of Daedalus and Icarus. One of the most telling moments in *A Portrait* is when Stephen informs Davin that he will try and fly by the nets of 'nationality, language, religion' (*P* 203). And hearing the word 'nets' we find ourselves conjuring up the image of Daedalus and his son held by the Minotaur against their will on the island of Crete and how the cunning craftsman prepared to escape his clutches. In this way Joyce calls on the Greek story to give depth to his own bid for freedom.

At the end of Chapter 2, Stephen wanders into a 'maze of narrow and dirty streets' (*P* 100), and we recall the labyrinth on Crete. The myth is so powerful that we tend to forget that Icarus disobeys his father and falls into the sea and drowns. So Joyce, the modern-day craftsman and maker of things, constructs a narrative where the identity of his main character moves between the two mythological figures, allowing his own story to reshape the myth. Ayrton's search for the underlying story began with drawings for paintings and studies for bronzes. Joyce found the myth waiting to be fastened to a narrative. But both the artist and the writer show us how fertile and capacious the myth remains.

Ayrton's novel, *The Maze Maker* (1967), is equally of interest to the student of Joyce's novel.[28] When we encounter the word 'Bull' toward the end of chapter 4 in *A Portrait*, we might be reminded not only of the North Bull Island, the sandy island in the mouth of the River

---

27 Michael Ayrton, *The Testament of Daedalus* (1962; London: Robin Clark, 1991), 65-7.

28 Michael Ayrton, *The Maze Maker: A Novel* (1967; Chicago: University of Chicago Press, 2015).

Liffey, where Stephen is heading, but also the Minotaur, with his head of a bull and the body of a man. The reference to Bull, which is a shortened form of North Bull Island, is followed by the realisation that Stephen has indeed escaped the sentries of his youth with his future prospects expressed simply, again with the addition of an articulate exclamation mark, as 'The university!' (*P* 165)

Ayrton's lightness of touch helps us see the Greek myth in a new light, and some of his comments find a strange echo in *A Portrait*. At one point, when Icarus is hungry he eats figs from a hanging tree and is 'quieted'. We might recall Cranly eating figs and using the stems to clean his teeth and wonder if this is a deliberately Cretan image on Joyce's part and if there are other images of the island in the novel. Ayrton also tells us that Icarus 'never became a man although he became an immortal' (92). 'I do not think he ever discovered who he was.' (132) Such an insightful way of thinking can serve to remind us of a modern sensibility completely at home in the world of an ancient myth. They also prompt us to think about Stephen, especially in the context of heroes, and if he ever did discover who he was.[29]

TO BE FREE

Throughout *A Portrait* we sympathise with the protagonist's bid for freedom especially in the way it evokes for us, though perhaps not for Stephen, a common plight. 'Away with Systems! Away with a corrupt World!' is the cry of the hero in George Meredith's

---

29 If Stephen Dedalus is an odd-sounding name, it is worth thinking about *Stephen Hero* and the reference in *A Portrait* to 'Turpin Hero' (215). Stephen says the old English ballad begins in the first person and ends in the third person, which is certainly true of one of the versions, 'Rare Turpin'. See Arty Ash and Julius E.Day, *Immortal Turpin* (London and New York: Staples Press, 1948), 128. Execution ballads, though, often work the other way round, beginning in the third person and ending on the gallows in the first person. In *May It Please the Court* (1951), Eugene Sheehy recalls listening to Joyce at their family socials singing 'Brave Turpin Hero'. As for the hero status of Dick Turpin, this came largely through the popularity of Harrison Ainsworth's novel *Rookwood* (1834). In George Meredith's novel *The Ordeal of Richard Feverel* (1859; London: Chapman and Hall, 1889) there is a passing reference to Turpin and to the phrase he used as a highwayman 'Money or life' and how Feverel would substitute 'happiness' for 'life'. (296) But sustaining a comparison between Stephen/Joyce and Dick Turpin can only be achieved with difficulty. Ordeal is another matter.

influential Victorian novel, *The Ordeal of Richard Feverel* (1859).[30] The word 'system' appears twice in *A Portrait*, once in connection with the nervous system and once in reference to Aristotle's system of philosophy. (*P* 206-8) When Stephen thinks of system in Meredith's sense, he uses 'nets' (*P* 203) or 'fetters' (*P* 180). But Joyce clearly understood the term's ideological import in the context of patriarchy, for in his letter to Nora Barnacle in August 1904 telling her about his mother's death, he 'cursed the system which had made her a victim' (*Letters II* 48).

Unsurprisingly, contemporary Irish writers also focus on the theme of freedom. *The Whiteheaded Boy* (1921), a play by Lennox Robinson, is now of historical interest, but it contains exchanges of dialogue which we might well compare and contrast with the struggle inside Stephen. Significantly for our purposes, the play was staged at the Abbey Theatre in December 1916, the same month *A Portrait* was published in New York. Denis Geoghegan, the youngest son in the family, is the whiteheaded boy of the title, a symbol here of Ireland. As he mulls over thoughts of emigration to Canada, he is asked to explain himself in the presence of a group of family and friends including John Duffy, Chairman of the Rural District Council:

> Denis: I only want to do what I like with my own life – to be free.

> Duffy: Free?... Bedad, isn't he like old Ireland asking for freedom, and we're like the fools of Englishmen offering him every bloody thing except the one thing?[31]

In the year of the Easter Rising when the play was first performed, the message would not have gone unnoticed. His family and friends have offered him everything by way of material goods and incentives, but Denis has only freedom in mind, just 'to be free'. And it is the appeal every generation since has sought, 'to do what I like with my own life'.

---

30 George Meredith, *The Ordeal of Richard Feverel* (1859; London: Chapman and Hall, 1889), 132. According to Constantine Curran, Meredith was 'the touchstone of emancipated intelligence' for himself and his generation. See *James Joyce Remembered* (London: Oxford University Press, 1968), 30.

31 Lennox Robinson, *The Whiteheaded Boy* (New York and London: Samuel French, 1921), 158.

Stephen's bid for freedom is more sophisticated; it is after all more than simply an expression of general dissatisfaction with his lot. Denis, on the other hand, seems incapable of moving from a personal form of rebellion to a more political one. Indeed, it is Duffy who makes us aware of Denis's position when he draws our attention to the parallels with how England treated Ireland in the past, particularly through bribery. The British Empire failed to get the measure of the Irish desire for self-determination. Freedom was an ideal, which expressed itself at times in simple emotional terms, but, with separate nation status at its heart, it was also a political idea that resisted compromise with the present or the future or indeed the past.

Unlike Denis, Stephen comes to see his predicament as belonging to this wider history of oppression, convinced that emigration means something more than just going abroad. Such a line of thinking can cope with historical set-backs even as it recognises what was best expressed by the Fenian John O'Leary in his old age. According to O'Leary, the failures of various attempts to break the English connection in the nineteenth century merely showed that 'Ireland is still at its heart's core firm to be free.'[32] This is what the presence of John Casey in the Christmas Dinner scene is telling us and what contributes to Stephen's make-up as a person.

Joyce has been frequently looked upon as a champion of freedom. In the early 1950s, Sean O'Faolain called him 'the great literary rebel of our time', a view that still holds today.[33] Throughout *Invisible Man*, Ralph Ellison's insightful study of racial oppression in America and the difficulty of forging an identity of one's own, Joyce's *A Portrait* can be heard. This is Ellison's protagonist recalling his Literature tutor, Woodridge:

> 'Stephen's problem, like ours, was not actually one of creating the uncreated conscience of his race, but of creating the *uncreated features of his face*. Our task is that of making ourselves individuals. The conscience of a race is the gift of its individuals who see, evaluate, record... We create the race by creating

---

32 John O'Leary, *Recollections of Fenians and Fenianism* Vol 2 (London: Downey, 1896), 227. O'Leary was the Fenian who influenced the whole of Yeats's generation.

33 See his commentary in James Joyce, *A Portrait of the Artist as a Young Man* (New York: Signet Books, 1954).

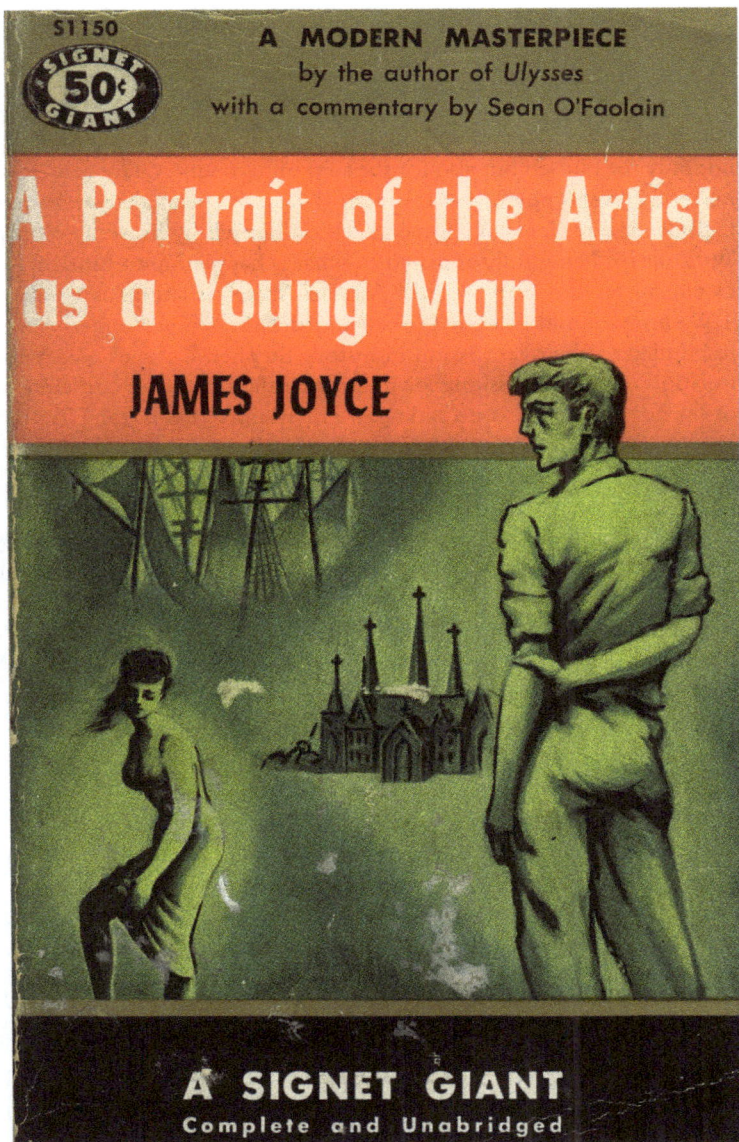

S1150

A **MODERN MASTERPIECE**
by the author of *Ulysses*
with a commentary by Sean O'Faolain

SIGNET GIANT
50¢

A Portrait of the Artist
as a Young Man

JAMES JOYCE

A SIGNET GIANT
Complete and Unabridged

The cover to the 1954 Signet Classic paperback of *A Portrait* shows the back of a young man, his head turned toward an attractive young woman, her left hand reaching down to lift her skirt, while in the middle distance looms a forbidding-looking church and in the background the sails of an emigrant ship..

ourselves and then to our great astonishment we
will have created something far more important: We
will have created a culture.'[34]

Reading *Invisible Man* reminds us that Stephen is involved in a struggle
not only for himself but also for the soul of his country. The nameless
hero of Ellison's novel, invisible man that is, discovers that he is not
invisible and is repeatedly forced back on himself by his skin colour.
Without his being fully apprised of what is happening to him, he in
fact recreates the story of how African-Americans such as Booker
T. Washington and Marcus Garvey and the great blues singers have
responded to their oppression in history. Stephen can seek solace in
isolation or the confessional or in creating the uncreated conscience
of his race, but there is no hiding, no invisibility that is, for Ellison's
hero. And yet, for Ellison, Joyce has shone a light on the meaning of
freedom in the context of his race. Woodridge's explanation clouds
the issue, so the search by Ellison's protagonist continues.

With comments on his struggles to find a voice and on 'artistic
scrupulousness', and in his sharply critical diagnosis of 'Negro
American consciousness' in 'The World and the Jug', Ellison's essays
also remind us in part of the common ground he shares with Joyce.[35]
Both writers saw themselves not as ambassadors of their culture
but as physicians diagnosing what was wrong with their culture.
In *Dubliners*, Joyce alights on paralysis, in *A Portrait* on the need
to escape. All of Joyce's energies went into writing. He signed no
petitions. Ellison, on the other hand, never relaxed in his unceasing
search for justice and personal satisfaction, and at the end of *Invisible
Man*, a novel that is about the sympathetic imagination, he wonders
if 'on the lower frequencies, I speak for you' (469).

In spite of his fame, or indeed because of it, Joyce's reputation
will always need to be supported, and this is no exception today.
In a recent interview John Banville, Ireland's leading contemporary
novelist, argued for the significance of Henry James as a novelist over
Joyce: '[H]e brought the novel to its fullest potential as an artistic
medium.... a true modernist, a true revolutionary.... an entirely new
kind of prose, more revolutionary than Joyce's.'[36] What the Wexford-
born novelist particularly objected to was the way 'Joyce devoured

---

34 Ralph Ellison, *Invisible Man* (1952; London: Penguin, 1986), 286.
35 Ralph Ellison, *The Collected Essays of Ralph Ellison* (ed. John F. Callahan)
(New York: Modern Library, 2003), 56, 183 and 171.
36 Interview: John Banville, *The Scottish Review of Books* 18 November, 2017.

the city, and left his successors only a few dried bones and a scrap or two of bloodstained fur. For a novelist to mention anywhere in Dublin is to strike a Joycean echo.' The complaint follows a similar objection in his memoir *Time Pieces* (2016): 'For me, as a writer in the making, the fact was that Joyce had seized upon the city for his own literary purposes and in doing so had used it up.'[37]

That is certainly one point of view. But to my mind, part of the attraction in reading Joyce today, something that is on display throughout the chapters of this book, is that his work belongs not only to the present but also to another country we call the past. In this respect, if we have the eyes to see, Joyce reminds us of a country always waiting to be discovered or revealed. All these are nice ironies, where not everything is used up or points in a single direction. Even plagiarism still has a part to play in Joyce's wake for we live in a relentlessly self-reflexive age. Plagiarism not by Joyce but of Joyce takes several different forms, and some of it is rendered in terms which are explicit and quite amusing.

This is the case with Julia O'Faolain's first novel *Three Lovers* (1970). One of the lovers is Fintan McCann, an expatriate Irish painter living in Paris who is modelled in part on Stephen Dedalus.[38] He is a plagiarist involved in pirating an edition of a book of poetry and at the end of the novel he is forced to flee Paris. O'Faolain has fun in particular with her protagonist's physical appearance and his negative qualities such as scrounging or thinking the world owes him a living because he is an artist. McCann, it transpires, comes from a large family of eight children and from a home where there was no indoor plumbing so 'you relieved yourself in the yard in all weathers' (138). His eyes, we are told, were 'pallid as a goat's' (16) and his body prone to tics. He has bad teeth and his underwear is 'a disgrace' (152). At the same time, in an insightful observation by O'Faolain on Joyce, McCann believes he is a 'seer' (235), that is, not someone who divines but a person whose observations are acute and wholly persuasive. As for McCann's way with words, these were 'his strength' (23), but, unfortunately, he mistakenly assumes reading verse to a woman will seduce her, which in its own way looks like a pointed comment on Stephen's writing verse to Emma Clery in *A Portrait*.

---

37 John Banville, *Time Pieces: A Dublin Memoir* (photographs by Paul Joyce) (Dublin: Hachette Books, 2016), 80.
38 Julia O'Faolain, *Three Lovers* (1970; New York: Coward, McCann and Geoghegan, 1971).

On a more serious note, we might consider the sequence in *Station Island* (1984) where Seamus Heaney steps down from the jetty after returning from his pilgrimage on Lough Derg, and grasps the helping hand of someone who seemed blind and who is walking with an ash plant. Almost immediately he recognises the voice, a voice 'eddying with the vowels of all rivers'. Heaney continues by describing the figure as 'cunning', the adjective used by Stephen Dedalus when he is determined to embark on exile from his country with 'silence, exile and cunning' (*P* 247).[39] Yeats was Heaney's example but he finds in the Catholic-educated Joyce encouragement and a helping hand. Writers, then, and Irish writers in particular, often latch onto something in Joyce not to criticise him, as Banville does, or even to identify with him or bring him up to date. Rather, as Heaney the 'convalescent' recognises, Joyce can be a surprisingly comforting figure, especially when it comes to getting through difficult times. After the self-flagellation he experienced on pilgrimage to Lough Derg, Heaney is told by the Joyce figure, 'You've listened long enough. Now strike your note.' It was good advice.

---

39 Seamus Heaney, *Station Island* (London: Faber, 1984).

Photograph of Joyce in Zurich taken around 1915.

A German map of Dublin in 1905 printed in Leipzig. Bray, 13 miles south
of Dublin, is off the map, but other places where the Joyce family lived such
as Rathgar and Rathmines in the south or Drumcondra in the north, can
be identified. With the varying depth of the sea carefully marked, the map
reminds us that Dublin is an 'aquacity', a city on water, and that *A Portrait*
is a novel surrounded by water.

CHAPTER 2: THE LIFE AND TIMES
OF JAMES JOYCE

Joyce's life began inauspiciously enough in a small terraced house in Brighton Square in Rathgar, a respectable suburb on the south side of Dublin. It was here that his father peered down at him through a monocle and told him a story about baby tuckoo and a cow coming down along the road from the nearby mountains. His life ended 59 years later amidst the snowy Alps in the Fluntern Cemetery in Zurich within earshot of the roaring lions in the nearby zoo. February 1882 to January 1941. In terms of a wider political history, he was born three months before the assassination of Lord Cavendish, the Chief Secretary to Ireland, in the Phoenix Park in Dublin in May 1882, an event that heralded another sharp downturn in Anglo-Irish relations. He died in neutral Switzerland, having luckily escaped the previous month from German-occupied France. If complications arising from a duodenal ulcer had not proved fatal soon after he arrived in Zurich, he might have continued writing into old age.

1882 Birth of James Augustine Joyce on 2 February in Brighton Square, Rathgar, Dublin, the eldest surviving son of John Joyce and Mary Joyce (*née* Murray). He is born a week after Virginia Woolf, the novelist often linked with Joyce in the movement known today as modernism. In *A Portrait*, Stephen cannot remember if his mother had nine or ten children, but probably neither figure is correct. From 1881 until her death 22 years later May Joyce had perhaps 13 children, more than one every two years, and that doesn't include the pregnancies, possibly in 1883 and 1885, which didn't come to term.

41 Brighton Square, Rathgar, Dublin, where Joyce was born.
The terraced house is larger than it looks.
Photo is from Herbert Gorman, *James Joyce* (1948).

On 11 March Ernest Renan delivers a lecture at the Sorbonne in Paris entitled 'Qu'est-ce qu'une nation?' (What is a nation?). The relevance of the question to his own country intrigued Joyce, as we can see from responses by two of his key characters, Stephen Dedalus and Leopold Bloom. Stephen in *A Portrait* has no doubt about his national identity, but, given how the Irish in 1890 had betrayed their own leader, Charles Stewart Parnell, he is wary of any nationalist agenda. In the 'Cyclops' episode of *Ulysses*, Leopold Bloom, the Jewish outsider, is forced to respond to a slight as to his own national identity. When asked to define what is his nation, Bloom blocks the line of attack by innocently replying, 'Ireland... I was born here'. May: the Chief Secretary of Ireland and his Under-Secretary are assassinated by unknown assailants in the Phoenix Park, Dublin.

The same month in the United States there is the premiere of Henrik Ibsen's *Ghosts*, a play in part about syphilis. This was a theme that was also to intrigue Joyce. In *Stephen Hero* Lynch warns Stephen of the dangers of catching the disease. Some critics have suggested that in the opening story of *Dubliners*, the priest suffers from the disease. Throughout Joyce's early letters when commenting on the stories of *Dubliners*, the theme of paralysis as a cultural phenomenon is particularly in evidence.

In a lecture tour of the United States in April Wilde discovers anew his feelings for his country of origins. In 'The Irish Poets of '48', he celebrates the nationalist poetry of his mother, who wrote under the name 'Speranza', and tells his California audience that 'The Saxon took our lands from us and left them desolate. We took their language and added new beauties to it.'

This year also sees the publication of W.W.Skeat's *Etymological Dictionary of the English Language*, a book, as we learn from *Stephen Hero*, Stephen studied 'by the hour'.

1884 Birth of Joyce's brother, Stanislaus Joyce. Joyce family move to Castlewood Avenue, Rathmines in Dublin, where they stay until 1887. May: *Against Nature* (*A rebours* in French or alternatively 'Against the grain'), a novel by Joris-Karl Huysmans is published. The so-called bible of the Decadents caused a stir on its first appearance. Des Esseintes, the hyper-sensitive anti-hero, looks to find an escape from the banality of life. The novel's attraction to the antinomian Joyce is discussed more fully in Chapter 3. First edition of the *Oxford English Dictionary* (completed 1928). The OED Online includes 103 entries for which Joyce is the first source. November: the Gaelic Athletic Association formed by Michael Cusack to promote Irish sport and nationalism. Cusack is a model for The Citizen in the 'Cyclops' episode of *Ulysses*. In *A Portrait* we learn that Davin 'had sat at the feet of Michael Cusack, the Gael'.

1885 September: birth of the English novelist, D.H.Lawrence, whose fiction was also, like Joyce's, to suffer at the hands of the courts for so-called obscenity. October: birth of Ezra Pound, a key figure in ensuring Joyce's career took off. Walter Pater's *Marius the Epicurean: His Sensations and Ideas*, a novel in Joyce's Trieste library, is published.[40] As we will see in the next chapter, *A Portrait* carries many echoes of Pater's novel, both in its narrative structure and in its themes. In the same year, Emile Zola's *Germinal*, an influential naturalist novel set in a mining area in northern France during an industrial strike, is published.

1886 June: Gladstone's Home Rule Bill, which would have granted to Ireland a measure of independence, is defeated at Westminster.

1887 March: the *Times* of London, making use of letters forged by Richard Pigott, launches an attack on Parnell, leader of the Irish Parliamentary Party at Westminster. Pigott falsely claimed that Parnell supported violence. May: the Joyce family move to Martello Terrace, Bray, County Wicklow, where they stay until 1891. This is the setting for the Christmas Dinner scene in *A Portrait*.

1888 April: death of Matthew Arnold. June: Joyce sings with his parents in an amateur concert at Bray Boat Club, his first public performance. September: he enrolls as a boarder at the Jesuit-run Clongowes Wood College, Salins, County Kildare, which he attends until December 1891. He is slightly older than six-and-a-half years and attracts the moniker 'half-past six'. Among his contemporaries (who are given a fictional presence in *A Portrait*) are Rody Kickham, Christopher 'Nasty' Roche, Charles Wells, Cecil Thunder, and his rival Jack Lawton ('Heron'), who was dead by the time Joyce came to write the novel. Two of Pigott's sons were enrolled at Clongowes for the academic year 1888-9. September: birth of T.S. Eliot, a constant presence throughout Joyce's career. *Fairy and Folktales of the Irish Peasantry*, edited by W.B.Yeats, published.

---

40 For a list of the 600 or so books in Joyce's library before he moved to Paris in 1920, see the Appendix in Richard Ellmann, *The Consciousness of Joyce* (London: Faber, 1977), 97-134.

Class of Elements 1888-89. Joyce, with arms crossed, is sitting on the grass in front of Fr William Power ('Fr Arnall'). In the back row, sixth from left, is Roddy Kickam; Christopher 'Nasty' Roche is fifth from right; Wells is second from right on front row. *Courtesy of Fr Bruce Bradley S.J.*

1889 January: the publication of *The Wanderings of Oisin*, Yeats's first volume of verse, constitutes an important moment in the emergence of the Irish Literary Revival. March: Joyce is punished at Clongowes by his (percipient) masters for using 'vulgar language'. Death of Gerard Manley Hopkins, the English Jesuit poet who taught at the Royal University of Ireland (the National University, now University College Dublin). He is buried in the Jesuit plot at Glasnevin Cemetery. His so-called 'Terrible Sonnets', which were composed in Ireland, date from 1885. In June William Archer's translation of Ibsen's *A Doll's House* is given its first performance at the Novelty Theatre in London.

1890 July: Oscar Wilde's influential novel *The Picture of Dorian Gray* is published in installments in *Lippincott's Monthly Magazine*. It is extensively revised for publication the following year with many so-called decadent and homo-erotic passages removed.

The National Library of Ireland, formerly the Library of the Royal Dublin Society, is removed to its present building. According to the one-time librarian, T. W. Lyster, writing in *The Literary Year Book 1897*, the Library 'contains about 125,000 volumes, and is open weekdays (from 10 am to 10 pm) to all persons over fourteen years of age and suitably introduced.' As is clear from the final chapter of *A Portrait,* this Library became the focal point for Joyce and his contemporaries while studying at the Royal University of Ireland.

Death of Cardinal John Henry Newman, first Rector of the National University of Ireland, and acclaimed by Stephen Dedalus as the greatest writer of prose in English. *Principles of Psychology* by William James published. Along with Édouard Dujardin, James provided a new understanding of consciousness as flow, and his phrase, 'stream of consciousness', was later exploited by Joyce as a powerful technique in his fiction.

The emergence of the New Woman can be felt throughout this period as in Ibsen's play *Hedda Gabler* (1890), Henry James's *Portrait of a Lady* (1881), George Bernard Shaw's play *Mrs Warren's Profession* (1893), and Kate Chopin's novel *The Awakening* (1899). By comparison, in its depiction of women *A Portrait* is fairly backward-looking.

December: Parnell, cited in a divorce case involving Captain O'Shea, one of his M.P.s at Westminster, is driven from office.

1891 6 October: death of Parnell in Brighton. The nine-year-old Joyce writes 'Et Tu Healy', a poem attacking those M.P.s such as Timothy Healy who betrayed Parnell. Only a fragment of the poem has survived. 'Ivy Day in the Committee Room', Joyce's story in *Dubliners* and written in 1905, offers a critical view of Ireland after the fall of Parnell. Ivy Day, when, formerly, people sported a sprig of ivy in his memory, commemorated the day of Parnell's death. The reference to 'Committee Room' is to room number 15 in the House of Commons, where his fellow M.P.s turned against Parnell in December 1890. Joyce's early view of contemporary Irish politics and history was governed by a feeling of betrayal associated with 'the chief', as he is called by John Casey in *A Portrait*. In this sense he wrote under Parnell's star.

Later in the year Joyce is withdrawn from Clongowes for financial reasons. Christmas: row in family over religion and politics, after which Mrs Conway ('Dante') leaves the Joyce household. Shaw's study, *The Quintessence of Ibsenism*, a sign of Ibsen's growing importance, published this year. Ten years later Joyce is writing essays and reviews about Ibsen, including a review, published in the prestigious *Fortnightly Review*, of Ibsen's last play, *When We Dead Awaken*. Novels this year included Thomas Hardy's *Tess of the D'Urbervilles*, a tragic novel about the plight of women set against the break-up of rural England, and George Gissing's *New Grub Street*, a naturalist novel about a struggling journalist set in London.

1892 September: publication of Yeats's play, *The Countess Cathleen*. November: Douglas Hyde delivers an influential lecture in the development of cultural nationalism in Ireland entitled 'The Necessity of De-Anglicising the Irish Nation'.[41] Late in year the Joyce family move to 14 Fitzgibbon Street, not far from Mountjoy Square, where they stay for a year. As Vivien Igoe points out this was the last 'good' address the family were to occupy.[42]

1893 Early in year Joyce attends for a short while the Christian Brothers' School, a school for less well-off pupils, in North Richmond Street. Joyce's life and fiction constantly crisscross, and we can often hear Joyce's father throughout his fiction. Thus when Stephen's father makes some derogatory comments about the Christian Brothers in *A Portrait*, we are listening to the voice of John Joyce. April: Joyce enters Belvedere College, Great Denmark Street, Dublin, as a day pupil. The Jesuit College served children from better-off homes, but it was less

41 This lecture is reproduced in my *Irish Writing in the Twentieth Century: A Reader* (Cork: Cork University Press, 2001).
42 Vivien Igoe, *James Joyce's Dublin Houses and Nora Barnacle's Galway* (Dublin: Lilliput, 2007).

pretentious than the more up-market Clongowes Wood. Summer: Joyce accompanies his father to sell off his remaining property in Cork, an episode that informs one of the key episodes in *A Portrait*.

The Gaelic League is founded to promote the Irish language, with Hyde as its first president. Joyce later attends Gaelic language classes but tells his friend, Frank Budgen, that he stopped going because his teacher, Patrick Pearse, insisted on denigrating English in favour of Irish. In *Stephen Hero* we learn that Stephen is lured into taking language classes by his attraction to 'Emma Clery'.

First performance of Ibsen's *The Master Builder*, a play that Joyce stayed up all night to read when the print version arrived at the family house in Dublin. Throughout *Finnegans Wake* we hear echoes of Ibsen's tragic protagonist, 'bygmester', who, like the hod-carrier Tim Finnegan in the song 'Finnegan's Wake', suffers a fall, but in his case it proves fatal, and when the curtain falls there is no resurrection.

1894 Wilde's *Salome,* with illustrations by Aubrey Beardsley, published. The appearance of George Moore's *Esther Waters* coincides with the demise of the three-decker or three-volume novel, the form that dominated nineteenth-century fiction. Moore's novel exposes the evils of the wet-nurse situation whereby the middle class used poorer women to breast-feed their babies. Autumn: the Joyce family, continuing their financial decline, move to 2 Millbourne Avenue, Drumcondra, on the north side of Dublin.

1895 Early this year the Joyce family move to 17 Richmond Street and remain there until 1898. February: first performance of Wilde's much-loved play, *The Importance of Being Earnest*, at St James's Theatre in London. May: Wilde, tried and found guilty of gross indecency, is sentenced to two years imprisonment in Reading Gaol. Hardy's *Jude the Obscure*, a tragic novel about social class and aspiration and designed to shine a light on those obscured by history, published. In 1896 Joyce sends his brother to borrow a copy of the novel from the library, and Stanislaus mistakenly asks for *Jude the Obscene* from a prudish librarian. Joyce wishes he had been present to enjoy the moment. For some bishops and members of the English establishment Hardy's novel was indeed obscene.

1896 Joyce is stirred by Father Cullen's sermons during the annual November retreat at Belvedere College.

Group photo of the Sodality of the Blessed Virgin Mary at Belvedere
College. Joyce is seated in a prominent position next to the priest, but he is
wearing a jacket which looks a size too big for him.

A studio portrait of Joyce, cap in hand, with his close
friends at university, George Clancy and J.F.Byrne.

1897 Joyce spends Sunday evenings with the Sheehy family at Belvedere Place, the home of David Sheehy M.P. and his children Eugene and Mary. Mary Sheehy is one of the female figures Joyce used for the character of 'Emma Clery'. Joyce plays charades and, with his mother, entertains in their comfortable middle-class home.

Yeats's *The Tables of the Law: The Adoration of the Magi* published. These stories have a strong impact on Joyce and he learns passages by heart. Joseph Conrad's *The Nigger of the 'Narcissus'*, a novel about racism and identity and 'written to make you see', is published. Joyce, too, writes to 'make you see'. In his last year(s) at Belvedere Joyce begins reading Dante Alighieri, a writer whose work he will come to read in its entirety.

1898 Joyce leaves Belvedere College and enters the Royal University to read modern languages. His contemporaries include Eugene Sheehy, Thomas Kettle, Francis Sheehy Skeffington ('McCann'), Arthur Clery, George Clancy, the model in part for the character of 'Davin', Vincent Cosgrave ('Lynch'), John Francis Byrne ('Cranly'), and Constantine Curran. Sheehy, Byrne and Curran have all left valuable accounts of Joyce at this time (see Bibliography). Family move to 29 Windsor Avenue, Fairview, a poorer district on the outskirts of Dublin near Drumcondra, where they stay until May 1899. Centenary celebrations in Dublin for the 1798 Rising against Ireland's union with Britain. After visits to the red light area Joyce goes to confession at the Carmelite Church in Dublin. This year sees the publication in February of Wilde's *Ballad of Reading Gaol*.

1899 February: Joyce is elected to the executive committee of the Literary and Historical Society at university. April: Yeats's *The Wind Among the Reeds* is published. Joyce refuses to sign a petition denouncing Yeats's play *The Countess Cathleen* for blasphemy. The Countess is criticised for selling her soul to the devil to feed her starving peasants. In *A Portrait* Stephen similarly refuses to sign such a petition.[43]

Arthur Griffith returns from South Africa, where he was campaigning with the Irish Brigade against the British, and in March, with William Rooney, he founds *United Irishman*, a nationalist newspaper, later

---

43 A letter to *The Freeman's Journal*, a Dublin-based Irish newspaper, reminds us of the prejudices among some of Joyce's contemporaries. 'The subject is not Irish. It has been shown that the plot is founded on a German legend. The characters are ludicrous travesties of the Irish Catholic Celt.' Signed by 'Dublin Catholic students of the Royal University'. 10 May 1899.

read with interest by Joyce when he was abroad. The Irish nationalist newspaper *Claidheamh Soluis* (Sword of Light) is launched by the Gaelic League and is edited at first by Eoin MacNeill and then in 1903-9 by Patrick Pearse.

Publication of *Heart of Darkness*, a novel of empire, which is based on Conrad's experience in the Belgian Congo. While in Africa, Conrad became friends with Roger Casement, the British diplomat, who was later executed by the British authorities for Irish republican activities in 1916. Joyce followed Casement's career with interest and he appears in the 'Cyclops' episode of *Ulysses*. While Conrad's response to imperialism is at the other end of the spectrum to Joyce's, both shared a life of exile and an aesthetic of suspicion.

1900 January: Joyce reads a lecture on 'Drama and Life' to the Literary and Historical Society at university. In April he has an essay on 'Ibsen's New Drama' published in *Fortnightly Review*. With the twelve guineas he received for the essay he took his father to London in May or June this year. Attends a meeting of the Gaelic League with his close friend Byrne. During a trip to Mullingar Joyce writes a (non-extant) play entitled 'A Brilliant Career'. A copy of D'Annunzio's *The Child of Pleasure* bears Joyce's signature and includes the date and place 'Mullingar July.5.1900'. November: death of Wilde in Paris. Sigmund Freud's *The Interpretation of Dreams* published.

Around this time Joyce begins writing epiphanies, brief sketches of what he had seen or heard. The epiphanies, some 70 plus in total, were composed for the most part in the years between 1900 and 1903. They are about ordinary people and, as Stanislaus Joyce informs us, concerned 'the very things they were most anxious to conceal'. They are short pieces of prose, some narrative, others dramatic, some ironic, others banal, some pious, others cold or emotionless. The role of epiphanies in Joyce's work is discussed more fully in Chapters 5 and 6.

1901 January: Queen Victoria dies and is succeeded by Edward VII. February: Joyce writes to Ibsen on his 73rd birthday making use of Dano-Norwegian, the language Ibsen spoke. July: accompanies his father to Mullingar to sort out the voting lists. August: completes a translation of Hauptmann's play *Michael Kramer*. September: William Archer, Ibsen's translator and theatre critic, responds with some criticism of a selection of poetry Joyce sent him the previous month. October: family move to 32 Glengariff Parade, and now only one float ('caravan') is needed to remove all their belongings. 'The Day of the Rabblement', Joyce's essay attacking the Irish Literary Theatre's new programme, is published in *Two Essays* along with Sheehy Skeffington's pro-feminist essay on 'A Forgotten Aspect of the University Question'. In October at the Gaiety Theatre in Dublin Hyde's *Casadh an tSugáin* (*The Twisting of the Rope*) is performed by the Gaelic League Amateur Dramatic Society under the direction of William Fay. It is the first play in Irish to be produced on the professional stage in Dublin.

1902 In February Joyce reads an essay on 'James Clarence Mangan' to the Literary and Historical Society. Mangan was a poet Joyce returned to in 1907 in a lecture delivered in Trieste, describing him as 'the type of his race' and by rights the national poet of Ireland.

March: Joyce's brother, George, is taken seriously ill with a form of typhoid, and in May, at the age of 15, he dies from peritonitis. In the weeks leading up to his death Joyce sings to him a setting of Yeats's poem 'Who Goes with Fergus'. Epiphany no 19 concerns George's worsening medical condition, when Joyce's mother discovers 'matter coming away from the hole in [his] stomach'. This scene resurfaces in *Stephen Hero* in connection with the death of Isabel, but for whatever reason Joyce does not include it in *A Portrait*. The day of George's death is recorded with feeling but matter-of-factly in epiphany no 20. The epiphany includes the lines: 'He lies on my bed where I lay last night: they have covered him with a sheet and closed his eyes with pennies.... Poor little fellow!' Joyce's eldest son, Giorgio, was named after George, and there is a suggestion his death prompted Joyce to apply to study medicine in Paris.

In April Yeats's *Cathleen ni Houlihan*, a highly charged nationalist play with Maud Gonne in the leading role, is performed in Dublin. Looking back in the 1930s, Yeats, in his poem 'The Man and the Echo', wonders if his play encouraged his fellow countrymen to take up arms in the Easter Rising of 1916: 'Did that play of mine send out / Certain men the English shot?' Joyce graduates from university in the summer. He is just 20. In this year Joyce purchases two novels by Flaubert in original French, *Madame Bovary* and *L'Éducation Sentimentale*. In October he meets Yeats for the first time, and reads him some poems and epiphanies. He also perhaps tells him, though this is disputed: 'I have met you too late. You are too old.' A collection of epiphanies, written in the period between 1900 and 1902, is shown to George Russell and friends in Dublin. Also in October the Joyce family move to 7 St Peter's Terrace, Phibsborough (Cabra), and stay here until March 1904.

December: Joyce travels to Paris to study medicine, meeting Yeats in London on the way. To support himself he begins reviewing for the Conservative and pro-British Dublin *Daily Express*.

Lady Gregory's *Cuchulain of Muirthemne* published. This becomes an influential book of translations of Irish myths centering on the figure of the warrior Cuchulain in the Ulster Cycle of sagas. It is written in an attractive style later termed 'Kiltartanese' after her local village of Kiltartan in County Galway.

1903 Early this year Joyce composes 'I Hear An Army', a poem based on a dream and later chosen as the final poem in *Chamber Music*, the volume published in 1907. The poem is later included in *Des Imagistes* in 1914, an imagist anthology edited by Pound, H.D. (Hilda Doolittle), and Richard Aldington. In March he writes to his brother, Stanislaus, that he has composed 15 new epiphanies. The epiphanies have now a decided order and arrangement, ready for incorporation into *Stephen Hero*. Also in March Joyce meets the Irish playwright, John Millington Synge, in Paris. After being shown the manuscript of his new play, *Riders to the Sea*, Joyce is duly impressed even if at first he imagines Synge might be a rival. In Zurich in March 1918 Joyce's wife, Nora Barnacle, plays Cathleen in Synge's play. Also in March he tells his mother: 'I am at present up to the neck in Aristotle's Metaphysics and read only him and Ben Jonson (a writer of songs and plays)'.

1 April: Joyce is called home, where his mother is dying of cancer. He remains in Dublin, and, as he did for his dying brother, George, he sings her the lines 'Who Goes With Fergus' from Yeats's play *The Countess Cathleen*. His mother dies in August. On the day of her funeral, Joyce attempts with his sister, Margaret, to call up her spirit, and it is recorded that Margaret did indeed have an apparition of her in a brown habit, a scene Joyce perhaps has in mind in 'Telemachus', the opening episode of *Ulysses*.

July: Edward VII visits Ireland. Moore's collection of short stories, *The Untilled Field,* is published. This volume played a part in Joyce's own collection of stories, *Dubliners*. *The Way of All Flesh* by Samuel Butler, a semi-autobiographical novel written in the early 1880s, is published. This is a novel that Joyce had in his library in Trieste and can be usefully compared with *A Portrait*. Between September and November Joyce is responsible for fourteen reviews in the Dublin *Daily Express*, including a hostile review in March of Lady Gregory's *Poets and Dreamers*.

1904 A defining year for Joyce. In January he writes 'A Portrait of the Artist', an essay-story dealing with aesthetics. He submits it to *Dana*, a freethinking magazine edited by John Eglinton (pseudonym of W. K. Magee) and Fred Ryan, but it is rejected. On his 22nd birthday, 2 February, Joyce tells his brother Stanislaus that he has embarked on a semi-autobiographical novel, now known as *Stephen Hero*. He writes the first chapter in just eight days, and optimistically declares it will be 63 chapters long.

In the spring he teaches for a short while at the Clifton School, Dalkey, an experience he makes use of when writing the 'Nestor' episode of *Ulysses*. Late March: the Joyce family move to 60 Shelbourne Road, Dublin. 16 May: sings at the *Feis Ceoil* (Festival of Music) in Dublin and receives a bronze medal.

On 10 June he meets his future wife, Nora Barnacle, and is attracted to her immediately. They walk out together for the first time probably on 16 June, the day Joyce made famous in *Ulysses* and now known as Bloomsday after its leading protagonist Leopold Bloom. Although they live together all their lives, Joyce and Nora do not marry until 1931.

July and August: prompted by George Russell, Joyce writes 'The Sisters', 'Eveline', and 'After the Race', stories which appear in the *Irish Homestead,* a weekly magazine which supported Horace Plunkett's Irish Agricultural Organization Society. Also in July/August, Joyce writes 'The Holy Office', a stinging attack on the hypocrisy of his contemporaries. In August, at the height of his singing career, he shares a platform with John McCormack at a concert given at the Antient Concert Rooms in Dublin.

1–2 September: stays with James H. Cousins at 35 Strand Road, Sandymount. 10 September: he spends six nights with Oliver St John Gogarty in the Martello Tower at Sandycove, the location for the opening episode of *Ulysses*. On 8 October he departs with Nora for the continent and finds employment teaching at a Berlitz School in Pola (today Pula in Croatia). October 11–19: Joyce finishes Chapter 12 of *Stephen Hero*. Chapters 1–11 are no longer extant. 1 November: Shaw's *John Bull's Other Island*, a telling critique of Anglo-Irish relations and insufficiently appreciated by the European-bound Joyce, opens at the Royal Court Theatre in London.

In November in his Commonplace Notebook (formerly known as the Paris and Pola Notebooks) he cites two sentences by Thomas Aquinas in Latin and then translates: *Bonum est in quod tendit appetitus*. 'The good is that towards the possession of which an appetite tends: the good is the desirable.' *Pulcera[e] sunt quae visa placent*. 'Those things are beautiful the apprehension of which pleases.' The second quotation should read *pulcra enim dicuntur ea quae visa placent*, that is, roughly translated, those things are said to be beautiful which please the eye. Joyce's omission of '*dicuntur*' (are said) is revealing. Not 'are' but 'are said to be'. The mistake is repeated in *A Portrait*. One conclusion we might draw is that Aquinas's qualification has the hallmark of a more circumspect thinker than Joyce.[44] November-December: Joyce writes Chapters 12-14 of *Stephen Hero*. 27 December: the opening night of the newly formed Abbey Theatre includes a performance of Yeats's *On Baile's Strand,* the first play in his Cuchulain Cycle of ancient Irish myths.

1905 February: Joyce is working on Chapter 17 of *Stephen Hero*. In March he moves from Pola to Trieste to take up a teaching post at the Berlitz School. His son, Giorgio, is born on 27 July. Stanislaus joins the Joyce household in October. Joyce completes all but one of the stories of *Dubliners* and submits them to Grant Richards in London for publication, but without success.

November: Griffith launches Sinn Fein with an advanced nationalist programme advocating independence for Ireland. Sinn Fein can be translated as 'We Ourselves', 'Ourselves Alone' or simply 'Ourselves'. Joyce's attitude to Griffith and Sinn Fein was fairly mixed, but in September 1906 he tells his brother, Stanislaus, that Griffith's *United Irishman* is the only newspaper of any pretensions in Ireland.

This year Moore's symbolist-inspired novel, *The Lake,* is published. In contrast with his naturalist novel, *Esther Waters* (1894), *The Lake* makes use of sustained symbols and imagery in a way that provides a useful comparison with what Joyce does in *A Portrait*. For the connection between Moore and Joyce see Chapters 3 and 4. First performance of Synge's play, *In the Shadow of the Glen*, at the Abbey Theatre. The play, written in a style closer to the people than Lady Gregory's Kiltartanese, was designed to give voice to the country people of Ireland. The publishing house, Maunsel and Company, is launched in Dublin by George Roberts, Stephen Gwynn, and Joseph Hone.

---

44 According to Fran O'Rourke the two 'errors' in Joyce's quotation from Aquinas on beauty 'confirm that he was working from memory rather than with the text.' See 'Joyce's Early Aesthetic' in *Journal of Modern Literature* 34:2 Winter 2011, 100. To my mind, they look more like mistakes, though why Joyce never corrected them for later editions is a mystery, unless he was happy to see them as Stephen's mistakes.

This photo of Arthur Griffith appeared in *The Voice of Ireland* (1923), a celebratory book which carries on its front cover 'A Memorial of Freedom's Day'. Griffith led the Irish delegation in 1921 which negotiated Ireland's independence from Britain. Two decades earlier, the ground for independence was being laid by Griffith and other advanced nationalists.

1906 May: first number of Griffith's new paper, *Sinn Fein*, appears. By June Joyce has almost completed *Stephen Hero*, the bulk of which was written between October 1904 and June 1906. July: Joyce takes his family to Rome, where he works as a foreign correspondent in a bank. Rome reminds him of 'a man who lives by exhibiting to travellers his grandmother's corpse'. September: Joyce conceives another story for *Dubliners*, to be called 'Ulysses'. In October, Joyce follows with interest the Italian socialist congress in Rome, and in a letter to Stanislaus he draws a comparison between Arturo Labriola and Arthur Griffith.

1907 January: riots take place at the Abbey Theatre when Synge's *Playboy of the Western World* is first staged. The audience object to the stain on Irish womanhood and, more generally, to the image of the country people of Ireland broadcast to the world. Joyce watches these events from a distance but with interest, and he composes 'The Dead' that summer in its wake. Synge's play and Joyce's short story belong together as important literary responses to defining Irish identity at this time.

February: defeated by the experience of Rome and failing to secure a job in Marseilles, Joyce returns to Trieste. He is employed again at the Berlitz school until autumn, but leaves over a financial disagreement with the management. His brother, Stanislaus, continues at the school and eventually is promoted to deputy director. March: Joyce meets Ettore Schmitz (aka Italo Svevo) at the Berlitz school and becomes his private tutor. Their friendship flourishes and Joyce makes effective use of him in his portrait of Leopold Bloom in *Ulysses*, while the figure of Anna Livia Plurabelle in *Finnegans Wake* is indebted to Svevo's wife, Livia.

Early May: *Chamber Music* is published by Elkin Mathews in London. Joyce writes articles for *Il Piccolo della Sera*, a Triestine newspaper. Lucia, their daughter, is born on 26 July. November: Elkin Mathews decides against publishing *Dubliners*. In 1907 Joyce embarks on a dramatic course to reshape *Stephen Hero*, and, by the end of November, he has rewritten the first chapter. This is not Chapter 1 of *A Portrait*, for much of that was inserted later. Edmund Gosse's much-admired autobiography, *Father and Son*, is published with a title that would not be out of place when we think about *A Portrait*. Taking its cue from the later work of Paul Cezanne, Cubism, a short-lived but influential artistic movement, begins under the leadership of Georges Braque and Picasso, and the first Cubist exhibition is held in Paris. A generation ago, the North American critic, Hugh Kenner, enigmatically declared that *A Portrait* was the first Cubist novel in the language.

1908 By April the third chapter of what became *A Portrait* is finished. Then follows the darkest period of the 'seven lost years' of *A Portrait*, about which we know little.[45] September: Patrick Pearse opens St Enda's school for boys in Rathfarnham, Dublin.

1909 March: Joyce writes an article on Wilde for the Triestine newspaper, *Il Piccolo della Sera*. According to Joyce, Wilde was a 'court jester to the English' in the tradition of Irish writers stretching from Sheridan to Shaw, a tradition that Joyce would never follow. The same month Synge dies of cancer at the age of thirty-seven.

July: in search of an Irish publisher for *Dubliners* and to investigate the possibility of a post at University College Dublin, Joyce returns to Ireland with his son, Giorgio. 26-7 August: he visits Nora's family in Galway and listens to Nora's mother singing 'The Lass of Aughrim', the song that Bartell D'Arcy sings in 'The Dead'. During his time in Dublin he composes a series of personal letters to Nora, the so-called 'dirty letters'. September: he returns to Trieste with his sister Eva. October: he makes a subsequent visit to Dublin in connection with the Volta cinema project, a project which proves fruitless. However, the burgeoning of early cinema is put to good use in Joyce's fiction, especially in how he constructs the narrative voice as well as in the technique of juxtaposition and in deliberately and abruptly switching angles. The first chapter of *A Portrait* owes much to cinematic techniques.

1910 Returns to Trieste on 2 January with his sister, Eileen. Maunsel and Company postpone publication of *Dubliners*. Death of Edward VII in May; succeeded by George V.

1911 In February, overcome with frustration over publishing and writing, Joyce throws a draft of the manuscript of *A Portrait* into the stove, but, fortunately, it is immediately retrieved by his sister, Eileen, and Nora. Home Rule Bill, which promised a greater degree of Irish

---

45 For the background sources to *A Portrait*, which includes a detailed analysis of the various notebooks including the Paris Notebook Joyce composed in 1902-3 and the Pola Notebook he composed in 1905, see Robert Scholes and Richard M. Kain (eds.), *The Workshop of Daedalus: James Joyce and the Raw Materials for A Portrait of the Artist* (Evanston, Illinois: Northwestern University Press, 1965).

autonomy, is passed in House of Commons, but is rejected in the Lords. The first volume of George Moore's autobiography, *Hail and Farewell*, published.

1912 May: on the passage of the Third Home Rule Bill at Westminster and no doubt with the Christmas Dinner scene in *A Portrait* fresh in his mind, Joyce writes an article on 'The Shade of Parnell' for *Il Piccolo della Sera*, a tribute to the 'uncrowned king' of Ireland.

July-August: Joyce's last journey back to Ireland. Visits Nora's family in Galway and cycles out to Oughterard, some 17 miles from Galway, to see for himself the graveyard where he imagined Michael Furey was buried. The visit inspires his poem, 'She Weeps Over Rahoon'. His attempt to persuade George Roberts of Maunsel to publish *Dubliners* again proves unsuccessful, this time because the printer refuses to handle the unpatriotic sheets. On his way home to Trieste he composes his most vitriolic poem, 'Gas from a Burner'.

Publication of George Saintsbury's *A History of English Prose Rhythm* (1912), a book Joyce raided when he composed the 'Oxen of the Sun' episode of *Ulysses*.

1913 January: Third Home Rule Bill is defeated in the House of Lords. Political events in Ireland reveal a sharpening of divisions most evident in the establishment of the Ulster Volunteer Force in the North and the Irish Volunteers in the South. Dublin lockout of workers by employers, led by William Murphy. On Yeats's suggestion, Pound writes to Joyce seeking material to publish. Lawrence's novel, *Sons and Lovers*, which draws heavily on his own life and sexuality, is published. Publication of the first volume of *À la recherche du temps perdu* (Remembrance of Things Past), a novel in seven volumes by Marcel Proust and completed in 1927. When Joyce meets Proust in Paris in 1922 they complain about their aches and pains, Joyce telling Frank Budgen 'Our conversation consisted solely of the word "no".'

1914 An important year for Joyce's career as a writer. On 2 February the serial publication of *A Portrait* begins in the *The Egoist*, a literary magazine edited by the anarchist Dora Marsden and the socialist Harriett Shaw Weaver. Only four extracts were published because the editors feared legal action on account of obscene material. (See above for the advert in *The Egoist* May 1917.) Joyce begins writing *Exiles*, a play indebted in part to his youthful hero, Ibsen. He also turns his attention to writing *Ulysses*. June: *Dubliners* is published by

Photo of Ezra Pound possibly taken in Sussex when he was wintering with Yeats at Stone Cottage in 1913-5.

Grant Richards in London. The same month sees the first issue of Wyndham Lewis's modernist magazine *Blast*. August: outbreak of the Great War. September: Third Home Rule Bill receives royal assent, but its operation is suspended because of the War. Irish Republican Brotherhood secretly appoints a committee to launch a military rising in the belief that 'England's difficulty is Ireland's opportunity'.

1915 January: Stanislaus Joyce is arrested in Trieste and interned by the Austrian authorities for his outspoken Irredentist (pro-Italian) views. June: Joyce and his family move to neutral Zurich. Finishes *Exiles*. With the help of Yeats, Pound, and Gosse, Joyce is awarded a pension from the Royal Literary Fund, to be followed in 1916 by a Civil List pension. June: Eliot's 'The Love Song of J. Alfred Prufrock', a poem that defined an age, published in the magazine *Poetry*. *The Rainbow*, Lawrence's novel about the emergence of the modern world seen through the eyes of three generations of the one family, is published. The same year sees the publication of Ford Madox Ford's *The Good Soldier*, a highly original modernist novel.

1916 March: Yeats's *Reveries Over Childhood and Youth*, the first volume of his autobiography, published by Macmillan. April: the Easter Rising in Dublin by the Irish Volunteers under Patrick Pearse and the Irish Citizen Army under James Connolly. Sheehy Skeffington, who had been attempting to stop looting in the centre of Dublin, is summarily executed by a British army captain. The Rising is brought speedily to an end but not without considerable destruction to central parts of Dublin. May: execution of leaders of Rising (de Valera's American background saves him). The mood in the country swings behind those who sought to break the link with Britain; soon the Rising is known as the Sinn Fein Rising. August: Roger Casement hanged for treason for his part in a gun-running episode in Ireland. Between July and November the Battle of the Somme, one of the key battles in the Great War, waged. One million soldiers were either killed or wounded. Meanwhile, in December *A Portrait* is published by Benjamin Huebsch in New York. In Zurich the Dadaist movement takes off.

1917 12 February: British edition of *A Portrait* published by the Egoist Press in London. 22 February: Joyce receives his first gift of money from an anonymous donor, Harriet Shaw Weaver. She continues supporting him even though she disapproves of his drinking habits among others. When Joyce died she became the executrix and administrator of Joyce's estate. She also assumed the role of guardian for Lucia, the mentally ill daughter of Joyce. In 1951 Weaver was responsible for Lucia's admission to St Andrew's Hospital (now Healthcare) in Northampton, where she lived out the rest of her life until her death in 1982. March: Russian Revolution. August: Joyce's first eye operation. July: de Valera, in prison in England, elected in landslide victory as Sinn Fein candidate for East Clare. November: Yeats's *The Wild Swans at Coole* is published by the Cuala Press, a small press run by Yeats's sisters, Elizabeth and Lily. On doctor's advice, Joyce winters in Locarno in Switzerland.

1918 March: *The Little Review* in New York begins serialization of *Ulysses*. Thirteen or so episodes appear until stopped by a court action brought by the New York Society for the Prevention of Vice in December 1920. April: Joyce takes over management of English Players; row with Henry Carr, an English actor, after a performance of Wilde's *The Importance of Being Earnest*. May: *Exiles* is published in London and New York. June: Nora plays Cathleen in a production of Synge's *Riders to the Sea*. In the autumn Joyce considers having an affair with Marthe Fleischmann, who lives in a flat opposite and whom he mistakenly imagines to be Jewish. November: end of the Great War. December: Sinn Fein wins landslide victory in general election in Ireland.

1919 January: War of Independence (the Anglo-Irish War) begins; ends July 1921 with Anglo-Irish Treaty. April: de Valera elected President of Dáil Éireann, the lower house in the provisional government in Ireland. October: Joyce and family return to Trieste.

1920 July: encouraged by Pound, Joyce moves to Paris with his family. March: Pound's *Hugh Selwyn Mauberley*, a significant contribution to modernist verse, is published. March: the Auxiliary Division, a paramilitary unit of the Royal Irish Constabulary, made up of former British officers, is responsible for the murder on 7 March of George Clancy, Mayor of Limerick. To help the Auxiliary Division, a Black-and-Tan force of temporary soldiers, the brainchild of Winston Churchill, is formed. In an attempt to break the will of resistance during the War of Independence, they terrorise the local population, burn down villages, and commit acts of reprisals against anyone they deem is harbouring members of the IRA. To this day, as if the trauma still lingers, the atrocities of the Black and Tans are remembered.

October: Terence MacSwiney, Mayor of Cork, dies in Brixton Prison on hunger strike. Lawrence's novel, *Women in Love*, a sequel to *The Rainbow*, is published.

1921 Sylvia Beach agrees to publish *Ulysses* in Paris. *Nouvelle Revue Française*, one of France's leading French literary magazines of the twentieth century, helps to publicise it. June: rift between Joyce and Budgen develops and lasts for three years. December: Anglo-Irish Treaty is signed in London. A split opens in the ranks of Sinn Fein, between those who accept the Treaty and those who oppose it, with de Valera leading the anti-Treaty faction.

1922 *Annus mirabilis* for Joyce and other modernist writers. The Shakespeare and Company edition of *Ulysses* appears on 2 February, Joyce's fortieth birthday. Civil war develops in Ireland between those who accepted the Treaty and the Republicans (as they came to be called) who did not. April: Nora and children, while on board a train to visit to her family in Galway, come under fire from both sides. August: death of Griffith. Michael Collins, a leader of the pro-Treaty side, is killed in an ambush in County Cork. In November Erskine Childers, who took the Republican side in the civil war, is convicted of possessing an illegal weapon and executed by the new Provisional Government. Childers, the author of the popular novel, *The Riddle of the Sands* (1903), was a late convert to Irish nationalism. With Griffith he helped to front the Irish delegation who negotiated the Anglo-Irish Treaty with the British government in 1920. The link with Joyce focuses particularly on the name of his cousin, Hugh Culling Eardly Childers, who was a leading nineteenth-century British politician and who attracted the nickname 'Here Comes Everybody' on account of his size. In *Finnegans Wake* the name of the male protagonist is Humphrey Chimpden Earwicker, and, throughout the text, Joyce plays with his initials, HCE.

Eliot's *The Waste Land*, the most famous poem of the twentieth century, is printed in *The Criterion* magazine in London. Mussolini marches on Rome. Also in November Howard Carter discovers the nearly intact tomb of Tutankhamun. *Finnegans Wake* never stops reminding us of Joyce's general interest in those who are dead to the world and also, in particular, in the Egyptian Book of the Dead.

1923 March: Joyce begins writing *Finnegans Wake*. May: end of civil war in Ireland. Figures for those killed are difficult to determine, but

THE TAXI-CAB OF MICHAEL COLLINS PASSING INTO THE CASTLE YARD TO " TAKE OVER " FROM THE VICEROY.

Michael Collins here arriving by taxi at Dublin Castle to take back control from the British. The photo and caption are from *The Voice of Ireland* (1923). In retrospect, we can see that *A Portrait*, too, belongs to this wider movement of taking back control.

one recent estimate puts the total below 2,000, with 750 members of the National Army, around 400 members of the IRA, and 200 civilians. For several generations thereafter bitterness overshadows Irish politics. Some critics have suggested that *Finnegans Wake*, with a prominent place allocated to the warring bothers, Shem and Shaun, constitutes or resembles a civil war text. Joyce spends summer vacation at Bognor Regis in Sussex.

1924 First fragment of 'Work in Progress' appears in *Transatlantic Review* in Paris. Joyce suffers severe eye trouble. March: French translation of *A Portrait* appears under title *Dedalus: Portrait de l'artiste jeune par lui-même* (Dedalus: portrait of the young artist by himself). In the summer, while staying at Saint-Malo, Joyce visits Renan's birthplace at Tréguier in Brittany.

1925 Several more fragments of 'Work in Progress' published. Publication of Yeats's *A Vision*, a complex study from an occult perspective outlining his theory of history, religion, people, and the world.

1926 Publication of a pirated edition of *Ulysses* in the United States. First German translation of *A Portrait*. First French translation of *Dubliners*. February: riots break out at the Abbey Theatre during the first performance of *The Plough and the Stars*, Sean O'Casey's tragi-comedy set during the Easter Rising of 1916.

1927 The first of seventeen installments of 'Work in Progress' appear in *transition*, a literary magazine edited by Eugene Jolas in Paris. *Pomes Penyeach* is published by Shakespeare and Company in Paris. First German translation of *Ulysses*. Virginia Woolf's visionary novel, *To The Lighthouse*, is published.

1928 *Anna Livia Plurabelle* published by Crosby Gaige in New York. First German translation of *Dubliners*. Yeats's *The Tower* published. Publication of Lawrence's *Lady Chatterley's Lover*, a novel which, together with *Ulysses*, constitutes one of the most influential, sexually explicit, 'underground' novels of the twentieth century. The novel was banned until 1960.

1929 *Tales Told of Shem and Shaun* is released by Black Sun Press in Paris. *Our Exagmination round his Factification for Incamination of Work in Progress* is published by Shakespeare and Company. The volume includes an important essay by Samuel Beckett. First French translation of *Ulysses,* honoured by a special 'Déjeuner Ulysse', hosted by Sylvia Beach and Adrienne Monnier. William Faulkner's *The Sound and the Fury*, a novel indebted in part to *Ulysses*, published.

1930 *Haveth Childers Everywhere* published in Paris and New York. Joyce undergoes an eye operation in Zurich. May: Beckett is refused access to Joyce household after being accused of trifling with Lucia's feelings. Marriage of Giorgio Joyce and Helen Kastor Fleischman. Joyce spends time promoting the Irish tenor, John Sullivan.

1931 Marriage of James and Nora Joyce at Kensington Registry Office on 4 July. September: rift between Joyce and Sylvia Beach over an American publication of *Ulysses*. Death of Joyce's father, John Joyce, on 29 December.

1932 15 February: birth of Stephen Joyce, son of Giorgio and Helen Joyce; Joyce's poem 'Ecce Puer' (behold a boy) written the same day. Lucia has her first breakdown caused by schizophrenia. Paul Léon becomes Joyce's secretary. De Valera, leader of Fianna Fáil, comes to power in Ireland (continues as Taoiseach until 1948).

1933 Lucia is hospitalized in Switzerland. Court in New York lifts ban on *Ulysses*. An English edition of *Ulysses* is published by the Odyssey Press in Hamburg and printed in Leipzig. Yeats's *The Winding Stair* published. Hitler becomes German Chancellor.

1934 *Ulysses* published in the United States by Random House. May: Giorgio and his family leave for the United States, where they remain until November 1935. In June, *The Mime of Mick, Nick and the Maggies* is published. Joyce takes Lucia to see Carl Jung for therapy.

1935 Lucia stays with relatives in Ireland and with Weaver in England, but her mental health continues to decline. She is admitted to St Andrew's Hospital, Northampton, for blood tests.

1936 Joyce's *Collected Poems* published in New York. Spanish Civil War begins. Joyce's final estrangement from his patron, Weaver.

1937 *Storiella as She is Syung,* the last fragment of 'Work in Progress' to be published. New constitution of Eire approved. In July Picasso's painting, 'Guernica', is exhibited for the first time in Paris.

1938 In January, after Beckett is stabbed by a pimp in a street in Paris, Joyce arranges for a private room at the hospital where he is taken. 'Work in Progress' completed; in July Joyce reveals its title: *Finnegans Wake*. Hyde becomes first President of Ireland. May: Yeats's *New Poems* published.

1939 Death of Yeats on 28 January. May: *Finnegans Wake* published by Faber and Faber in London and the Viking Press in New York. *At Swim-Two-Birds*, Flann O'Brien's extraordinary novel, is also published this year. When war is declared, Joyce is preoccupied with Lucia and her continuing hospitalization. De Valera pursues a policy of neutrality for Ireland.

1940 Yeats's final volume, *Last Poems and Plays*, is published. In December, forced to flee Nazi-occupied France, Joyce returns to Zurich, helped by his friends including the art critic, Carola Giedeon-Welcker.

1941 On 13 January Joyce dies in Zurich from a perforated duodenal ulcer. Two days later he is buried in the Fluntern Cemetery in Zurich.

Two editions of *Stephen Hero*, the more restrained one published by Jonathan
Cape in 1944 and the more enticing paperback version by Ace Books
at the beginning of the 1960s. Not surprisingly Joyce has created
his own audiences.

A street sign in Paris confirming the arrival of the Irish. Photo: the author.

On 25 January the Irish Minister of Supplies, Sean Lemass, declares, 'We in this country have a right to be neutral if we so decide.' 28 March: Virginia Woolf takes her own life by drowning in the River Ouse near her home at Rodmel in Sussex.

1942 April: death of Joyce's secretary, Paul Léon, in the concentration camp at Auschwitz.

1944 The surviving manuscript of *Stephen Hero* is published. In turn the publication contributes to a reassessment of *A Portrait*.

1947 This year sees the publication of *Under the Volcano*, a beautifully crafted novel by the English writer Malcolm Lowry about an alcoholic British consul living in Cuernavaca, Mexico. Set on one day, the Day of the Dead, in 1938, it takes forward the experimental fictional path pioneered by *Ulysses*.

1949 James Joyce Exhibition at La Hune Gallery in Paris, the first major retrospective for Joyce in post-war Europe. Ireland (now Eire) formally declares itself a republic and ceases to be a member of the British Commonwealth.

1951 10 April: Nora Joyce dies in Zurich. Lucia is admitted as a mental patient to St Andrews Hospital in Northampton, where she remains until her death in 1982.

1953 Beckett's *En attendant Godot* is given its first performance in Paris, followed in 1955 by *Waiting for Godot* in London. Without Joyce and Beckett, the Irish writers who found a home in Paris, modern literature would be unimaginable.

1955 Death of Stanislaus Joyce in Trieste.

'Some Persons of "the Nineties"', a caricature by Max Beerbohm from his book *Observations* (1925). Figures on back row include Richard Le Gallienne, George Moore (third left), the suitably attired Wilde and Yeats airily gesticulating; on front row Arthur Symons, Henry Harland, editor of *The Yellow Book*, Beerbohm himself, and Aubrey Beardsley.
Copyright to the Estate of Max Beerbohm.

CHAPTER 3: *A PORTRAIT* IN PERSPECTIVE: THE AESTHETIC MOVEMENT

The word 'Artist' in *A Portrait of the Artist as a Young Man* invites a wide-ranging response, and the same can be said for the artistic contexts which surround and inform the novel. Omit the word 'Artist' from the title and we are left with 'A Portrait of a Young Man', which might recall Henry James's *Portrait of a Lady* (1881), an Anglo-American novel of fine consciousness, or of George Moore's autobiographical reflections on his time in Paris with leading French artists in *Confessions of a Young Man* (1888). By rights, Moore's account should have included somewhere in the title the word 'artist'. Joyce is more explicit, for his *bildungsroman*, or novel of education, assigns a prominent place to 'Artist', and serves as a forceful illustration not only of the individual's growth as a person but also of a discourse on art which became increasingly insistent as it gathered momentum throughout the nineteenth century.

In the closing decades of that century, the discourse on art in France and Britain issued in the aesthetic movement and in the late flowering of symbolism. With a protagonist who is an artist in the making and whose mind turns readily to literature for comfort and inspiration, *A Portrait* emerges against a sophisticated artistic background and in turn speaks to it. When we listen to the Jesuit-educated Stephen Dedalus defining art and beauty in terms deriving from Aristotle and Aquinas, we are conscious at the same time of the currents of a contemporary debate which included, among many others, Joris-Karl Huysmans, Walter Pater, William Morris, Oscar Wilde, George Moore, and Yeats himself. Indeed, even if he resisted an invitation to join them, Joyce not only followed in the wake of his predecessors, but he also carried forward their programme.

If we list in chronological order from the 1830s to the 1890s key quotes by influential writers at the time, we can observe how the course of that debate on art and aesthetics has a processional quality. Not everything contributed to the unfolding procession, but it is remarkable how, in retrospect, we can track a movement emerging and acquiring legitimacy in the post-romantic period.

• 'The only things that are really beautiful are those which have no use.' Théophile Gautier, Preface to *Mademoiselle de Maupin*, 1835.[46]
• 'Poetry...has no goal other than itself...and no poem will be so great, so noble, so truly worthy of the name of poetry as that which will have been written solely for the pleasure of writing a poem.' Charles Baudelaire, Essay on Théophile Gautier, 1859. [47]
• 'Art for art's sake first of all, and afterwards we may suppose all the rest shall be added to her...but from the man who falls to artistic work with a moral purpose, shall be taken away even that which he has.' Algernon Swinburne, *William Blake: A Critical Essay*, 1868.[48]
• 'To regard all things and principles of things as inconstant modes or fashions has more and more become the tendency of modern thought.... Not the fruit of experience, but experience itself is the end.' Walter Pater, *Studies in the History of the Renaissance*, 1873.[49]
• '*Vivre? Les serviteurs feront cela pour nous.*' ('As for living, our servants

---

46 Théophile Gautier, *Mademoiselle de Maupin* (trans. Helen Constantine) (intro. Patricia Duncker) (1835; London: Penguin, 2005), 23. For an alternative translation, 'There is nothing really beautiful save what is of no possible use.' See *The Romances of Théophile Gautier, Mademoiselle de Maupin* (trans. F.C.De Sumicrast) (1835; Boston, MA: Little Brown, 1912), 82.
47 Charles Baudelaire, *Baudelaire As A Literary Critic* (trans. Lois Boe Hyslop and Francis E.Hyslop) (University Park, PA: Pennsylvania State University Press, 1964), 162.
48 Algernon Swinburne, *William Blake: A Critical Essay* (London: John Camden Hotten, 1868), 91.
49 Walter Pater, *Studies in the History of the Renaissance* (1873; London: Oxford University Press, 2010), 118-19.

will do that for us.') Villiers de l'Isle Adam, *Axël*, 1890.[50]
• 'All art is at once surface and symbol.... All art is quite useless.'
Oscar Wilde, *The Picture of Dorian Gray*, 1891.[51]
• 'What distinguishes the Symbolism of our day from the Symbolism
of the past is that it has now become conscious of itself.' Arthur
Symons, *The Symbolist Movement in Literature*, 1899.[52]

When we reflect on the origins and course of the aesthetic movement,
we frequently encounter the ubiquitous phrase 'art-for-art's sake'.
This was the cry Gautier popularised in the 1830s, and, a generation
later in Swinburne's monograph on William Blake, it is again to the
fore. In the art world in Britain, Dante Gabriel Rossetti and the Pre-
Raphaelites were among the pioneering spirits. In France in the 1870s,
Impressionism, which took its name from Claude Monet's painting
Impression, Sunrise (1874), came to prominence. It was followed in the
1880s by the deliberately confrontational figure of Huysmans, author
of *Against Nature* (1884).[53]

Whether explicitly or implicitly, the stress on subjectivity, on
impressions for example or on moods, especially evident in Joyce's
volume of poems, *Chamber Music*, pushed aside traditional certainties
and began to transform our idea of ourselves as well as our view of
culture and society. Artists and, by implication, writers were not to
involve themselves in anything but their art. Art was independent
of the world of morality, religion or politics. Let the artist draw

---

50 Villiers de l'Isle Adam, *Axël* (Paris: Maison Quantin, 1890), 283. Yeats
chose this quotation as an epigraph to *The Secret Rose* (1897). *Axel's Castle*
by the American critic, Edmund Wilson, and first published in 1931, was a
pioneering critical study exploring how modern literature, including writers
such as Yeats, Eliot, and Joyce, emerged out of late-nineteenth-century
symbolism and the aesthetic movement.
51 Oscar Wilde, *The Picture of Dorian Gray*, (1891; Richmond, Surrey: Alma
Classics, 2017), 4. One of the classics in Joyce studies is by Robert M. Adams
and is entitled *Surface and Symbol: The Consistency of James Joyce's Ulysses*
(London: Oxford University Press, 1962). Many other studies in the 1950s and
1960s also explored Joyce's writings by yoking together realism and symbolism.
52 Arthur Symons, *The Symbolist Movement in Literature* (intro. Richard
Ellmann) (1899; New York: E.P.Dutton, 1958), 2. Symons dedicated his study
to Yeats, whom he called 'the chief representative' of the symbolist movement
in 'our country'.
53 Joris-Karl Huysmans, *Against Nature* (*A rebours*) (trans. Margaret Mauldon)
(intro. Nicholas White) (London: Oxford University Press, 2009). 'Against the
grain' is an alternative translation.

a line around art and the beautiful and concentrate on the world within. Or, as Joyce expressed it in an early essay attacking the Irish Literary Theatre, an essay with the provocative title 'The Day of the Rabblement': 'No man, said the Nolan, can be a lover of the true or the good unless he abhors the multitude; and the artist, though he may employ the crowd, is very careful to isolate himself.' (*CW* 69)[54]

Today the term 'art-for-art's sake' has been emptied of much of its force. But throughout the nineteenth century in France, Britain and elsewhere, art-for-art's sake had both its advocates and its detractors. That art had no moral purpose or should embrace inconstant fashions was quite alarming for some. On the other hand, when writers insisted on the immorality of art, this was not to celebrate licentious behaviour (although there was an element of this to it). Rather, it was to underline that ethics and aesthetics occupied different terrain, and that only by separating them could new art take shape or new forms of writing emerge. To consider art as useless, as Gautier or Wilde imply, or as evanescent, as Pater suggests, has always had the potential to unsettle polite opinion, but such a disturbance became particularly acute with the break-up of traditional values in the nineteenth century. At the inaugural dinner of the literary magazine, *The Yellow Book*, held in London's Soho in 1894, 'People were puzzled and shocked and delighted, and yellow became the colour of the hour, the symbol of the time-spirit.' As Holbrook Jackson, the historian of the Nineties, noted, yellow became 'associated with all that was *bizarre* and queer in art and life, and with all that was outrageously modern.'[55]

In this chapter the focus is on four aspects which have a direct or indirect bearing on *A Portrait*: Huysmans's novel *Against Nature*, Walter Pater, symbolism, and Oscar Wilde. The aim is to better appreciate the nineteenth-century literary contexts behind Joyce's novel. Joyce's rebelliousness is both home-grown and part of a European movement, and it worth spending time on how Joyce learned his trade from

---

54 The 'Nolan' refers to one of Joyce's favorite philosophers, Giordano Bruno of Nola, who was burned at the stake in 1600 for heresy. In his 1903 review, 'The Bruno Philosophy', Joyce writes enthusiastically about Bruno's active brain, his vehement temper, and his rapturous mysticism. (*CW* 132-40) For Joyce, the artist and the heretic had much in common. Bruno features prominently in *Finnegans Wake*.

55 Holbrook Jackson, *The Eighteen Nineties: A Review of Art and Ideas at the Close of the Nineteenth Century* (1913; reprinted London: Grant Richards, 1922; Brighton: Edward Everett Root, 2017, intro. Christophe Campos), 46.

others both in Britain and in continental Europe. In a public lecture delivered to an audience in Trieste in 1907, Joyce suggested that 'Ireland's contribution to European literature can be divided into five periods and into two large parts' (CW 176). He had clearly given some thought to this, though we can leave aside the periods and the parts and concentrate on Joyce himself. The particular comment came in a lecture on James Clarence Mangan, a neglected Irish poet from the 1840s. Joyce identified with Mangan, and, at times, as when he suggests that Mangan wrote 'without a native literary tradition' (182), he could almost be addressing his own position outside the emerging Literary Revival. In 1907, three years into his sojourn in Europe, the contribution Joyce is defining for his native country is not to English literature but to European literature. As much as the essay is about Mangan and Irishness, it is also, then, about Joyce and his European home.

Joyce's European identity began with his entry at baptism into the Holy Roman Catholic Church, whose liturgy was in Latin, whose saints were largely European, and whose theologians and heresiarchs were also for the most part continental. His favourite saint was St Thomas Aquinas, his favourite heretic was Bruno of Nolan, and both were Italian. Saint Aloysius Gonzaga, a Jesuit priest from Rome and a model for young boys on account of his purity, was the name Joyce chose for his confirmation. The hell, fire, and damnation sermon, which Stephen hears in A Portrait, was plagiarised by Joyce from a seventeenth-century tract by an Italian Jesuit.[56] Twenty years later, in conversation with Frank Budgen, Joyce made a celebrated if arcane distinction: 'You allude to me as a Catholic. Now for the sake of precision, and to get the correct contour on me, you ought to allude to me as a Jesuit.' (JJ 27)

As an undergraduate at what is now University College Dublin, Joyce studied modern languages, and, under his Italian tutor, the Jesuit priest, Charles Ghezzi, he read Dante in the original. He also bought copies of Flaubert's novels in French for his own use, and translated two of Hauptmann's plays from German into English. Much of his reading was outside the formal curriculum, and he

---

56 See *Hell Opened to Christians, To Caution Them from Entering into It*, which was written by Giovanni Pietro Pinamonti, a seventeenth-century Jesuit. The English translation was printed in Dublin for J. Nolan in 1823. A later edition was published in 1845 by T.Richardson and Son for the Catholic Truth Society..

Postcard of a lively street scene in Trieste in 1910. It is not unreasonable to assume that, for the most part, when he stepped out of his flat of a morning, whether in Trieste or Zurich or Paris, Joyce would have heard every language but his own.

put it all to good use. Thus, he learned Norwegian in order to be able to read Ibsen in the original. There was always an element of winning out against his rivals, but Joyce's facility with languages was commented on favourably by his contemporaries. In addition, his language learning was accompanied by an interest in different literatures and by the ideas informing those cultures. *A Portrait* never ceases being unmistakably Irish, but its direction of travel is away from Ireland and towards continental Europe.

AGAINST NATURE

At the Marquess of Queensberry libel trial in 1895, Wilde was cross-examined by Edward Carson, Queensberry's prosecutor. Among other accusations, Carson claimed that the 'poisonous' book in Wilde's possession was Huysmans's *Against Nature*.[57] Subsequently, Wilde withdrew his libel case against Queensberry and the courts gained their first victory over Wilde, a victory which was felt throughout Europe. *Against Nature* was a novel composed against the grain of contemporary opinion, so much so that when it was published in Paris in 1884 it became the bible of the Décadents. In retrospect, it was, according to the social and art historian, Arnold Hauser, 'the principal document of…anti-natural and anti-practical aestheticism'.[58] Huysmans's hyper-sensitive and critical anti-hero, Des Esseintes, seeks an escape from the banality of life, and in the process he subverts everything dear to the bourgeoisie, not least their dependence on a hierarchy of significance. For Des Esseintes, 'artifice was the distinguishing characteristic of human genius' (20), 'obsessions both libertine and mystical mingled together' (91). As for his frankness with regard to sexuality or attitudes to mistresses and

---

57 The Marquess of Queensberry, the father of Wilde's young lover Bosie, had accused Wilde of 'posing as a sodomite', which resulted in Wilde bringing a libel case against him. For a recent discussion of the 'poisonous' book, see Peter Raby, 'Poisoned by a Book: The Lethal Aura of *The Picture of Dorian Gray*' in Kerry Powell and Peter Raby (eds.), *Oscar Wilde in Context* (Cambridge: Cambridge University Press, 2013). For a recent biography of Wilde, which seeks to situate him in his time and thereby to rescue him from the bias of later interpretations, see Matthew Sturgis, *Oscar Wilde: A Life* (London: Hodder and Stoughton, 2018).

58 Arnold Hauser, *The Social History of Art: Naturalism, Expressionism and the Film Age Volume 4* (1951; London: Routledge and Kegan Paul, 1977), 173. Hauser also has in mind Villiers de l'Isle-Adam's *Axël* (1890).

prostitutes, this must have delighted readers wanting to get away from respectability and a diet of moralising fiction.

One of the phrases in the novel, 'devout and blasphemous' (132), is missing from *A Portrait,* but expressions such as this might well have contributed to Joyce's views when confronting the Church's authority in Ireland. He would almost certainly never have heard the phrase on the lips of his Jesuit teachers, but in Catholic France disaffection and rebellion against the dominant religion had a long history, and with it came a complex set of unorthodox or irreligious responses. It would be surprising if Huysmans's novel did not have a liberating effect on an Irish Catholic boy, a boy who in his own country couldn't be both 'devout and blasphemous'. At Clongowes Wood College Joyce had been confined, in the words of Kevin Sullivan, to such a 'fervid religious atmosphere' that he later imagined he might have a vocation to the priesthood.[59]

Interestingly, it would have been natural for Joyce to draw a line under his past, but Stephen's intense religious phase after the retreat at Belvedere is not dismissed out of hand but rendered with honesty and sensitivity. In turn the reader allows Stephen space to travel such a road, even if we know it will prove to be a cul-de-sac. So *A Portrait* is not a novel which could be called 'against nature'. In many respects it lacks extremism. Indeed, in the face of convention and of the clamour of 'the rabblement', Joyce avoids recourse to what might be considered outrageous. Instead, he insists on courage and the integrity of the individual as well as on the paramount importance of listening to (and obeying) the sexual demands of the body, even if that led to exile away from Ireland.

When juxtaposing the two novels, therefore, we need to be conscious of how they are similar and where they differ. It is true that *A Portrait* is set against the grain of contemporary opinion, particularly in Ireland, but it never achieved the status of notoriety that accompanied the publication of *Against Nature.* It might seem surprising to some, but, in advancing his cause, Joyce respected certain limits as to what was possible in the English-speaking world. Its most rebellious moment should be the cry *Non serviam* (*P* 117) (I will not serve), Lucifer's defiant utterance on exiting heaven, but in *A Portrait* this phrase is embedded in the priest's words in the retreat sermon. When it finally appears on Stephen's lips, it is almost lost in the outline

---

59 Kevin Sullivan, *Joyce Among the Jesuits* (New York: Columbia University Press, 1958), 119.

of a programme ending in the more memorable and quieter triplet of 'silence, exile, and cunning' (P 247).

No sooner have we embarked on reading *Against Nature* than we learn that the protagonist's passion for women was spent, that he was an expert at distinguishing between genuine and deceptive shades of colour, and that he had acquired a reputation for eccentricity. The accumulation of one wry observation after another must have struck a chord with Joyce, who went on to create his own kaleidoscope of misrule in *Finnegans Wake*, but Huysmans's appeal to Joyce went further:

> Many times had Des Esseintes reflected upon the thorny problem of how to condense a novel into a few sentences, which would contain the quintessence of the hundreds of pages always required to establish the setting, sketch the characters, and provide a mass of observations and minor facts in corroboration. (162)

Eventually, after devoting over nine hundred pages to writing *Stephen Hero*, Joyce embarked on a process of cutting, condensing his opening, for example, into a short sequence rather than spending time on character and setting. Like Huysmans, Joyce in his apprentice years was a voracious reader, ruthlessly determined to cast aside anything which he couldn't use. 'My god! How few books there are that are worth rereading,' muses Des Esseintes with a sigh. (158) The tone is not Stephen's, but, like Huysmans, Joyce as a writer had no interest in marking time. And, like Des Esseintes, he read to sample and then, more often than not, to discard. Thus, he criticised a story in Moore's collection *The Untilled Field* (1903) when a woman, who has been living for three years on the line between Bray and Dublin, is told by her husband that there is a meeting in Dublin at which he must be present. She looks up the timetable to see the hours of the trains. 'This on D and WR where the trains go regularly: this after three years.' (*L II*, 71)[60]

As we reflect on the list of quotations above outlining the course of the aesthetic movement, we can also discern another current at work, where writers and artists sought above all else the autonomy of art in its confrontation with bourgeois society and the market-place. This was a battle that continued to be waged by artists and writers

---

60 Letter to Stanislaus Joyce, 19 November 1904. The D and WR was the Dublin and Wexford rail line.

into the modern period, none more so than by Joyce himself.[61] It was fine for Des Esseintes to rebel, but for writers or artists without any form of patronage the future was bleak. As is apparent from the chronology outlined in Chapter 2, during the second half of his life, Joyce needed financial support from Weaver and others. Even though he was in receipt of a pension from the Royal Literary Fund and the Civil List pension, without the patronage afforded in particular by Weaver it is difficult to imagine how he could have completed *Ulysses* and *Finnegans Wake*. One of Weaver's gifts in 1923 was for £21,000, or over £750,000 in today's money.[62] In 1919, after another patron, Edith Rockefeller, refused to fund him any longer, Joyce needed to sell some of his manuscripts to the wealthy New York lawyer, John Quinn. His involvement in the market led him in June 1925 to tell Weaver not that he has written 60,000 words but that he has 60,000 words to sell. Independence for the artist in Joyce's case came at a price, and, perhaps not surprisingly, his letters betray a constant preoccupation with money matters. The irony of all this was almost certainly lost on him.

WALTER PATER

Pater is a central figure both in the background and in the development of modern literature, and he had a particular influence on Joyce.[63] Pater writes, 'Not the fruit of experience, but experience itself is the end.' At the close of *A Portrait*, Stephen reminds us of the distinctive aura surrounding the word 'experience': 'Welcome, O life! I go to encounter for the millionth time the reality of experience and to forge in the smithy of my soul the uncreated conscience of my race.' (252-3) For both Pater and Joyce, experience is another word for intensity. Pater holds back from telling us what lies ahead after experience, but Joyce represents it as an opening onto a future in which he/Stephen will play a part in 'the uncreated conscience of his race', as he rather grandly puts

---

61 For a high-level discussion exploring these tensions in the context of French writers and artists in the nineteenth century, see Pierre Bourdieu, *The Rules of Art: Genesis and Structure of the Literary Field* (trans. Susan Emanuel) (Cambridge: Polity, 1996).

62 For these figures and equivalences, see Roger Norburn, *A James Joyce Chronology* (Basingstoke: Palgrave Macmillan, 2004).

63 When confronted by his peers at school to name the best prose writer in English, Stephen replies, 'Newman'. On reflection, he might have said 'Pater' and then drawn us into the role of another father-figure in the novel.

it. In paying attention to the 'reality of experience', then, Joyce insists not on a past set of experiences behind his protagonist's departure from Ireland, for his concern is not with the fruit of experience but with experience as an end in itself. From the moment Stephen, at the onset of adolescence, describes Dublin as a 'new and complex sensation' (66) to 'Welcome, O Life!', we know we are on a journey in pursuit of experience *per se*, and it is a journey which pushes back against the nets that would seek to fashion or contain it.

In Pater's portrait of *Marius the Epicurean: His Sensations and Ideas* (1885), an historical novel that was in Joyce's personal library in Trieste, we learn that, as a young boy, Marius:

> lived much in the realm of the imagination, and became betimes, as he was to continue all through life, something of an idealist, constructing the world for himself in great measure from within, by the exercise of meditative power. A vein of subjective philosophy, with the individual for its standard of all things, there would be always in his intellectual scheme of the world and of conduct, with a certain incapacity wholly to accept other men's valuations.[64]

This could be a description of the dreamy boy in *Reveries Over Childhood and Youth*, Yeats's autobiography published at the same time as *A Portrait*.[65] Both Yeats and Stephen construct the world from within and both resort to a subjective form of philosophy, which is occult and romantic in the poet's case and Aristotelian and classical in the case of Joyce and Stephen. Neither of them came to accept the valuations of others, although Yeats occasionally suffered humiliation at the hands of his father. According to Curran, a close friend of Joyce's at Belvedere College and university, 'Joyce lived a withdrawn life.... He was self-centred and centripetal.'[66] There was more, since, like Marius, Joyce had 'a peculiar expression of intellectual confidence, as of one who had indeed been initiated into a great secret' (157).

The confident-sounding tone Joyce adopts in his early essays, a tone close to a pose, recalls the prose of Pater in *Studies in the History*

---

64 Walter Pater, *Marius the Epicurean: His Sensations and Ideas* (1885; London: Penguin, 1985), 12.

65 W.B.Yeats, *Reveries Over Childhood and Youth* (London: Macmillan, 1916).

66 Constantine Curran, *James Joyce Remembered* (London: Oxford University Press, 1968), 21.

of the Renaissance. In Pater the tone reflects a mind at ease with its judgements, in Joyce a mind learning the skills of the aesthetic critic. [67] However, when we turn to Pater's influence in his fiction, we find constant echoes of Pater's novel in its narrative structure, in its themes, and in passages of lyrical intensity. Both *Marius the Epicurean* and *A Portrait* are novels of development, both concern sensations and ideas, both are about the individual versus society, both have protagonists who live much in the realm of the imagination, and both value language and integrity in a changing world. Where Pater returns to the classics for enlightenment, and in *Studies in the History of the Renaissance* for inspiration, Joyce adds Aquinas and medieval scholastic philosophy to the mix. Reading *A Portrait* in the light of *Marius the Epicurean* reminds us that both are novels not of opinions but of ideas. This is something which is particularly apparent in the final chapter, but throughout the novel Stephen is wrestling with ideas and his place in the world. Simon Dedalus, we might notice, has opinions, but Stephen recognizes his life depends on ideas.

In terms of ideas, their use of the past yields special insights into their similarities and differences. The past weighs heavily in both novels, but in Pater the present tends to be displaced or filtered through the lens of the past. Stephen's past is all around him, but he lives for the most part in the turmoil of the present. In the opening to the novel the present dominates our view even though the tense of the first three verbs is past: 'was', 'was', 'was', followed by his father's 'told'. Paradoxically, even when it feels up-close and personal, time present in *A Portrait* is always time past. By way of contrast, the present in Pater's historical novel is in dialogue with the past. If we followed Stephen into his next incarnation in *Ulysses*, we would be struck by his anger against both history and dialogue: 'History, Stephen said, is a nightmare from which I am trying to awake.' (*U* 2:158) Such a view would be wholly foreign to Pater's epicurean.

SYMBOLISM

According to Yeats's friend, Arthur Symons, author of *The Symbolist Movement in Literature* (1899), an influential study both at the time

---

67 Compare for example passages in 'The Poetry of Michelangelo' in *Studies in the History of the Renaissance* (1873; London: Oxford University Press, 2010), 52ff with the opening of Joyce's essay 'James Clarence Mangan' (1902) where he writes about the opposition between the classical and romantic schools. (*CW* 73-74).

and subsequently, the distinguishing mark of symbolism in the modern world was that it became conscious of itself. With a slight twist, we might then say of symbolism that it became conscious of its artfulness. Conventional wisdom believed that *ars est celare artem*, that art should hide its art or artfulness, but the new movement insisted on the *how* alongside the *what*, on how something is conceived or realised as much as the finished product. This led in turn to a certain distance between the artist and the world and to the frequent recourse to irony or doubt. After symbolism came modernism and then high modernism in the period around the Great War. Late-nineteenth-century symbolism possesses this transitional quality, but its conscious parading of self-reflexivity was intensified by modernism, for now works of art and literature were accompanied by an imaginary sign saying 'This is a painting' or 'This is a novel' or 'This is a poem'. At its most extreme or treacherous, such a move led to René Magritte's famous painting *Ceci N'est Pas Une Pipe* (1929), literally 'this is not a pipe'.[68]

In its use of symbols, *A Portrait* is positioned in the middle of these on-going changes. The novel is a half-century away from Baudelaire's 1850s idea of a 'forest of symbols'.[69] Equally, it is some way from the scepticism as expressed by Beckett in the 1950s when he suggested in a final note to his novel, *Watt* (1953): 'no symbols where none intended'.[70] We are not facing the unknown in Joyce, nor the unknowable. His symbols have a signature and vitality of their own, so we should not underplay or dismiss the many symbolic references

68   For a short informative survey of symbols and symbolism, see *Princeton Encyclopedia of Poetry and Poetics* (ed. Roland Greene *et al*) (fourth edition) (Princeton and Oxford: Princeton University Press, 2012), 1395-8. Michael Wachtel, the author of this entry, distinguishes symbolism from decadence and naturalism: 'In contrast to decadence and naturalism, both of which denied the existence of a world beyond the quotidian, symbolism considered physical reality either a distorted reflection or a too-faint echo of the world of essences.' There is merit in this distinction but it is not one I follow here. We both agree, however, that Huysmans is a decadent and not a symbolist.

69   Taken from Charles Baudelaire's poem 'Correspondances' in *Les Fleurs du Mal*, first published in 1857. For a modern edition including translation, see Charles Baudelaire, *The Flowers of Evil* (trans. James McGowan) (intro. Jonathan Culler) (London: Oxford University Press, 1998), 18. The line in French is *L'homme y passe à travers des forêts de symbols* (we thread our way through a forest of symbols).

70   Samuel Beckett, *Watt* (Paris: The Olympia Press, 1953), 254.

The epoch-making book on the French symbolists which strongly influenced the poetry of Yeats and Eliot

The symbolist movement in literature ARTHUR SYMONS

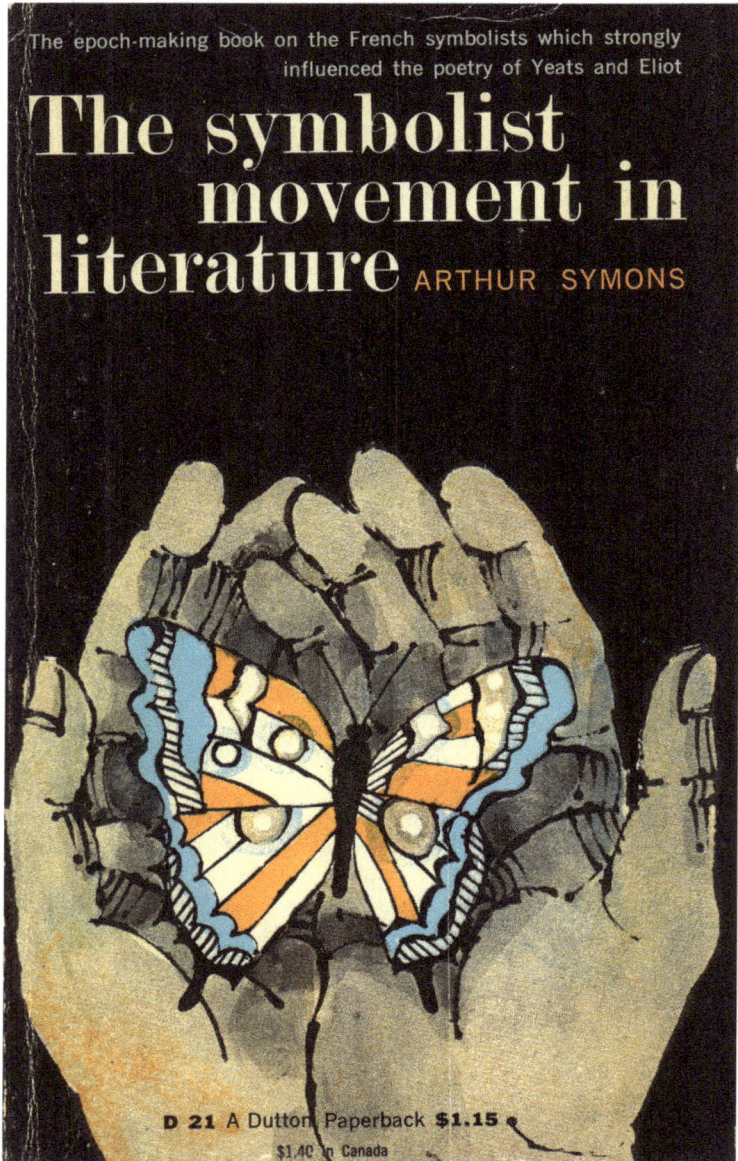

D 21 A Dutton Paperback $1.15

$1.40 in Canada

Seymour Chwast's striking cover design for the paperback version of *The Symbolist Movement in Literature* published by E.P.Dutton in 1958. A butterfly in cupped hands.

in the novel. Thus the bird motif or the symbolic representation of women or the presence of the pre-Socratic four elements are designed to enhance our understanding of Stephen the artist as well as to add coherence to the narrative. As such, they are different from the wholesale integration of symbols in the fiction of Henry James, or from Hardy's ability to render an object as both itself and also a symbol of something else as if they exist isolated from each other but in apposition, or from the frequent use of discordant symbols in the verse of T.S.Eliot.[71] All these attest to the judgment of Symons that symbolism in the modern world became conscious of itself. Symbols in *A Portrait* share in this general outlook, but their special character requires further attention.

A comparison with Moore's symbolist-inspired novel, *The Lake* (1905), can help in this regard. Moore was an Irish novelist read with interest by Joyce. *The Lake* concerns a Catholic priest in the west of Ireland losing his faith and in the process discovering his authentic self. The similarities with Joyce's youthful novel of exile are striking. Indeed, Moore's significance for Joyce was that he provided texts to be improved upon. Both novels are profoundly inner-directed works, where the values of a public world are tried and tested in the only crucible of authentic life they acknowledge, namely the privacy of conscience. In both there is an emphasis on working through, on undergoing, a religious view of the world, and both novels explore, through the pressure of sexuality, the continuity or otherwise of the self through time.

Like Stephen, Moore's protagonist, Fr Oliver, feels acutely the loneliness of exile among his own people. In one of his letters to Rose Leicester - whom he has earlier publicly driven out of his parish, an action he now regrets - he complains about his fate in accents that an older, more chastened Stephen might have employed, looking back on his life:

> I had suffered so much in the parish. I think the places
> in which we have suffered become distasteful to us,
> and the instinct to wander takes us. A migratory bird
> goes, or dies of homesickness; home is not always
> where we are born - it is among ideas that are dear

---

71   On Hardy, I am thinking here of a comment by John Bayley in *An Essay on Hardy* (Cambridge: Cambridge University Press, 1978): 'Hardy puts metaphor and description in apposition, so that each ignores the other instead of complementing it.' (38)

to us: and it is exile to live among people who do not
share our ideas.[72]

The explanatory mode is not Joyce, but the passage can serve to recall
Stephen's last conversation with Cranly, where the latter remarks: 'It
might be difficult for you to live here now' (*P* 245). As ever, Joyce does
something more with the symbolic aspect of birds as well as with the
symbolic associations with Stephen's surname. One day on the shore of
the lake Fr Oliver finds a dying curlew, its legs tied, and the symbolism
is not lost on the priest:

> From long pondering whether it was a tame bird
> that had escaped from captivity, or whether it had
> fallen into a fowler's net and been let loose after its
> legs had been tied together from sheer love of cruelty,
> this strangely-fated curlew came to occupy a sort of
> symbolic relation towards my past and my future life
> and it was in thinking of it that the idea occurred to
> me that, if I could cross the lake on the ice, I might
> swim in it in the summertime when the weather was
> warm, having, of course, hidden a bundle of clothes
> amid the rocks on the Joycetown side. My clerical
> clothes will be found on this side, and the assumption
> will be, of course, that I swam out too far. (272)

To Stephen on the steps of the National Library the swallows represent
freedom, but the priest focuses on his identity with the dying curlew.
This is not something that Stephen would overtly do in *A Portrait*. We
watch Stephen watching the swallows flying, but he draws back from
his own identification with the symbol:

> Then he was to go away for they were birds ever
> going and coming, building ever an unlasting home
> under the eaves of men's houses and ever leaving the
> homes they had built to wander. (*P* 225)

The use of 'wander' reminds us of Fr Oliver's 'instinct to wander' and of
Joyce's instinct, whether consciously or unconsciously, to involve Moore
in his intertextual import business. Equally, we pause on the phrase
'unlasting home', for this, too, we realise is Stephen's fate, leaving his
home to wander abroad. Symbols in *The Lake* insist on their presence in

---

72 George Moore, *The Lake* (London: William Heinemann, 1905), 273-4.

a way that contrasts with Joyce's more sparing treatment, for Joyce allows the symbol (and the allegorical figure of Icarus or Daedalus) to emerge in the reading experience. Both writers affirm the self-consciousness of symbols in the modern period, as suggested by Symons. Moore's protagonist even refers to 'a sort of symbolic relation towards my past', but, with Joyce in mind, we might agree that this is doing the work of the reader. The force of 'unlasting home' is precisely because it works by inference, and if what is inferred were spelt out it would lose its lustre and appeal. Swallows spend most of their time on the wing and have homes which don't last; Stephen's home-life is 'unlasting' and his future home might also become 'unlasting'. As for the everlasting home he would have heard in sermons, that comforting thought he will have to leave behind. Joyce, then, insists on the spaces in the reading experience between narrator and character and between author and both narrator and character. He constantly insists on a new departure for fiction, for he is an intelligent writer who not only attracts an intelligent audience but who also makes his readers intelligent in the process.

As Stephen watches the flight of birds, he wonders if he is observing 'a symbol of the artist forging anew in his workshop out of the sluggish matter of the earth a new soaring impalpable imperishable being' (169). Here the run of the adjectives before 'being' tends to undercut whatever is soaring, while 'forging' recalls artifice as much as creation. Or consider Stephen's self-reflexive comment when observing the flight of swallows. What follows is a sentence without a verb, as if we are listening to his thoughts as they come to him in note form: 'Symbol of departure or of loneliness?' (226). Stephen has just been reflecting on 'an augury of good or evil' (224). Partly because of its self-conscious, distancing turn, the use of the word 'symbol' has a peculiar resonance for the reader. It tells us how far we have travelled from the colour symbolism in the first chapter of the novel. By this stage we realise that A Portrait is so saturated with images and symbols of flight that we wonder at times about the author's motivation. Thus, in cautioning against a simple correlation between word and image or symbol and reality, Joyce shows a modern sensibility at work, reminding us of a literary tradition in need of updating and no longer functioning in the same way as before.

Some critics focus on the content of symbols, such as the colour green at the beginning of A Portrait and what it represents. Few critics notice, say, the colour yellow or how most of the nineteen times the word occurs in the novel come with an unpleasant or negative association. In Blake's symbology, green represents vegetation, or 'instinctive life' if we follow the account in the Blake edition by Edwin Ellis and Yeats.[73] Joyce is not so prescriptive and his originality lies not so much in an exercise in matching symbol and reality as in his self-conscious use of symbols. In one respect the colours green and maroon serve to highlight Dante's changing political attitudes, particularly to Parnell, and this might lead us to reflect on the inescapable and divisive presence of politics in the homes of Irish middle-class families in the 1880s. But we need to weigh this against the prejudice and sentimentality of a character who, as we have seen, uses brushes, neatly placed on her press, to proclaim her political allegiance. It is as if the author, in advancing from the outset a political reading of his novel, is also seeking to qualify how we respond to the symbols in Dante's brushes and the 'little green place' in the line from the song.

Such a form of cancelling out continues in the scene in the classroom when the boys are divided into the Houses of Lancaster and York, lining up behind the red rose or the white rose. In terms of history, we are reminded of the English Wars of the Roses in the fifteenth century and the heraldic badges worn by the participants. The irony in the teachers getting their pupils to wear little silk badges pinned to their jackets and cheer for opposing sides in a long-forgotten English war of succession to the crown is not something raised by Stephen in the novel. And something else suffers a reduction in this scene. Visiting Clongowes in July 1869 a Jesuit priest, Fr Richard Campbell, who later joined the staff at the college and who appears in Joyce's novel as 'Lantern Jaws' (*P* 161), listened to a debate on 'The Wars of the Roses', which 'left an impression of prepared dullness'.[74] To some extent the Jesuits wished to challenge an English worldview. At the same time they were keen on ensuring Clongowes became a leading Irish public school for the education of the wealthy and

---

73 Edwin Ellis and William Butler Yeats (eds.), *The Works of William Blake: Poetic, Symbolic and Critical* Vol 1 (London: Bernard Quaritch, 1893), 322.

74 'My final recollection of the day was a "Debate". A table and four chairs were placed in the centre of the hall, and at this table sat four boys, two with white roses in the buttonholes of their coats, and two with red roses. The subject of this "Debate" could scarcely be called modern, nor could it be said to enter into political questions: "The Wars of the Roses". Each of the four boys made a well-learned speech on the subject, and then proceedings abruptly ended. This was one of the last of the Academy days, and left an impression of prepared dullness.' See Fr Richard F. Campbell, S.J., 'Clongowes Forty Years Ago' in *The Clongownian*, June 1924, 24.

Classroom at Clongowes Wood College with AMDG given
prominent space on the blackboard under the crucifix.

the professional Catholic middle class.[75] Two or more forces seem to
have been in play. Presumably, in importing an English history and
an English house system, together with an English curriculum and
sport such as cricket, the Jesuits at Clongowes, which was a college
modelled on Stonyhurst in Lancashire, learned not to stray too far
from reassuring similarities with their English counterparts.

In attending to these particular colours, Joyce reveals how the
combination of 'history and symbols' works differently from 'patterns
and symbols'. To some extent, the two sets of oppositions between
green and maroon and red and white tend to raise more issues than
they resolve. On one level, the Wars of the Roses in history are brought
into the same field of play as the political turmoil in Ireland in the years
before and after the fall of Parnell. We are not absolutely sure whether
history is being foregrounded or patterns in history. Or is it about a boy
becoming conscious of 'beautiful colours' (12) and of a world where
people take sides and wear colours to express their identity? This might
then prompt other lines of inquiry, how, for example, one war belongs

75 Kevin Sullivan summarises the contrasts between Belvedere and Clongowes
in terms of social class. At Belvedere the Jesuits taught boys from the middle
class and lower middle class, in contrast to the 'pretensions of the Clongowes
gentry'. See *Joyce Among the Jesuits*, 69. In *Stephen Hero* the connection between
the Jesuits in their work in the parish and the 'insecurely respectable middle
class' of their parishioners comes in for strong criticism. (*SH* 119)

to the past and the other is continuing, or how history eventually leads to paralysis or a dead end in one case, and to artificial commemorations in classrooms under the banner of education in the other case. For the son of a supporter of Parnell, green should trump every other colour, but the red and white further qualify such a view. And we cannot quite forget the lingering impression of 'prepared dullness' that greeted 'Foxy Campbell' (*P* 161) in 1869, for this, too, may lie behind Joyce's gentle satire on his schooling.

OSCAR WILDE

On virtually every page of Wilde's *The Picture of Dorian Gray* can be found something of interest for the student of Joyce's *A Portrait*. Joyce's title begins with the indefinite article as if to insist on the provisional nature of what is to follow. 'There may be other portraits I could come up with, but this is the one I'm giving you. So don't hold me to anything too definitive.' Joyce called his first attempt *Stephen Hero*, but his new title is so plain and unassertive that it is at first difficult to remember the run of words or to get right the alternating course of indefinite and definite articles. Joyce's title to some extent doesn't deceive, and neither does it give too much away. But there is something odd about it, for it seems to concern a young man writing a novel about someone who as a young man had a past. The question naturally arises as to what past or whose past is the subject of attention. And, except as a student, we never properly get to observe the young man.

The title, then, offers us many perspectives and false starts on what is to follow. In this respect, the novel reminds us of an object seen from different angles, not unlike a sculpture in a gallery which requires the visitor to walk round it to obtain the full experience. Wilde also makes effective use of his title, giving it a Faustian twist with Dorian seeking to retain his youth in exchange for his portrait aging. Unlike *A Portrait*, *The Picture of Dorian Gray* requires the definite article; otherwise, we might entertain the idea of another portrait of Dorian or of a biographical study of a person called Dorian Gray. The definite article shifts the focus onto more intriguing ground where two meanings, one literal, another metaphoric, are held in play. If Joyce had employed the definite article, the relationship between the author and reader would have set in train thoughts of a third-person narrative, where the reader would become a passive recipient and come to rely on a narrator to make sense of what was happening.

Joyce's debt to Wilde was in many ways considerable, not least in how to be wise before the event. On the relationship between art and life Wilde opened the eyes of a whole generation of writers. When it came to incisive observations about culture and social class and or about the close connection informing polar opposites, few could match him. According to Richard Le Gallienne, his near-contemporary and author of *The Romantic 'Nineties* (1925), his humour was 'cleansing', his wit 'drastic, purifying'.[76] 'Cleansing' is such an unusual adjective to apply to a person's humour, and yet in the case of Wilde it is just. Always we are faced with defining our response when encountering Wilde and his beautifully composed sentences. Joyce, too, must have been similarly affected. He would have taken particular note of Hallward's cautionary remark early in the novel: 'We live in an age when men treat art as if it were meant to be a form of autobiography.' (4) Others were less responsive, for this was precisely how *A Portrait* was read by critics at the time and since. Indeed, taken together, the Wilde comment and Joyce's novel should continue to caution those writing about fiction today, for few things are more tiring than critics who assume their primary task is to reduce a text to the author's life.

While *A Portrait* provides an echo or a play on Wilde's title, the differences also stand out. So, 'portrait' as a word is not quite interchangeable with 'picture'. Wilde remains committed to the physical canvas on which the portrait is painted and which is assigned a central role in the novel. The picture can be 'indifferent' to the viewer (97), the expression on the face can alter and convey 'lines of cruelty round the mouth' (84), and at the end of the novel the knife that killed the painter can kill 'the painter's work' (202).[77] In contrast to what occurs in *A Portrait,* the picture is incorporated into the plot and narrative, and the conceit drives everything forward to its dramatic conclusion. Joyce's novel, on the other hand, depends on realistic settings and on a plot that relies on the character of Stephen for its momentum. In this regard Joyce insists on how we see the subject rather than on a physical canvas in an artist's studio, 'see' being the operative word. *A Portrait* also includes a theoretical discussion on beauty as conceived in terms of neo-scholastic philosophy. But, whether 'picture' or 'portrait', the concrete or the abstract, the novels share a concern with pictorial appeal. And, contrary to what is sometimes suggested about Joyce's

---

76 *The Complete Works of Oscar Wilde: The Poems* (intro. Richard Le Gallienne) (New York: Wm. H. Wise), 1927), xl.
77 Quotations are from Oscar Wilde, *The Picture of Dorian Gray*, (1891; Richmond, Surrey: Alma Classics, 2017).

novel, we should not forget that *A Portrait* constantly depicts portraits of life that are as vivid as anything we read in *The Picture of Dorian Gray*.

A Portrait is full of emotion, but we perhaps need to distinguish between emotion and feeling. Thus, when Basil Hallward remarks that 'every portrait that is painted with feeling is a portrait of the artist' (9), we wonder what Joyce would have made of 'with feeling', for it is not a phrase that immediately springs to mind on reading *A Portrait*. *The Picture of Dorian Gray*, on the other hand, is full of feeling, and the impression created is so personal that it cannot be denied or fully expressed. Joyce, on the other hand, follows Flaubert in championing the invisibility of the artist and comparing him or her to God, 'refined out of existence, indifferent, paring his fingernails' (P 215). Wilde recalls his predecessors in the aesthetic movement. Basil, the painter, tells his sitter and subject, Dorian, in a long and informative passage on art: 'It often seems to me that art conceals the artist far more completely than it ever reveals him.' (106) Although Joyce would generally have agreed with such a sentiment, in one important respect he would not, for *A Portrait* lacks such a encounter in the artist's studio. Wilde, on the other hand, conveys an aesthetic viewpoint within the more natural surroundings of a studio and inside a novel that shares as much with a Socratic dialogue as with a modern novel.

The Picture of Dorian Gray comes complete with Wilde's striking aphorisms and memorable quotations, many of which we respond to immediately as if we were hearing them recited by an actor on the stage, for the theatre and theatricality are ever present in this novel. 'Buck' Mulligan in *Ulysses*, who has much in common with the figure of Wilde, claims, 'We have grown out of Wilde and paradoxes' (*U* 1:554). What he means is we have outgrown Wilde, not that we have our origins in him. Harold Nicolson, in a review of St John Ervine's study of Oscar Wilde in 1951, wondered if 'any intelligent or educated person in this year 1951 regards the works of Oscar Wilde as possessing any interest or significance other than those of a period piece?'[78] How wrong they were, for Wilde has outlasted his supercilious detractors whether in fiction or in the world of Sunday newspapers, and his aphorisms and paradoxes continue to delight us and to move us.

Indeed, for all its liveliness and brilliance, both in conception and execution, the novel is a study also in more serious matters including, for example, the pain of old age. When Lord Henry tells Dorian 'you

---

78 Harold Nicolson's review of St John Ervine, *Oscar Wilde* (London: George Allen and Unwin, 1951) appeared in the *Sunday Times*, 9 December 1951.

must keep your good looks' (96), we know this is a delusion, and it is fitting that towards the end of the novel we finally arrive at the statement we have been awaiting: 'The tragedy of old age is not that one is old, but that one is young.' (196) Such a thought must have come to many on entering a care home as a visitor or resident. The theme of old age is largely absent from *A Portrait,* a novel which remains single-mindedly committed to the qualification in the title 'as a young man'. If anything proves it is Stephen's novel, it is this. At the same time, pithy remarks by Stephen, as for example with 'Ireland is an old sow that eats her farrow' (*P* 203), often serve to remind us as much of the character himself as the world he shares with his audience or reader.

In the article on Wilde which Joyce wrote for the Triestine newspaper, *Il Piccolo della Sera* in March 1909, Joyce referred to Wilde in unflattering terms as a 'court jester to the English' in the tradition of Irish writers stretching from Sheridan to Shaw. Joyce is careful with his words. Wilde was a 'dishonoured exile', someone who is not dishonourable, which is how he was conventionally viewed, but someone who has been dishonoured. Joyce, however, warmed to something else which he might have imagined lay outside Wilde's imaginative grasp or sympathy. This was Wilde's understanding of the truth inherent in the soul of Catholicism that 'man cannot reach the divine heart except through that sense of separation and loss called sin' (*CW* 201-5). The theology behind such a view also found expression at the time in Yeats's *Where There Is Nothing* (1902), a Nietzschean play about an outcast monk who finds a way to God through nothingness. Hence where there is nothing there is God.[79] In his own life – and presumably this is how he arrived at such a view - Wilde understood

---

[79] Yeats's title echoes the Church's motet *Ubi caritas et amor, Deus ibi est.*' ('Where there is charity and love, there is God'). The hymn is sung at the Maunday Thursday service and commemorates Jesus washing the feet of his disciples. Yeats and Wilde had a privileged access to Catholicism via their Irishness and, in Yeats's case, via his uncle's Irish servant, Mary Battle. But neither of them were Catholics. When he was staying in Rome in 1900 Wilde made frequent visits to the Vatican to have sight of the Pope. In a letter to More Adey, six months before he died, he confessed, 'I am not a Catholic; I am simply a violent Papist.' (*The Letters of Oscar Wilde*, 825). Wilde's father, an ear and eye surgeon and one of Queen Victoria's oculists, was a proud Protestant, who was part of a generation of Irish Protestants, such as Lady Gregory and Douglas Hyde, who collected Irish folktales from the mainly Catholic rural poor. The Wildes lived in Merrion Square, which was a desirable area in central Dublin, where Yeats lived for a time in the 1920s.

the place of sin in a believer's life. This was something Joyce, in moving away from his religion, could appreciate but perhaps not share. However, he never stopped sharing with Wilde, the fallen father, the theme of guilt, shame, and confession.

Joyce's remarks on Wilde's novel reflect his ambivalent attitudes to his compatriot, as we see from a letter he wrote to Stanislaus in August 1906:

> I have just finished *Dorian Grey* [sic.]. Some chapters are like Huysmans, catalogued atrocities, lists perfumes and instruments. The central idea is fantastic. Dorian is exquisitely beautiful and becomes awfully [sic] wicked: but never ages. His portrait ages. I can imagine the capital which Wilde's prosecuting counsel made out of certain parts of it. It is not very difficult to read between the lines. Wilde seems to have had some good intentions in writing it - some wish to put himself before the world - but the book is rather crowded with lies and epigrams. If he had had the courage to develop the allusions in the book it might have been better. (*SL* 96)[80]

Joyce picks up on Wilde's treatment of homosexuality, but he holds back from full approbation. Instead, he suggests candour became ammunition to the prosecuting counsel in a court of law. Five years after Wilde's death, a death that followed two years imprisonment, we see Joyce distancing himself from his fellow writer. Wilde confirmed for Joyce, who was an expert in innuendo, that it was wise not to be too explicit when it came to writing about sexuality. In retrospect, Joyce appears to be drawing a line under the aesthetic movement that coursed its way through the nineteenth century. In *A Portrait* the references to 'smugging', or to what is implied by Cranly touching Stephen, which is characterised by Joseph Valente as a form of 'homosexual panic', or to the composition of the villanelle possibly after masturbating, all these essentially require the reader to infer what

---

80 As for Wilde's death-bed conversion, Joyce in an interview with Yeats is supposed to have said that 'he hoped his conversion was not sincere'. Cited in Richard Ellmann, *The Identity of Yeats* (New York: Oxford University Press, 1954), 87.

is happening.[81] One conclusion we might well draw is that Wilde is a more honest or less cunning writer than Joyce, but such integrity had terrible consequences.[82]

If the nineteenth century is seen as a century increasingly preoccupied with art, the twentieth century turned its attention to the life which underpinned or ignored art. Joyce, too, discovered something else about himself in writing: that he had outgrown the aesthetic movement and that he was by nature temperamentally drawn to the ordinary and the everyday. The movement from *A Portrait* to *Ulysses* is, therefore, towards and away from art. The lyrical impulse on display in both novels finds its counterweight in the detailed attention to ordinariness as with Cranly habitually chewing figs or closely observing what Bloom has for breakfast. The sheer weight of ordinariness is what is impressive about *Ulysses*, and we witness its beginnings in *A Portrait*.

What we might well ask is the reference at the beginning of the second chapter to Uncle Charles visiting the family outhouse to 'enjoy his morning smoke' (*P* 60) doing in a novel about art and writing? One conclusion worth pondering is that habit is Joyce's true Penelope.[83] He began with art and defiance, the 'reality of experience' and writing the self, and with the path between home and exile, but in the end he came upon something more ordinary, the reality and texture of our daily lives, whether that was lived in Ireland or Europe, at home or abroad. Joyce, then, began his career inside the folds of one century but emerged largely unscathed into the twentieth century. He has now become our contemporary.

---

81 Joseph Valente, 'Will to Artistry in *A Portrait of the Artist as a Young Man*' in the *James Joyce Quarterly* 50 (1-2) September 2012. Joyce's disputes with printers and publishers over the publication of *Dubliners* tended to be on account of his reluctance to change a word or phrase or their impugning his motives. Unlike *Ulysses* or passages in his personal correspondence with Nora in 1909, there is little in *Dubliners* or *A Portrait* that is explicitly sexual. The priest in the first story might have syphilis and the boys in 'An Encounter' might have encountered a pedophile. It is for the reader to decide.

82 The recent publication of an edition of the novel based on the original manuscript version suggests Wilde was concerned about what he could and could not say about the homo-erotic passages, especially in the dialogue between Basil and Dorian. See *The Picture of Dorian Gray* (foreword Merlin Holland) (London: SP Books, 2018).

83 This is an echo of Pound's remark in *Hugh Selwyn Mauberley* how 'His true Penelope was Flaubert'.

Joyce among the Jesuits. A group photo of the class of 1902 taken in the garden of Newman House on Stephen's Green. Joyce is standing second left with hands in pockets. Constantine Curran is at the front on the right. George Clancy ('Davin') is seated in front of Joyce. The ash tree is still standing. *Courtesy of the Beinecke Rare Book and Manuscript Library, Yale University.*

CHAPTER 4: PORTRAITS AND REVERIES

When we juxtapose Joyce's *A Portrait* with Yeats's *Reveries Over Childhood and Youth* we are struck by a certain irony, for it was the poor-sighted Joyce, lacking in artistic skills, who made use of an analogy from painting for a title to his novel, while Yeats, in spite of being an 'artist's son', avoided titles with references to painting.[84] In his choice of 'Portrait' Joyce draws attention to the late-nineteenth-century European discussion of art-versus-life, while in choosing the word 'Reveries' Yeats returns us to the Celtic Twilight and to the dreamy self out of which he emerged. 'Portrait' suggests something contained within a definite space or frame. The word implies something more deliberate, more selective, more conscious, than 'Reveries', which gives the impression of randomness, of thoughts which are less structured, of a deliberate refusal in this case to provide an interpretation of one's life as a whole. 'Reveries' belongs to the language of desire, to Pater and the aesthetic movement, to the years Yeats spent as a boy with his family in the artistic enclave of Bedford Park in west London. It represents an escape from the world of conscious thought processes, and recalls an underground stream or stored memories welling up into consciousness. As Yeats wrote to his father the day after finishing *Reveries*: 'The book is…less an objective history than a reverie over

84 W.B. Yeats, *Reveries Over Childhood and Youth* (London: Macmillan, 1916), 76.

such things as the full effect on me of Bedford Park and all it meant in decoration.'[85]

Throughout his career as a writer, Joyce always had Yeats in his field of vision. As we have noticed, passages from Yeats's occult story 'The Tables of the Law' he could recite by heart. To comfort his dying brother and mother, Joyce recited 'Who Goes with Fergus?', a strangely haunting poem from *The Countess Cathleen. Chamber Music* is full of Yeats's cadences. Without Yeats, Joyce's early career would have lacked an important focus. More widely, although he was often mocked for his manner and style, Yeats was a central figure for every Irish writer who came after him. He was for Heaney an 'example', which as a term he did not use lightly.[86] Difference in age mattered. In his late thirties, Yeats entertained the belief that he had the measure of Joyce in his early twenties: 'He is from the Royal University, I thought, and he thinks that everything has been settled by Thomas Aquinas, so we need not trouble about it. I have met so many like him.'[87] In the subsequent volume of his autobiography, 'The Trembling of a Veil', there is a reference to 'a young Irish poet, who wrote excellently but had the worst manners' and who told him, 'You do not talk like a poet, you talk like a man of letters'.[88] Yeats took notice of Joyce, and he was also protective of him, as when, away from the public eye, he came to his defence when attacked by Gosse in the Savile Club in London on the publication of *Ulysses* in 1922.

There is a memorable phrase in *Finnegans Wake* when Joyce and Yeats are compared to a 'daintical pair of accomplasses'. 'You, allus for the kunst and me for omething with a handel to it (*FW* 295.27-9). The portmanteau words betray a childlike playing with words and cross-gendering: 'daintical' includes dainty and identical; 'accomplasses' accomplice, compass, and lasses. The stress on identity, gender, and, for some reason, transgression is continued in Joyce's use of the German word *kunsthandel* or art dealer. Yeats was for 'kunst', for art that is and, possibly because Joyce is full of innuendo, for women. Joyce sides with music, as represented by George Frideric Handel, but, more down-to-

85 J.B.Yeats, *Letters to His Son W.B.Yeats and Others 1869-1922* (ed. Joseph Hone) (preface Oliver Elton) (London: Faber and Faber, 1944), 203. Letter from Yeats to his father, 26 December 1914.

86 Seamus Heaney, 'Yeats as an Example?' in *Finders Keepers: Selected Prose 1971-2001* (London: Faber, 2002).

87 Cited in Richard Ellmann, *The Identity of Yeats* (New York: Oxford University Press, 1954), 87.

88 W.B.Yeats, *Autobiographies* (London: Macmillan, 1977), 166.

earth, he is also for anything with a handle to it, and hence commerce (*handel*), or perhaps it is the male body or friendship, or something without an s, 'omething' that is.

At times it is nothing more than innuendo, but we cannot always be sure what Joyce intends in co-opting the separate items in the construction of his kaleidoscope or portmanteau words. What sort of crime, for example, have they both committed, or is crime behind the confessional mode of every writer since St Augustine? Joyce's protagonist, Stephen Dedalus, would have identified with art, not business, but, by the time he came to write *Finnegans Wake* in the 1920s, the union of art and commerce was clearer to him. In retrospect, however we interpret *kunsthandel*, we can discern that, between them, the dreamy Yeats and the ever-alert Joyce divided a large part of the spoils of modern writing in English. Indeed, without these two Irish accomplices we would be looking at a very different landscape.

FATHERS AND SONS

A Portrait of the Artist as a Young Man, which was published in the same year as the Macmillan edition of Yeats's *Reveries Over Childhood and Youth*, reminds us that, before entering the major phase of their respective careers as writers, the two Irish authors turned to quarry their own lives. For some years before 1916 Yeats had been applying his thoughts to writing an autobiography, and it was always linked in his mind with family and the dynastic theme. As he was to write in the introductory poem to *Responsibilities* at the beginning of 1914:

> *Pardon, old fathers....*
> *Although I have come close on forty-nine,*
> *Pardon that for a barren passion's sake,*
> *I have no child, I have nothing but a book.*
> *Nothing but that to prove your blood and mine.*[89]

A book was a poor substitute for a child, and it was to be five years before his first child was born. As we move through the lines here, we can almost hear the poet thinking, from 'no child' to 'nothing but a book' to nothing to prove his family ties but a book. With *Reveries* in our hands we can recognise, therefore, the proximity between writing about his life and Yeats at the onset of middle age worrying about ties to his family.

---

89 W.B.Yeats, *Selected Poetry* (ed. Timothy Webb) (London: Penguin, 1991), 72.

It will come as no surprise that Joyce had no such dynastic ambitions or, indeed, inhibitions. His father was a fallen father, responsible for the family's decline. Stanislaus was his severest critic and described him as 'a man of absolutely unreliable temper' (*MBK* 35). Indeed, their long-suffering mother, May Joyce, 'was often terrified to be alone with him' (*MBK* 36). Joyce himself was always more forgiving as we witness in his moving poem 'Ecce Puer', written to coincide with the birth of his grandson in 1932. Here his considerable tenderness towards his father makes itself felt, even if it is to apologise for having forsaken him by living abroad. 'O, father forsaken / Forgive your son.' The irony is not lost on us for when he wrote these lines John Joyce was dead. At the close of *Finnegans Wake* he seems to recall a tender moment from his childhood which, like the opening of *A Portrait,* is also expressed in the language of a child: 'Yes. Carry me along, taddy, like you done through the toy fair' (*FW* 628:8-9). By contrast, perhaps the most compelling image in *A Portrait* of the family's ancestry is the sale of Simon Dedalus's mortgaged properties in Cork. Joyce had a family history but in one important respect he had nothing to inherit except what lay in his imagination.

The theme of dispossession can also be seen in how he rewrote the role of his closest brother in his two novels. Stanislaus has a significant part to play in *Stephen Hero* in the character of Maurice, but by the time of *A Portrait* his presence has shrunk considerably. This might well be because the portrait of Stephen in the second novel emphasises not connection with family but the isolation of the artist confronting his fate. At the same time with regard to their father, Joyce was always more forgiving than his brother. That said, the portrait we have of Simon Dedalus in *A Portrait* is not one that would lend itself to anyone contemplating a dynastic theme. Apart from the Christmas Dinner scene, when we see the fire banked high, his father wearing coattails, Stephen in his Eton jacket, and servants in attention, interior shots of the family tend to be marked by poverty, straightened circumstances and shouting orders. Only once in the novel are his sisters, Katey, Boody, and Maggie, mentioned by name, and this is when Stephen, now at university, issues a demand: 'Fill out the place for me to wash.' (*P* 174) When he gets his mother to wash him, and to stop her complaining, he calmly, if cruelly, quips, '[I]t gives you pleasure' (*P* 175). As soon as Stephen wins an essay prize at College, there follows 'a swift season of merrymaking' (*P* 97), with meals out and trips to the theatre for the family. In case we might be tempted to sit in judgment on the feckless lifestyle of the Dedalus family or the Joyces, we might remember that this is what many of those facing the daily grind of poverty do: live for today, and give no thought for tomorrow. Either way, Stephen does in fact buy his mother a 'mantle' or cloak to protect her from the cold.

While their own fortunes were declining, the Joyces were not without hope. They took pride, for example, in their family history and their links with the great nineteenth-century Irish leader, Daniel O'Connell. In the Christmas Dinner scene, Simon Dedalus takes care to point out to Mr Casey the portrait hanging on the wall of his grandfather, who was condemned to death for being a Whiteboy, a member that is of an eighteenth-century secret agrarian organisation founded to protect tenants against unscrupulous landlords. But whatever heirlooms the Joyces inherited, it was never enough to counter the reality of debt and financial ruin. Once, the family owned property in Cork and had a toe-hold in the rentier class, but by the time Joyce arrived at his mid-teens they owned nothing and sometimes they couldn't even afford the rent.

In 1907 Yeats's father left Ireland for New York, never, as it happened, to return. In reading through the letters between father and son, we come to realise their importance in giving a focus to Yeats's ideas about the self, character, and personality. In one letter he writes, 'Poetry is the last refuge and asylum for the individual of whom oratory is the enemy.' And in another, complete with underlining for his son's attention, he declares: 'There is one thing never to be forgotten. *That the poet is the antithesis of the man of action.*'[90] The letters were also occasions for learning from his father about the family. Yeats tells his father that someone thought he might have called his own memoir 'Father and Son' if Gosse had not already used it.[91] His father is invariably direct. He tells Yeats the poet's 'benign quality' he inherited from whose family were '"the Good people", in a sense the fairies are not.'[92] Paradoxically, distance forced the two into closer intimacy and into expressing what may have gone unrecorded if they had lived in the same city.

It was at this time that Yeats became increasingly dissatisfied with

---

90 .J.B.Yeats, *Letters to His Son W.B.Yeats and Others 1869-1922*, 178 and 187. The first was written on 20 April 1914, the second on 18 August 1914. In the second letter Yeats's father is humorously mocking his son's interest in fairies.
91 Ibid., 203. Letter dated 26 December 1914 and sent from Lady Gregory's estate at Coole Park.
92 Ibid., 117. Letter to Yeats written 24 March 1909.

the public world of politics and the theatre, and he wanted to invest more in the theme of family to compensate for the loss he felt both in the public world and also in his own family. Such a theme must have impressed itself on him with the death of his uncle, George Pollexfen, in 1910. George had played host to Yeats when he returned to Sligo, so his death marked the end of family visits as he would have known them since childhood. In addition, on reading Moore's *Hail and Farewell* (1911-4), with its satire on Yeats and the Literary Revival, Yeats must have also felt that there was a need to set the record straight and to counter the cavalier treatment of the course of his life. After all, Moore had mocked and broadcast to the world his social pretensions. Once in conversation with George Russell, Yeats expressed the opinion that if he had his rights he would be Duke of Ormonde, to which Russell replied 'I am afraid, Willie, you are overlooking your father.'[93]

In *Reveries* Yeats's struggle with his father is played out against a background of fear and religion. In many respects his father represented a more potent figure of authority than the English. *Reveries* was written in the aftermath of Gosse's *Father and Son* (1907), a powerful autobiography about the severity of the author's upbringing among the Plymouth brethren. 'I remember little of childhood but its pain,' (14) remarks Yeats, and we cannot help recalling Gosse's upbringing. The suffering began with his grandfather, the paterfamilias William Pollexfen, the person in the family it was 'the custom to fear and admire' (4). Yeats is candid but at the same time declines outright condemnation and even allows for his own responsibility: 'I think I confused my grandfather with God' (7).

The scene in *Reveries* when Yeats's father flung a book at his head when he was being taught to read is one that most readers will not easily forget. Again, Yeats softens his outrage at such humiliation with a nicely honed sentence: 'Because I had found it hard to attend to anything less interesting than my thoughts, I was difficult to teach.' (38) Yeats did not learn to read until he was nine, and he never fully mastered English spelling, so he would not have appreciated the humour behind Joyce's remark in *Finnegans Wake* how 'every letter is a godsend' (*FW* 269.17). But what is intriguing about the reasoning that follows the word 'Because' is that it neatly shifts the focus from Yeats being a slow learner as a child to the author's beautiful prose as an adult.

---

93 George Moore, *Hail and Farewell: Ave, Salve, Vale* (1911-4; Gerrards Cross: Colin Smythe, 1976), 540. Russell added insult to injury by telling Yeats that 'We both belong to the lower-middle classes'.

Yeats's candour is often at the service of something else, but he is not to be condemned for being insufficiently truthful. Part of Yeats's charm as a writer of prose is not only the way he apparently glosses over difficult moments but also how he allows us to see him doing so. It is not surprising that one of his favourite sayings was 'wisdom is a butterfly/ And not a gloomy bird of prey'.[94] Being a victim, whether of the colonial encounter or of his father or of his given limitations as a person, was not something he over-indulged. Most of his friends, after all, were English, some of them with titles. Unlike Joyce, when he looked back on his upbringing he also saw the comforting image of 'memory harbour'.

RELIGION

As with Gosse's autobiography, Yeats's struggle with his father was in part connected to religion. 'My father's unbeliefs,' he tells us, 'set me thinking about the evidences of religion.' (42-3) His use of 'evidences' in the plural reflects not only his defence of religion but also his later interest in the occult and the practical ways through séances and magic of getting in touch with the spirit world. Most Victorians before and after Charles Darwin were interested in the theoretical evidence of religion, but Yeats, who was an active member of the Order of the Golden Dawn, was interested, with Madame Blavatsky and others, in practical evidences. Four days following his marriage to George Hyde Lees in 1917, he began a lengthy series of automatic writing sessions with her.[95] In the same chapter about evidences in *Reveries*, he records that, following the death of his brother, Robert, he heard the banshee wailing. (45) Yeats effectively spent his whole life looking for contact with the spirit world, and so familiar were the automatic writing sessions he conducted with his wife that 'controls' or intermediaries had individual names and personalities.

The struggle with the father in *A Portrait* assumes a different complexion, in part because the issue of religion is resolved by Stephen away from his father's influence. In rebelling against his father's unbelief, Yeats found religion; in rebelling against what was essentially his mother's religion, Joyce found himself. Moreover, it was

---

94 The lines are from his poem 'Tom O'Roughley', which appeared in *The Wild Swans at Coole* (1919).

95 For a further discussion on Yeats and the occult, see the chapter entitled 'Yeats's Female Daimons' in my *Yeats's Worlds: Ireland, England and the Poetic Imagination* (1995).

through sin, through falling, that his fictional counterpart begins the process of expunging religion and God the Father from the centre of his being. What is also striking about Joyce's novel in comparison with *Reveries* is how Stephen's father declines in significance and is overthrown almost without any major upheaval on Stephen's part.

The episode where Stephen accompanies his father back to Cork shows a child who is already capable of distancing his father and who is in his mind already beyond his father's influence. On the train journey, as suggested in the last chapter, we notice the 'silent sentries' (*P* 87) and imagine them guarding over his childhood and youth. As he watches his father drinking with his 'two cronies', the narrator tells us that Stephen's mind 'felt older than theirs' (73). The novel captures so well this kind of exposure and the accompanying sense of isolation and loneliness. His father at this juncture wants friendship with Stephen and not a father-son relationship. Stephen, on the other hand, betrays little or no affection for him, and has only accompanied him to Cork because he is bound to him by ties of blood. Needless to say, we are some distance from the earlier scene where Stephen, who is unable to absorb the fact that his father is vulnerable, sees his father at the dinner table crying over the fall of Parnell.

The idea of the soul in *A Portrait* is covered in more detail in my final chapter, but here we can notice how the issue of religion and apostasy also affected other writers such as Synge in Ireland and Ernest Renan in Catholic France. In his library in Trieste Joyce had a copy of Renan's *Souvenirs d'enfance et de jeunesse* (1883) (*Recollections of My Youth*).[96] And we should not forget that in 1924 he took time out from holidaying in Saint-Malo to visit Renan's birthplace in Tréguier in Britanny. Renan spent many years as a seminarian in St Sulpice in Paris, and his memoir, with its roots deep in the nineteenth century, is dominated by intellectual doubts and growing scepticism over theology and the role of the Church.

But even when he left the Church, Renan retained a fondness for what it had taught him: 'to love truth, to respect reason, and to see the serious side of life' (125). The Church imparted to him a moral compass, which he never abandoned for 'the Gospel gave me my moral law.' (28) What he regretted was that he was not 'born in a land where the bonds of orthodoxy are less tightly drawn than in Catholic countries' (281). Before him was 'a bar of iron...and you cannot reason with a bar of

---

96 Ernest Renan, *Souvenirs d'enfance et de jeunesse* (Paris: Calmann-Lévy, 1883).

iron' (281). As a consequence, Renan came to accept, reluctantly, that it was not possible to doubt one tenet of dogma without calling into question everything else.

The phrase 'bonds of orthodoxy' dramatically captures just how absolute the Church also appeared in Catholic Ireland. When doubts were raised with priests or teachers, they were deferred, or mystery was invoked. The rational was countered by belief, and the leap of faith called on. As he listens to the retreat sermons, Stephen registers the horror that committing one mortal sin is to risk the eternal damnation of his soul. On the other hand, unlike the account in Renan's *Recollections*, *A Portrait* only briefly explores the intellectual reasons for Stephen's apostasy. In the final chapter, his undergraduate friends listen but have little to contribute, as if there is a joint recognition that Stephen has already made up his mind. The central theology of redemption or salvation history or the resurrection of the dead or the Trinity or what he made of the historical Jesus, none of these, with the exception of the real presence in the Eucharist, are given air time in the novel. In discussions with the Dean he declares his support for the views of Aristotle and Aquinas on art and beauty. Serious logical thinking he reserves for his aesthetic theory, not religion.

Stephen's resistance, or 'revolt' (P 247) as he calls it in discussion with Cranly, gives the appearance of being bound by the absolute world described by Renan, and in Stephen's case resistance means flight rather than engagement. In terms of attitude, we can recognise an unholy alliance or a sequence composed of questioning, disbelief, loss of faith, disaffection, and ending in apostasy and rebellion. If you began asking questions in the Catholic Ireland of Joyce's day, you might discover it ended with unrest. So *A Portrait* is not an *apologia* in how that was conceived by one of Stephen's writing heroes, Cardinal John Henry Newman.[97] Plotting Joyce's withdrawal from the Church, however, is not straightforward for, unlike Renan, he refuses to spend time analysing his decision. He certainly does not feel himself to be a deserter or one of Dante's 'renegade Catholics' (P 34), but more like someone who stands apart, *apo stasis*, to recall the Greek etymology of apostasy, in order to arm himself for battles ahead.

---

97   See John Henry Newman, *Apologia Pro Vita Sua* (London: Longman, Green *et al*, 1864). An apology was not so much a confession as a defence of one's own position or, here, a defence by Newman of his life as an Anglican who became a Catholic.

Le Petit Journal
SUPPLÉMENT ILLUSTRÉ

TOUS LES VENDREDIS
Le Supplément illustré
5 Centimes

Huit pages : CINQ centimes

TOUS LES JOURS
Le Petit Journal
5 Centimes

Troizième Année

SAMEDI 22 OCTOBRE 1892

Numéro 100

ERNEST RENAN

Joyce took a particular interest in the celebrated French writer and thinker, Ernest Renan. Here he is on the front cover of *Le Petit Journal* in 1892.

Something else we might notice about how Joyce described himself after leaving the Church. Unlike Moore, the ex-Catholic would never count himself a pagan. In a final chapter in *Memoirs of My Dead Life* (1906), Moore provides a series of engaging reflections on death and mutability occasioned by the passing away of his mother. Surrounded by his Catholic relations, Catholic country people, and even, he imagines, a Catholic countryside, he feels especially conscious on his return to the family's estate in the west of Ireland of his own 'paganism' as he calls it.[98] Moore had the ability to put some distance between himself and his upbringing, but this was less true for Joyce, who always recognised the continuing power of the line he had crossed. His past was never going to be associated with his dead life. Only someone from inside the albeit outer orbit of the Church and with goodwill in his heart could collapse St Peter and St Patrick into 'thuartpeatrick' (*FW* 3.10) or refer to the four evangelists as 'mamalujo' (*FW* 398.04). A pagan would not have bothered.

When he reflects on the reason for not taking up a priestly vocation, Stephen reports he was obeying 'a wayward instinct' (*P* 165). This is such an unusual expression that it should cause us to delay. What, we might well ask, is a wayward instinct? Freud uses the term 'an underlying instinct', where the adjective implies an unconscious force, a force he later formulated as the 'id', which he set in triangular relation with the 'ego' and 'supergo' or conscience. Freud stressed the sexual nature of the instinct, which obeyed its own compulsion and was separate from the intellect. The relationship between the 'id' and the 'ego' he compared to a horse and rider.[99] The task of the rider is to control the horse or 'id'.

To some extent, the choice of 'wayward' resists an investigation along Freudian lines, for 'wayward' and 'underlying' suggest fundamentally differing approaches to how the psyche is conceived. On the other hand, although the Freudian association is distanced by the use of 'wayward', the presence of Freud can still be felt. *A Portrait* is about falling to earth. Constantly, Stephen tries to soar upward, but he is dragged back down, in part because of his sexual drives, as for example when he frequents a prostitute at the end of Chapter 2. In

---

98 George Moore, *Memoirs of My Dead Life* (1906; London: William Heinemann, 1925), 352.

99 Sigmund Freud, *The Standard Edition of the Complete Psychological Work of Sigmund Freud, Volume XIX (1923-26) The Ego and the Id and Other Works* (eds. James Strachey, Anna Freud, et al) (London: Hogarth Press, 1978), 19

declining the opportunity to join the Jesuit Order we are reminded of an underlying aspect of his character and personality. Thus, Stephen's refusal can be related to his growing rebellion against the Church. Equally, whatever is meant by 'wayward instinct' suggests the rider is not in full control of the horse.

In a move that Joyce would have resisted, Freud might have attempted to systematise the whimsical nature of 'wayward'. Joyce, however, knew what he was doing. As can be observed in the priest's retreat sermons, the Church tended to see the body as a site of evil or temptation, with instincts to be resisted. In obeying his instinct, Stephen advances the cause of freedom. At a rational level Joyce gave voice to what lay behind his leaving the Church. Nowhere is this expressed more forthrightly than in a letter to Nora at the beginning of their relationship:

> My mind rejects the whole present social order and Christianity – home, the recognised virtues, classes of life, and religious doctrines. How could I like the idea of home? My home was simply a middle-class affair ruined by spendthrift habits which I have inherited. My mother was slowly killed, I think, by my father's ill-treatment, by years of trouble, and by my cynical frankness of conduct. When I looked on her face as she lay in her coffin – a face grey and wasted with cancer – I understood that I was looking on the face of a victim and I cursed the system which had made her a victim. We were seventeen in family. My brothers and sisters are nothing to me. One brother alone is capable of understanding me. (*Letters II*, 48)[100]

Joyce wrote this letter within ten weeks of their first meeting and six weeks before he and Nora left Ireland for the continent in October 1904. Most of *A Portrait* was still to be written, and Stephen's character was still being imagined. 'A wayward instinct' is the kind of phrase that belongs to Joyce after his declaration to Nora; it would have been out of place in such a letter. But in its tentativeness it is precise. Albeit from a different direction, it is not unlike the '*Non serviam*', which looks more like a cry of the heart than a programme of action based on reason. Stephen's psychology is not Joyce's, and it exhibits

---

100 Letter to Nora Barnacle, 29 August 1904.

the appropriate mixture of assertiveness and vulnerability that we encounter in the myth of Icarus confronting the Minotaur. Stephen's whimsical nature even has a certain consistency, so that, when asked by Cranly if he believes in the Eucharist, he enigmatically replies, 'I neither believe in it nor disbelieve in it' (P 239). And the reader is left wondering if 'it' refers to the real presence or to religion as a whole, or if Joyce is qualifying his own beliefs as expressed in the letter to Nora.

Significantly, Yeats's upbringing in the Church of Ireland meant he did not have to confront Renan's 'bar of iron', and this partly explains his more relaxed attitude to where he prayed. Critics still argue over whether or not Yeats was a Christian. In 'A General Introduction for My Work', written in 1937, within two years of his death, Yeats declared: '[M]y Christ, a legitimate deduction from the Creed of St. Patrick as I think, is that Unity of Being Dante compared to a perfectly proportioned human body, Blake's "Imagination", what the Upanishads have named "Self".'[101] Such an amalgam of religious, poetic, and philosophical ideas to support his own singular outlook might recall a butterfly rather than his gloomy bird of prey, but at the same time we suspect there is a system behind it all. Indeed, the neo-Platonic tradition in western thought has attracted many followers over the centuries, but, it must be confessed, Yeats's combination of St. Patrick, Dante, Blake, and the Unpanishads will tempt few Christians away from their traditional beliefs.

To complete the picture, Synge's experience of religion belongs more decidedly to the nineteenth century and in particular to the Victorian world of faith and doubt. One of his family relatives, uncle Alexander, was the first Protestant missionary to the Aran Islands in the 1850s. Alexander had little time to adjust to his posting, and in a letter to his brother he writes: 'Here I am lord of all I survey...surrounded with dirt and ignorance'.[102] His nephew identified completely with the country people and the rural poor. Within a generation, therefore, social attitudes in Ireland had dramatically altered. The transformation in Synge began with his critique of religion. As he tells us in his autobiography, 'I was painfully timid, and while still very young the idea of Hell took a fearful hold on me.'[103] So it was not so much an intellectual critique

---

101 See W.B.Yeats, *Essays and Introductions* (London: Macmillan, 1961), 518.
102 David M.Kiely, *John Millington Synge: A Biography* (Dublin: Gill and Macmillan, 1993), 3.
103 *The Autobiography of J.M.Synge* (ed. Alan Price) (Dublin: Dolmen Press and London: Oxford University Press, 1965), 14.

as an emotional response to his religious upbringing. It was followed in his middle teens by a rational mind at work:

> By the time I was sixteen or seventeen I had renounced Christianity after a good deal of wobbling.... I felt a sort of shame in being thought an infidel.... Till I was twenty-three I never met or at least knew a man or woman who shared my opinions. (23-4)

Synge's isolation recalls Joyce's position, but in the latter's case rejection was a badge of honour worn not by an infidel but by someone with a higher calling. It helped that Stanislaus, who was always more extreme than Joyce, shared certain hostile attitudes to the church. Synge took a different path: 'Soon after I had relinquished the Kingdom of God I began to take a real interest in the kingdom of Ireland. Everything Irish became precious and had a charm that was neither quite human nor divine.' (26) This kind of crossover or exchange, which involved losing one kind of community and finding another, was essential for Synge to adopt before his plays could begin to emerge. In the cottages of the country people, where he stayed for weeks and month at a time, Synge learned how they spoke Hiberno-English. In turn, their way of speaking assumed the role almost of an essential character in his plays.

In the last third of the nineteenth century, if Protestants in Ireland were attracted to an All-Ireland position or a cultural initiative to unite all classes, they were obliged to confront the prejudices of their class. This was true of figures such as Standish James O'Grady, Douglas Hyde, Lady Gregory, or Yeats himself, figures who, with Synge, were indispensable in the emergence of the Literary Revival. Unlike the immersive Synge, they did not need to abandon their religion, and most did not, but, if they were to discover the 'kingdom of Ireland', there had to be some movement away from thinking they were superior to people from different backgrounds or religious persuasion.

The Jesuit-educated Joyce, his cudgels intact, experienced no such conversion. There was something uncompromising and egotistical about his revolt. Kevin Sullivan frankly admits as much:

> For if many of Joyce's intellectual virtues were the product of his Jesuit training, so it must be said were many of his vices – his pedantry, his perpetual seeking after first principles, his implicit sense of superiority that will not explain and cannot apologise, the sense

"I Don't Care a Rap."

Cartoon of a defiant Synge in the wake of the *Playboy* riots of January 1907.
From *The Abbey Row Not Edited* by W.B.Yeats, a publication edited by Page
Dickinson, Frank Sparrow and Joseph Hone in the same year.

that he leaves with even his most patient reader of
being party to a secret which he will not share.[104]

As his discussion with Bloom in the 'Eumaeus' episode of *Ulysses*
reveals, Stephen's sojourn in Paris merely reinforced his temperament.
'Ireland must be important because it belongs to me' (*U* 16:1160–
65). Stephen's mind sounds tired and nearly exhausted, but it is still
agile enough to restore a sense of equilibrium. The remark conveys
something Joyce might have inserted into Stephen's dialogue with
Davin or Cranly at the end of *A Portrait*. In *Ulysses*, it follows on
from another 'quote' by Stephen, which is equally relevant for our
purposes: 'I may be important because I belong to the *faubourg Saint
Patrice* called Ireland for short'. Ireland was never his fatherland, but
in the familiarity of the phrase, St Patrick's suburb, with Ireland
humorously depicted as a Paris suburb, we can appreciate how Joyce,
the 'paleoparisien' (*FW* 151.9)), never relinquished an affection
for his country. The last book he was reading before his death was
Gogarty's *I Follow St Patrick* (1938).

SEXUALITY

Joyce's title, with its qualification 'as a young man', recalls Moore's
title *Confessions of a Young Man* (1888). At the end of *A Portrait,* when
Stephen sets his sights on Paris, we are reminded of Moore, that other
Irish writer who went to Paris in the 1870s. *Confessions of a Young Man,*
which is couched as an autobiography but which is in fact more like
a novel, provided Joyce, if he wanted it, with an example of a text that
cut across different genres. However, its particular relevance derives
from another source, namely the way it interweaves a discussion about
French art with a confessional mode of writing. While Yeats's work
leans toward the language of desire, Joyce's impulse, if we were to leave
aside for a moment his suppressed lyricism, is towards the confessional.
Although 'confessions' does not appear in the title, there is a lingering
scent throughout *A Portrait* that Joyce – more so than Stephen - wishes
to reveal the truth about himself and that he needs an intermediary
to do this for him. We cannot be too precise about any of this, but
writing looks as though it is Joyce's way of confessing, not to a priest
in a church, but to his fellow mortals in a secular world. So *A Portrait*
is Joyce's account of how he wrote his way out of his former self, or,

---

104 Kevin Sullivan, *Joyce Among the Jesuits* (New York: Columbia University
Press, 1958), 10.

to put this another way, how he sought to recuperate the self from his own sins or from a fallen world.

In recalling their pasts, both Yeats and Joyce provide us with very different accounts of the awakening of sexuality in boyhood. One seems realistic, the other more evasive. 'The great event of a boy's life,' according to Yeats. 'is the awakening of sex.' (116) Joyce would have agreed but he would never have included such a sentence in a novel that never stops reminding us of that truth. When his family lived for a year or so in a house on the cliffs overlooking Howth, Yeats removed his bedroom window and in stormy weather 'the spray would sometimes soak my bed at night' (113). The reader delights in this sexually charged image but it goes almost unnoticed by Yeats. His innocence isn't so much beguiling or even reprehensible but naïve. He continues by describing the stirring inside him, and assumes that his interest in the outdoors is not part of this same awakening but merely the space wherein, like Percy Bysshe Shelley's solitary figure of Alastor, he can be alone to give his passions 'my whole attention' (117).

Yeats wrote a more honest account of his sexuality in *Memoirs* (1972), which he began compiling in the aftermath of *Reveries* and which remained unpublished until 1972. In section XXIII, which has masturbation for its focus, he tells us that the experience 'left me with exhausted nerves' and 'filled me with loathing of myself'.[105] He also innocently records that in his twentieth-seventh year he had 'never since childhood kissed a woman's lips' (72). As we can perhaps observe with 'smugging', a word which is explored more fully in my final chapter, *A Portrait* also deals with masturbation. Joyce's novel is more honest than *Reveries* but, surprisingly, it is less explicit than Yeats's *Memoirs*. But we can notice here something that is inseparable from the context of Joyce's sexuality, namely his Catholic education. When Stephen goes to confession he recalls his 'sins of impurity' with himself and with women (*P* 144). The priest's response will catch many readers, especially Catholic readers, by surprise, for he berates Stephen not so much for having sex with a woman but for 'that wretched habit', which is presumably masturbation. The priest's interest in the status of the women and whether they were married or unmarried is also curious, for they were almost certainly sex workers. In this priest's eyes, and perhaps more widely in the Church at that time, masturbation was a worse sin than frequenting brothels.

---

105 W.B. Yeats, *Memoirs: Autobiography-First Draft-Journal* (ed. Denis Donoghue) (New York: Macmillan, 1972), 72.

Yeats and Joyce grew up in a world where it was sinful to masturbate. For Wilde, homosexuality was the love that dared not speak its name, but for many Catholics, inside and outside Ireland, masturbation was the pleasure that dared not speak its name – except, that is, in the confessional. Many Victorians thought the practice was enervating. The Church added sin, for as the priest says, 'You cannot know where that wretched habit will lead you' (*P* 145). Indeed. In Joyce's case it almost certainly contributed to his leaving the Church. Yeats in *Reveries* sought to hide his shame, whereas Joyce's inclination, once he was beyond the Church's influence, was to tell all. However, he left a more explicit treatment of the subject to *Ulysses*, where he devotes a whole sequence in the 'Nausicaa' episode to Bloom masturbating on Sandymount strand opposite the Star of the Sea Church, where the exposure of the Blessed Sacrament is taking place during the service of Benediction. By the time he wrote this passage, Joyce had found a way of turning his sense of schoolboy shame into schoolboy humour.

The habit made Yeats ashamed of himself, but he had no recourse as a Catholic has in going to confession, and he must have lived with his shame for long periods of his youth. In his religious phase, Stephen/Joyce was penitent, succumbed to the overwhelming idea of hell as described by the retreat priest, and acknowledged his sin. But when he decided to go to confession, his shame followed him; he did not confess to one of his Jesuit masters but to a Capuchin priest in a chapel where he would not be recognised. In time, as *A Portrait* implies, Stephen found his own God within himself and outside Ireland.

Joyce influenced generations of Catholics who succeeded him, but he is not the only figure worth noticing. In *Twice Round the Black Church* (1962), which is among the most clear-sighted memoirs by an Irish writer after Joyce, Austin Clarke perceived something more disturbing in the culture as a whole, something that Joyce never explored:

> It is regrettable that theologians should have brought in this custom of confession at so early an age, when nature itself is endeavouring to protect the growth of personal consciousness. The curiosity and self-display of the infantile phase being quickly forgotten, a child becomes modest, reserved.[106]

---

106 Austin Clarke, *Twice Round the Black Church* (London: Routledge and Kegan Paul, 1962), 132.

MEMORY

The physical appearance of Joyce's novel, published in New York in 1916 by Benjamin Huebsch, is traditional and restrained, with a plain blue cloth cover, complete with gold lettering on the spine and title stamped blind on the front. It gives nothing away. To his lasting credit, Yeats, more than Joyce, was concerned with the visual impact of his books. *Reveries* was published by Macmillan in the same year as *A Portrait*.[107] By contrast, *Reveries,* which is indebted to the 1890s arts-and-crafts movement, has a striking front cover, printed in gold on mid-blue cloth. It carries a design by T.Sturge Moore, featuring the hand of God tickling the young infant into life.[108] In the lower half, the naked boy emerges through a stairwell as a shy young man on the threshold of life, with the motif repeated on the spine. This is one of Moore's most successful designs. The coyness of the theme is held in check by the panel motif and geometric space characteristic of his mentor, Charles Ricketts. The poetic design, however, stands in contrast with the book's contents, for, as his friend, George Russell, noticed, the boy in the story might have become a grocer as a poet.[109]

Opposite the title page there is an image of *Memory Harbour* (1900) from Jack B.Yeats's painting of that name.[110] The painting depicts the harbour at Rosses Point in County Sligo, where the Yeats brothers would spend time in the summer. The scene is dominated by a ship at anchor, with a metal man directing the boats in and out to sea, and in the foreground a blue-coated, bearded fisherman who accompanied Yeats on fishing trips as a boy. If the title to his brother's painting had not been used by Filson Young for a 1909 novel of that name, his own volume might have been called 'Memory Harbour'. This lively scene meant so much to the Yeats boys growing up and so much more in memory. Indeed, *Reveries* gathers together Yeats's love of Sligo, his early interest in the outdoor life, his enjoyment of being with country people and fisher folk, and how memory returns him to the harbour of his childhood and youth.

---

107 Yeats's sisters published an edition of the book, with separate plates, in 1915 under The Cuala Press.

108 This image can be found in my *Yeats's Worlds*, 174.

109 See John Eglinton [W.K.Magee], *A Memoir of AE, George William Russell* (London: Macmillan, 1937), 111.

110 This image is reproduced opposite the opening page to the first chapter of my *Yeats's Worlds*.

Joyce, too, enjoys inhabiting his past, but in *A Portrait* he deliberately sets his face against the image of 'memory harbour', 'reveries', or indeed conventional introductions to autobiographies or fictionalised autobiographies possibly along the lines of: 'When I reflect on how my life began, I recall my father looking into my pram and singing me a nursery rhyme and calling me all kinds of baby names. I remember also wetting the bed and how first it was warm and then it went cold.' Together with William Wordsworth and Proust, Beckett and Brian Friel, Joyce is one of the great writers of memory. His work is full of the past whether that includes personal memories of his childhood and education, or the history of Ireland, or the cultural memory that shelters inside the covers of Skeat's *Etymological Dictionary*. In the closing moments of *Finnegans Wake* Joyce plays on the word 'memory' in 'mememormee', and in so doing recalls the self-regarding 'baby tuckoo' focusing, slightly anxiously, on himself alone. It also speaks to the inter-subjective role of language affecting us all. Stephen's attraction as a young boy to the sound of words, those 'wonderful vocables' (*SH* 30), serves at the same time as an entry-point into the storehouse or memory of a culture. So Joyce is doing more than just taking up residence in the city of words; he is activating the past, making the past present, showing how what was is.

When we turn to how the two writers evoke the past, this is as intriguing as what they select from the past for their focus. *Reveries* concerns events that happened over twenty years before, where distance is part of the view. As we have noticed, *A Portrait* situates itself in the years from the 1880s and the era of Parnell to Stephen's university days at the beginning of the twentieth century. The events described by Joyce are much closer to the time when they were transmitted to paper, which gives the novel immediacy and leaves the future more open-ended or still to be written. Joyce's version differs in this respect from the more measured presentation of Irish history after Parnell in Lennox Robinson's play *The Lost Leader* (1918). In reflecting on the changes in Ireland after the death of 'the lost leader', Robinson shifts the debate away from Parnell's stature or achievements towards the popular imagination and the folk memory that refused to accept Parnell had died. Joyce, too, was familiar with the story. In the 'Hades' episode in *Ulysses* the mourners visit Parnell's grave in the cemetery at Glasnevin, and, Mr Power gives voice to a popular superstition at the time that Parnell might still be alive: 'Some say he is not in that grave at all. That the coffin was filled with stones. That one day he will come again.' (*U* 6.919–20) Robinson keeps the stress on the spiritual dimension, and how Home Rule has to be more than 'merely the exchange of government by English shop-keepers for government by Irish gombeen-men'.[111] In *Ulysses*, then, Joyce plays with some of these ideas; in *A Portrait* it is the iconic status and character of Parnell that is emphasised.

Joyce and Yeats exploit specific historical references. Their texts are associated with particular decades, but this needs a certain qualification. For, as Robinson can serve to remind us, the use to which the authors put the historical material differs. Joyce is much more aware of historicising his material, while Yeats tends to be more inert in his use of history, haunted one suspects in part by memories of the Fenians, waiting for something to happen (as it did in his poem 'Easter 1916'). The Land War of 1879-82, when tenant farmers in Ireland, led by Michael Davitt, took part in organised resistance against their landlords, obtrudes at one point momentarily into *Reveries*, but in *A Portrait* the historical and political context is given from the start of the novel. Thus, on the opening page, Dante's brushes are an oddly telling reminder of a public history in which two Irish leaders, Davitt and Parnell, are more than mere 'decoration' as Bedford Park was for Yeats. Stephen, we sense, is part of a known history, and perhaps the only sure way the aesthete has of escaping from the historicising process is to 'change the subject', as Stephen tells Bloom in *Ulysses*. (*U* 16:1174)

Our task with *A Portrait* is not, therefore, to place an 'unhistorical' text within an historical context; rather it is to bring out and give due weight to the historical context already there, or, alternatively, to understand how history and consciousness are being arranged.[112] With *Reveries* it is different. Yeats was brought up as a Sligo Protestant. His mother's family, the Pollexfens, owned warehouses and ships which regularly plied between Sligo and Liverpool and which also carried Yeats back and forth to school in London. They possessed an imposing house on the edge of Sligo town, an indication that although they were not gentry they were solidly middle-class. Yeats's father, John Butler Yeats, whose family owned land, was destined for the law, but he turned away from the workaday world and instead sought an uncertain

---

111 Lennox Robinson, *The Lost Leader* (1918; Belfast: H.R.Carter, 1954), 63. Gombeenmen were usurers who, during periods of famine or hardship, would make money out of the sufferings of the rural poor.
112 For further discussion along these lines, see Chapter 1 of *The Joyce Country* (2018).

career as an artist. *Reveries* is essentially a family history with glimpses of a world beyond occasionally intruding.

In the early chapters of *Reveries* Yeats gives expression to his Sligo Protestant upbringing and takes pride in his family history. It was his responsibility at night to lower the union jack flag in the front garden. In the eighteenth century his ancestors took part in hounding the United Irishmen, and always in the background to Yeats as a boy we sense, along with the orange songs, the presence of the Fenians. But any anti-Catholic sentiment was kept in check by his sympathetic imagination. From Mary Battle, who was a Catholic servant of his uncle George Pollexfen, he learned about the folklore of the country and their faery stories. More by way of texture than by sustained argument, *Reveries* gives us a flavour of this world, a world very different from Joyce's family, who were Catholic, downwardly mobile, and city-dwellers. Unlike Yeats's family in Sligo, Joyce's family were aware of religious divisions between Catholics and Protestants, as the opening to *A Portrait* affirms, but, in general, aside from Mrs Riordan, they suffered less from the kind of sectarianism Yeats experienced in Sligo. It is, therefore, not surprising that Joyce's father sought the separation of church and state, or, as that was often defined, the separation of priests and politics. Equally, John Joyce looked to a Protestant leader in Parnell to win a measure of Home Rule from the imperial parliament at Westminster.

Family background and the contrasts in their experience of mediation between family and the wider world help to explain some of the differences informing their writing. Nothing, however, fully explains Joyce's view of history as formative, for history is not noises off but central to his delineation of character. At the same time, in his shrewd choice of historical references, which are more than simply illustrative, Joyce undermines a naïve theory whereby literature simply reflects a known history. In this regard his view is more sophisticated. As much as he shows how an individual is determined by outside forces, the Jesuit-educated writer is also drawn to the space between the individual and history and to the idea of consciousness before the intervention of history. Yeats is less insistent, in part one suspects because he had the protection of family against the forces outside. He wasn't exposed as Joyce was at an early age to political debates then tearing families apart. Yeats was blessed with a kind-hearted and intelligent father, who helped him with making sense of the world and with managing differences, especially those between the Pollexfens and the Yeatses: 'We have ideas and no passions, but by marriage with a Pollexfen, we have given a tongue to the sea cliffs' (*R* 37). His use of 'we' is significant, for to John Butler Yeats his son was first and foremost a Yeats.

It is clear that Yeats was as interested in ancient Irish mythology as in contemporary Irish history, and he was equally interested not so much in the contrast between the two as in the continuity. What he sees in the General Post Office during the Easter Rising is the figure of the ancient Irish hero, Cuchulain. And in 'The Statues', a poem written towards the end of his life, he asks the question: 'When Pearse summoned Cuchulain to his side, / What stalked through the Post Office?'[113] He never lost his attachment to the link as he saw it between myth and history. Joyce, on the other hand, quickens ancient myth from within, so that Stephen, who shares a surname with a Greek mythological figure, is essentially someone with a modern sensibility confronting a modern problem. Where Yeats seeks an identity, Joyce more often than not reminds us of the trope of doubling, of moving in an out of ancient myth and the modern world. As he explained to Carlo Linati in September 1920 in connection with the myth of Ulysses: 'My intention is to transpose the myth *sub specie temporis nostri*' (under the aspect of our time). (*Letters* I 147) The crucial word here is 'transpose', not fusion or identity.

THE ENGLISH ISSUE

However we configure the relationship between history and myth, the English for Yeats and Joyce keep returning. As we see below in connection with the episode over 'tundish', Joyce was not overawed by the English. And neither was Yeats. In 'A General Introduction For My Work', a late essay written in 1937, Yeats was generous in his praise of English culture. But, twenty years earlier, in *Reveries*, the English are depicted as 'natives' under the critical eye and unsympathetic gaze of the outsider. He even takes care to enumerate their faults. The English lack reserve, they disclose their affairs to strangers, they swap wives, they eat dog-fish, and, to make matters worse, when he first arrived in England, Yeats once saw an old man put marmalade in his porridge. Such negative attitudes he shared with Moore, who was horrified by England's 'shameful and vulgar materialism'.[114]

Given his family background, which was not lower-middle-class as Russell alleged, it is not in the least surprising that Yeats felt no

---

113 W.B.Yeats, *Selected Poetry* (ed. Timothy Webb) (London: Penguin, 1991), 215.
114 Moore, *Hail and Farewell*, 222.

sense of inferiority towards the English. Ironically, his schooling in west London merely reinforced this. The heroes of history he was supposed to admire were English; he was a foreigner, among people who were not his own; he was an Irishman in England during the Land League agitation of 1879-82 when anti-Irish feeling was running high. His schooling may have been designed to stress the superiority of the English, but in his heart he had the family confidence, both from the Yeatses and from the Pollexfens, to believe that the opposite was the case.

The language issue was inescapable for Joyce, and he gave it a particularly sharp twist in a moment full of drama in his novel. The discussion between the Dean and Stephen in the physics theatre at Belvedere is one of the most memorable in *A Portrait*. They have been discussing Stephen's high-flown ideas of art and beauty in the context of Aristotle and Aquinas, but they become distracted by the Dean's use of 'funnel', a word which betrays the speaker's Englishness, for in Ireland, according to Stephen, the word that would be used is 'tundish'. It is a small point, and has nothing to do with art or beauty, but it makes Stephen uncomfortable:

> The dean repeated the word yet again.
>
> —Tundish! Well now, that is interesting!
>
> —The question you asked me a moment ago seems to me more interesting. What is that beauty which the artist struggles to express from lumps of earth, said Stephen coldly.
>
> The little word seemed to have turned a rapier point of his sensitiveness against this courteous and vigilant foe. He felt with a smart of dejection that the man to whom he was speaking was a countryman of Ben Jonson. He thought:
>
> —The language in which we are speaking is his before it is mine. How different are the words *home, Christ, ale, master,* on his lips and on mine! I cannot speak or write these words without unrest of spirit. His language, so familiar and so foreign, will always be for me an acquired speech. I have not made or accepted its words. My voice holds them at bay. My soul frets in the shadow of his language. (*P* 189)

As the chronology in my Chapter 2 reveals, in 1903 Joyce was reading Jonson and Aristotle in the Bibliothèque Ste. Génèvieve in Paris. In March, as we have seen, he told his mother: 'I am at present up to the neck in Aristotle's Metaphysics and read only him and Ben Jonson (a writer of songs and plays).' (*SL* 19)[115] When he drafted the passage in *A Portrait*, some of this moment must have come back to him. But he shifts the focus. For in Paris he read Jonson's poems with considerable interest, an interest that is also on display in the poems in *Chamber Music*. In the novel he seems to be allowing Stephen full vent to his feelings of being a stranger in language, the language which, on account of his being a native speaker, he should own, but which he now feels is or has become 'an acquired speech'. We might be reminded of a comment by Thomas Davis, the leader of the Young Ireland movement in the 1840s, how 'to lose your native tongue, and learn that of an alien, is the worst badge of conquest – it is the chain on the soul'.[116] We might also recall Wilde's comments about the Saxon taking the lands of the Irish in his California lecture in 1882, and how the Irish 'took their language and added new beauties to it'.[117] Stephen is not a spokesperson at this point for Joyce. Few would believe that Joyce, who in *Finnegans Wake* 'murdered all the English he knew' (43.2), would ever have fretted in the shadow of the language into which he was born. On the other hand, there must have been something he shared with his protagonist.

All this is reminiscent of a conversation Joyce had with Stefan Zweig, one of his German-speaking friends, who had expressed interest in 1919 in staging *Exiles* and translating *A Portrait*:

> When I became acquainted with James Joyce…he harshly rejected all association with England. He was Irish. True, he wrote in the English language but did not think in English and didn't want to think in English. 'I'd like a language which is above all languages, a language to which all will do service. I cannot express myself in English without enclosing myself in a tradition.'[118]

115 Letter to May Joyce, 20 March 1903.
116 Thomas Davis, *Literary and Historical Essays* (Dublin, 1846). The comment is from the essay 'Our National Language', which first appeared in *The Nation*.
117 See 'The Irish Poets of '48' in *The Annotated Oscar Wilde* (ed. H. Montgomery Hyde) (New York: Clarkson N.Potter, 1982), 379.
118 Stefan Zweig, *The World of Yesterday: Memoir of a European* (trans. Anthea Bell) (1943; Lincoln and London: University of Nebraska Press, 2011), 226.

Like Stephen, Joyce wrote inside a language which he felt marked him in some way. He did not want to think in English or be enclosed in an English tradition. So when we read *A Portrait* we should bear in mind that for him, too, it belongs to 'acquired speech' and that it reflects a stranger in language. But no sooner do we entertain such an idea than we realise how fluently the novel reads and how it issues from someone utterly familiar with the language he is using. Ironically, Stephen corrects the Dean in his choice of words, not because 'tundish' is a Gaelic word but because the Dean is not familiar with a dialect word which is spoken in the poorer district of Lower Drumcondra where 'they speak the best English'. The narrator then adds 'said Stephen laughing' (*P* 188).

Stephen's complaint is not the whole story, for, unlike the Dean, his ear is attuned to the 'acquired speech' which his fellow Dubliners speak and which is not Gaelic. There is a measure of irony in all this, and Joyce allows Stephen to exaggerate his claims to being a victim. In his diary notes at the end of *A Portrait* 'tundish' is recalled, and Stephen realises his mistake. The word is 'good old blunt English', he tells us (in fact it dates from the fourteenth century). Then, after cursing the Dean, Stephen adds 'what did he come here for to teach us his own language or to learn it from us?' (*P* 251)

Even when he's wrong, Stephen is reluctant to apologise, that word we first encounter on the opening page of the novel. Joyce is more cunning than the character he invented, for he flew by such nets including the narrowly-based one of linguistic imprisonment. The polygot Joyce draws attention to all the languages of Europe waiting to be learnt or acquired or voiced or just enjoyed. In addition, his writing has the potential to be more radical still, for it suggests how the subject is positioned in language, so that when we speak it is the language speaking us as much as we speaking the language.

FAREWELL

When his parents say goodbye to Stephen at the entrance to Clongowes Wood College, little did they imagine they were anticipating how *A Portrait* would end with their son's farewell not only to his family but also to the country of his birth. Everything in the novel points to the final goodbye, but, when we arrive there, the scene is drained of much of its poignancy. This is not the tender goodbye we find in Yeats's early poem 'Ephemera': 'our souls / Are love, and a continual farewell'.[119]

---

119 W.B. Yeats, *Selected Poetry* (ed. Timothy Webb) (London: Penguin, 1991), 17.

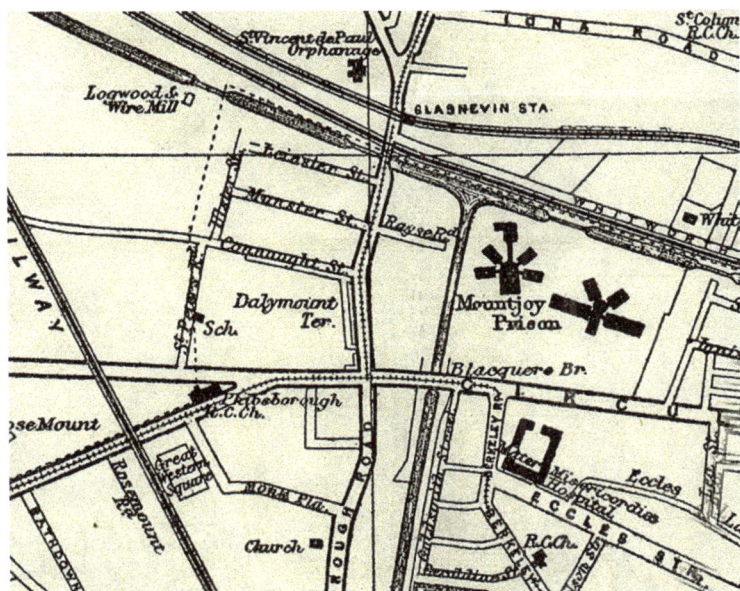

In his discussion with the Dean Stephen refers to the poorer district
of Lower Drumcondra. This is where the Joyce family once lived on
St Peter's Terrace (near sch or school). On this cut-out from the 1900
Bartholomew's map of Dublin we can see how his neighbours included
prisoners, orphans, and the inhabitants of the near-by Glasnevin cemetery
where the Jesuits have a plot and where Parnell is buried. The more
upmarket Eccles Street, also on the map, is a reminder of Joyce's next
novel, *Ulysses*, for this is where the Blooms live or lived at number 7.

An overdressed Joyce in the seaside town of Bognor in summer 1923. *A Portrait* and *Ulysses* behind him, his mind was turning to *Finnegans Wake*, a text that would allow him to say a final farewell to writing in his own inimitable style. *Courtesy of the Beinecke Rare Book and Manuscript Library, Yale University.*

And it is far removed from the sentiments expressed by his university friend, Thomas Kettle, in his essay 'On Saying Good-bye':

> But there is a constant heart-break in travel which comes from this that every departure is a sort of geographical suicide. To live anywhere even for an hour or a day is to become inwoven into a manifold tissue, material and spiritual. You cannot pluck yourself suddenly out without carrying a fringe of destruction, and it is your own personality that dies in every snapped fibre.[120]

A Portrait refuses sentimentality, for we realise that Joyce's is a story of emigration not tagged on at the end of something, but always in play from the beginning. Stephen has learned as a boy from the adults around him the attitude that will carry him abroad. In the Christmas Dinner scene, the Irish are described by Stephen's father as a 'Godforsaken race' (*P* 37). And the attitude seems to be pervasive, so we are not surprised when, towards the end of the novel, a similar phrase appears on Lynch's lips in his reference to 'this miserable Godforsaken island' (*P* 215). Earlier, Stephen addresses the theme of exile directly in conversation with Davin, the figure who is closest in sympathy to Ireland and its people:

> When the soul of a man is born in this country there are nets flung at it to hold it back from flight. You talk to me of nationality, language, religion. I shall try to fly by those nets. (*P* 203)

Then at the end of the novel, his decision already made, it is to Davin he somewhat cruelly remarks that 'the shortest way to Tara was *via* Holyhead' (*P* 250). Stephen is deliberately mocking a hallowed image from Ireland's past. In antiquity Tara was the hill in County Meath, not far from Dublin, where the kings of Ireland would meet in council with their advisers. At Tara in 1843 Daniel O'Connell, the leader of nationalist Ireland at the time, held one of his 'monster' meetings with around a million people in attendance. For Stephen, the shortest way to heaven is via the port of Holyhead in north Wales, where ships docked from Kingstown (now Dun Laoghaire). Joyce's story of emigration is

---

120 Thomas Kettle, 'On Saying Good-bye', *The Day's Burden: Literary and Political and Miscellaneous Essays* (Dublin: Maunsel, 1918), 103.

here displayed not in the plangent notes of the common plight of the Irish but in the personal account of an author who was determined, as he said about *Dubliners*, to 'write a chapter of the moral history of my country' (*SL* 83).[121]

When we next see Stephen at the beginning of *Ulysses*, he has returned from Paris a changed person. His wings have been clipped and he has fallen back to earth. The new novel begins with a comic imitation of the opening of the Catholic mass, with 'Buck' Mulligan in the role of celebrant and Stephen in the congregation, no longer at the centre of things. Gone is the Stephen of *A Portrait*, replaced by a less engaging figure, who occupies the first three episodes like a soul without a body or a soul searching for a body. Once upon a time he strode onto the stage of fiction as the defiant Icarus attempting to escape the clutches of the Minotaur with his father Daedalus. Now in the guise of Telemachus he suffers the taunts of suitors like Mulligan and worries about our knowledge of the external world. As he awaits the return of his father, Odysseus, from his wanderings after the Trojan Wars, it becomes apparent that he is being usurped of his rightful home. From our knowledge of his previous incarnation, we realise Stephen has broken free of the nets that once held him, but Tara has eluded him. Moreover, his author has become more interested in another fictional character, the more down-to-earth Bloom, who is joined by the sensuous figure of Bloom's wife, Molly, a modern-day Penelope. The artist has met his match in the citizen, the aesthetic movement has issued in *l'homme moyen sensuel*, the average man with average tastes and appetites. However, we cannot forget where the path began, so that, when Stephen says goodbye at the end of *A Portrait,* we know there is more to come.

---

121 Letter to Grant Richards, 5 May 1906.

César Abin's caricature of Joyce appeared in *transition* in March 1932. With Joyce's help it was designed to stress the author's unheroic side. As he escapes the cobwebs of his native country he leaves a black hole. His body is reshaped as a question mark, his black hat carries an unlucky number, his dark glasses suggest his near-blindness, his trousers are patched, and in his pocket can be discerned the title of a sentimental ballad, itself a reference to his often poor health.

CHAPTER 5: STEPHEN DEDALUS THE ARTIST

THE ART OF DEFAMILIARISATION

The concept of defamiliarisation was given a modern interpretation in the work of Russian Formalists in the years around the publication of *A Portrait* in 1916. One of the most succinct definitions can be found in the work of Viktor Skhlovsky:

> And art exists that one may recover the sensation of life; it exists to make one feel things, to make the stone *stony*. The purpose of art is to impart the sensation of things as they are perceived and not as they are known. The technique of art is to make objects 'unfamiliar', to make forms difficult, to increase the difficulty and length of perception because the process of perception is an aesthetic end in itself and must be prolonged. *Art is a way of experiencing the artfulness of an object: the object is not important.*[122]

Shklovsky coined the Russian word '*ostranenie*' as a way of highlighting how art makes things unfamiliar. In the above translation the word is

122 Viktor Shlovsky, 'Art as Technique' in *Russian Formalist Criticism: Four Essays* (second edition) (trans. and intro. Lee T.Lemon and Marion J.Reis) (Lincoln and London: University of Nebraska, 2012), 12. For a very brief account of Russian Formalism, see the entry in the *Princeton Encyclopedia of Poetry and Poetics* (fourth edition) (ed. Roland Greene *et al*) (Princeton and Oxford: Princeton University Press, 2012), 343.

'unfamiliar', but in some translations it is rendered as 'estrangement'. 'Estrangement' will evoke for some Bertolt Brecht's famous concept of '*Verfremdung*', which is sometimes translated as the alienation-effect or distancing device. 'Unfamiliar' is a less charged word and is closer to what Joyce is doing in his writing. He is not set on estranging the reader or on distancing the world, but making things that are familiar unfamiliar and vice-versa. As is apparent from my comments throughout this book, Joyce wants to make the stone stony, to give us the sensation of things, to ensure we pause or delay, and to prolong the perception, for this is an aesthetic end in itself. In this regard remember how Stephen 'kept repeating [words] to himself till they lost all instantaneous meaning for him and became wonderful vocables.' (*SH* 30)

Shklovsky is right: the object is sometimes not important. Listen to Byrne, his friend at university: 'James Joyce valued many words for their sounds and for their own sake as much as he did for their connotation. Indeed the meaning of a word or group of words often was less important to Joyce than the word itself, or the grouping.'[123] We might co-opt the last sentence in the Shklovsky quotation as a useful addendum to the list as outlined in Chapter 3 on the aesthetic movement. It also serves as a reminder of the line of continuity Russian Formalism enjoys with its nineteenth-century predecessors. In particular, 'Art is a way of experiencing the artfulness of an object' recalls the discussion on experience in the section on Pater and Joyce. Further afield, we might also be reminded in the English context, of William Morris and the importance the arts-and-craft movement attached to making things by hand.

Joyce is an expert in the art of defamiliarisation. He begins *A Portrait* with a formulaic opening to a children's story, 'Once upon a time', but then unexpectedly supplements it with 'and a very good time it was'. Such an opening is itself an example of defamiliarisation because we don't expect a novel for adults to start, unannounced, as if it were a children's fairy tale. He then continues with an adult speaking to a child in baby talk: 'there was a moocow coming down along the road and this moocow that was coming down along the road met a nicens little boy named baby tuckoo....'. At first Joyce puts the reader at ease, but in the second half of the sentence he disrupts the unfolding narrative. As the train bore her away from Paris and away from girlhood into 'the

---

123 J.F.Byrne, *Silent Years: An Autobiography with Memoirs of James Joyce and Our Ireland* (New York: Farrar, Straus and Young, 1953), 188.

unguessable country of marriage', the protagonist in Angela Carter's 'The Bloody Chamber', a story based on Charles Perrault's 'Bluebeard', begins within the conventions of fiction with 'I remember'.[124] The insertion of the delightful and completely unexpected word 'unguessable' is proof that Carter is operating within the conventions both of literary fiction and of classic fairy tales. *A Portrait,* on the other hand, works in a more straightforward direction, from fairy tale to a novel, but along a path without too many signposts for the reader.

Positioning the novel in the way he does – for it is a positioning and not just an opening - highlights Joyce's break with tradition in the novel as a form, for now the text is foregrounded in glorious isolation and the context is…what exactly? If we can trust first impressions, we might well imagine we were inside a fairy tale or listening into a fairy tale. Indeed, the appearance of a wicked stepmother in the guise of an aunt and of eagles waiting to pull out the boy's eyes supports the idea that we could be in a fairy tale, albeit a fairy tale with perhaps believable sources in a family history. In keeping with the convention of a fairy tale, Joyce shows how the child perceives the world in animistic terms, a world inhabited with living forces, and one which is, significantly, removed from an adult's worldview. Additionally, if we stretch things and think of the childhood of humanity, we might discern a crossover between traditional children's fairy tales and ancient classical myths, for, perhaps without our realising it, eagles introduce the novel's well-worked bird imagery and the theme of flight associated with Stephen's name 'Dedalus'. Joyce threatens disruption but only as much as we can take.

According to Bruno Bettelheim in *The Uses of Enchantment* (1977), the child asks him- or herself a number of questions: 'Who am I? Where did I come from? How did the world come into being? Who created man and all the animals? What is the purpose of life?'[125] The questions invite all kinds of responses, but we might concentrate here on one. Joyce holds back from a psychological reading of his protagonist, and it is left to readers to supply their own theory or explanation perhaps along the lines of Bettelheim. Later in the novel, Stephen does ask or formulate such questions, as when he wonders how God can be addressed as *Dieu*

---

124 Angela Carter, *The Bloody Chamber and Other Stories* (London: Gollancz, 1979).

125 Bruno Bettelheim, *The Uses of Enchantment: The Meaning and Importance of Fairy Tales* (New York: Random House, Vintage Books, 1977), 47.

in French, or when he lists his place in the universe beginning with his name and his class of elements at school.

There is, then, merit in highlighting a foundational role for enchantment. The novel later explores how the boy escapes the nets thrown at him by family, education, the Church, and politics. But, at first, Stephen belongs elsewhere, to a world before anything existed, before, that is, he is thrown into existence to meet a cow coming down along the road and a father who told him stories. Such a course is more familiar than we might think: start with enchantment and with education, move on to sociology, and, when looking back as an adult, don't neglect the ideological or psychological roots of enchantment. At the same time never forget that you cannot get inside my head and that I can never get inside yours. Enchantment is at once profoundly individual and what we all share.

In terms of narrative theory, then, Joyce distances himself from a conventional opening such as 'My earliest memories were of my father telling me stories about a moocow'. In this rendering the position of the narrator is clear, as is the narrator's relationship with the story s/he is telling. In terms of context, therefore, Joyce has something missing in mind. Not, that is, in his mind but in mind. Recall the reference to the word 'gnomon' in 'The Sisters', the first story of *Dubliners*, gnomon being in Euclidian geometry a figure formed by removing a similar parallelogram from a corner of a larger parallelogram. Joyce misses nothing, and he enjoys showing us how things get misreported or misremembered or misinterpreted. A man in a macintosh attends Paddy Dignam's funeral in *Ulysses*; later that evening in the newspaper report we read of someone called McIntosh attending the funeral.

At the start of *A Portrait*, Joyce refuses to furnish anything substantial by way of context, or, indeed initially, any signs of a moral universe. We are closer to atmosphere or something woven together than to the more defining word 'context'. Conrad, by contrast, gets to the heart of the issue in the opening sentence to *Lord Jim* (1900): 'He was an inch, perhaps two, under six feet'. Such a sentence governs a reading of the novel, and intimates that, even though he might be called a 'Lord' and spend his days struggling to achieve it, Jim will never assume heroic status and full height in the traditional sense. Equally, Muriel Spark in her opening to *The Girls of Slender Means* (1963) pulls apart our notion of context and asks us to reconsider how generalisations about the past are constructed: 'Long ago in 1945 all the nice people in England were poor, allowing for exceptions.' Not unlike Joyce, Spark plays with orientation and disorientation in equal measure and in the same sentence. And her wit is just below the surface as when she claims that 1945 was 'long ago', which was hardly the case in 1963 when the novel was published.[126] Like Joyce, Spark repays attention. As she tells us in this opening sentence, she is writing not about the poor but about 'nice' people who imagine they are poor.

Fairy tale v novel, narrator v character, text v context, author v reader, past v present: all these relationships are put into play by Joyce. According to Mark A. Wollaeger, text and context in this novel are 'mutually illuminating but do not fully disclose each other's secrets'.[127] In the sentence following the novel's opening Joyce sketches in another relationship, this time between a father and a son: 'His father told him that story: his father looked at him through a glass: he had a hairy face.' It would help if we knew exactly how the story continued for it must be longer than what is here. However, 'story' reminds us of the book we have in our hands, even if we don't know if it is the boy telling us the story or an author known as James Joyce writing it. So, from the outset of *A Portrait,* we find ourselves inside a story about a story told by one of the characters, a story told by a father who will himself become part of the story told by his son. The father is described up-close: he has a 'glass', which we assume is a word that the boy is familiar with from its contrast with, say, wool or paper. Equally, 'glass' does service for a word he is unfamiliar with, namely 'monocle'. This is the start of Stephen's relationship with the stony world of words as well as with his father and, by implication, with the reader. As it happened, John Joyce was, according to Eugene Sheehy, 'a dapper little man, with military moustache, who supported an eyeglass and cane, and wore spats.'[128]

The vocabulary of the young artist is expanding, but it is not yet secure. The adjective 'nicens' is baby talk but, later, as 'nice', it is

---

126 The tagged-on phrase at the end of Spark's sentence is reminiscent of a similarly ungrammatical phrase in the 'Eumaeus' episode of *Ulysses* where Joyce apologises to the writer of school textbooks in the nineteenth century for not writing a properly constructed English sentence: 'with apologies to Lindley Murray' (*U* 16.1475). See Lindley Murray, *English exercises, adapted to the Grammar lately published by L. Murray Designed for the benefit of private learners, as well as for the use of schools* third edition (York: Wilson, Spence, and Mawman: 1798).

127 Mark A. Wollaeger (ed.), *James Joyce's A Portrait of the Artist: A Casebook* (New York: Oxford University Press, 2003), 15

128 Eugene Sheehy *May It Please the Court* (Dublin: C.J. Fallon, 1951), 175.

deployed by Stephen to identify with his mother against rough boys. Even empty-sounding adjectives can acquire substance and protection as a child. The irony with the use of 'glass' is that, while it is transparent, this is less true of the opening to the story, which is more like seeing something darkly, as St Paul suggests in his letter to the Corinthians concerning a vision of God. Of course, children in an adult's arms resort to touching glasses not to destroy the transparency but to touch the fascinating object. So when we read about his father looking through a glass, this is only possible for a boy to record in retrospect. Indeed, seeing the world through his father's eyes requires a leap of the imagination, a leap the would-be artist possesses in abundance, although there is little sign he inherited it from his father.

As for his 'hairy face', this could suggest for some readers a figure from the Old Testament such as Esau or one of the prophets, or God himself, peering down at the child with all the accompanying authority. Whatever the case, the phrase distances the teller from the child, who resorts to a piece of contextual information as if, were he whimsically inclined, such a detail might help trace his father if he were ever lost or ensure the detail is accurate if he were to sit for a portrait painting. We might also notice the overlap between the boy at the time and, as the tense of the verb 'told' suggests, the boy, at some period in the future, relaying the scene. Crossing demarcation lines in Joyce's fiction implies a form of contamination, where nothing holds firm and where everything is subject to what he characterises in *Finnegans Wake* as the 'warping process' (*FW* 497.3). Another prominent aspect in this sentence is the switch from speech to a written narration, a switch accompanied by something else. For, whether in the form of speech or writing, we are conscious of being inside the mind of a child, a child who is capable of using colons, which are a highly sophisticated part of speech, correctly.

In turn, the next sentence raises another talking point: 'He was baby tuckoo.' This sentence suddenly exposes the tension between narrative and narrator. The problem is not that 'he' is without an identity, for we all know it is the boy, but who is telling us this? Who in other words is the focaliser? A number of possibilities suggest themselves, but none of them looks sufficiently compelling to resolve matters. One line of thought will identify 'he' as the father telling the boy that 'he', the boy, is the character in the story. But this is odd not least because it is not what the father would have uttered. 'You are baby tuckoo' sounds more plausible. So something interesting is happening here. The shift

A woodcut of Clongowes Wood College taken from
The Dublin Penny Journal, 7 July 1832.

in the narrative, especially evident in the point of view, captures something of the creative process, which in turn is close to the mind of the artist. Even though it is early days in Stephen's consciousness we might be reminded of something that Dorrit Cohn suggests, how psycho-narration can 'effectively articulate a psychic life that remains unverbalised, penumbral, or obscure'.[129]

The shifts in narrative point of view are always worth noticing. After his classroom punishment, Stephen seeks redress from the rector. Tension mounts as he summons up courage walking down a normally out-of-bounds corridor reserved for senior staff. Throughout this episode we are inside his mind; we see everything through him, for he is both the narrative voice and the focaliser. He notices bullet marks on the walls from a previous episode of history before Clongowes became a Jesuit college. He asks an old servant for the rector's room: 'the old servant pointed to the door at the far end and looked after him as he went on to it and knocked'. (*P* 56) The insertion of the phrase 'and looked after him' shifts the focaliser at this point, for now we see Stephen as the focus of someone else's observation. Alternatively, perhaps this is Stephen looking back and noticing the servant looking at him, or, more likely, a vulnerable Stephen feeling his back exposed: 'I'm being singled out. I can feel the eyes of the old servant on my back. There are bullet marks on the wall.'

These kinds of subtle modulations or doubts in the narrative voice constitute one of the delights in reading Joyce and should not

---

129 *Transparent Minds*, 46.

be missed. Think of the strange echo when we hear Stephen's parents bidding him goodbye on leaving him at school: 'Goodbye, Stephen, goodbye!' (*P* 9) For this is rendered not so much from the perspective of persons uttering the phrase as from inside an older Stephen/Joyce recalling what was possibly a traumatic moment from his childhood. There is so much going on when reading Joyce's prose that, in spite of the theory proposed by Shklovsky, we seem to lack the resources at times to describe it. As Jean-Paul Sartre, in one of his most enigmatic remarks, observed about Flaubert, how he steals language from men and returns us to silence and the secret goal of written language.[130]

Because he often has something missing in mind, Joyce emphasises gaps in our reading. This is not quite the same as Flaubert's emphasis on silence, for Joyce is less absolute and more accommodating. He is always ready to involve the reader in identifying the person speaking or thinking, whether that is a character, the narrator, the author, or some third person not specified. And sometimes these are half-thoughts where full consciousness is not on display. Joyce's preoccupation is initially on narrative perspective rather than character. With regard to the psychology of Stephen or his father, we can only surmise something of this at first, for, as suggested above, Joyce gives the impression that he is more interested in cognitive psychology than in the psychology of character. He signals as much by inserting the definite article in the title, so it is 'the Artist', not 'an Artist'.

The psychology of Stephen is shown as developing and maturing through time, but at first it remains on hold, as if something prior in the field of narrative viewpoint and cognitive psychology is being addressed.[131] Carter's insertion of 'unguessable' hints at the psychology of the protagonist and what might happen to her as the story unfolds. By contrast, when we encounter the word 'glass', we do not know if it might foreshadow the incident when Stephen's glasses are broken at school or serve as an image heralding the theme of sight and seeing in the novel.

---

130 Cited in Jonathan Culler, *Flaubert: The Uses of Uncertainty* (London: Elek, 1974), 71-2 and note 57 on pages 239-240. For Sartre's remark, see his *L'Idiot de la famille* II (Paris: Gallimard, 1971-2), 1617-8.

131 I write more about the idea of consciousness in my chapter 'A New Departure for Fiction: *A Portrait of the Artist* ' in *The Joyce Country: Literary Scholarship and Irish Culture* (Brighton: Edward Everett Root, 2018). For a recent collection of essays on Joyce and cognitive psychology, see Sylvain Belluc and Valérie Bénéjam (eds.), *Cognitive Joyce* (London: Palgrave, 2018).

As it happens, 'He was baby tuckoo' recalls what parents do all the time in speaking to their children, how the child's name becomes the subject of a sentence when 'you' is avoided. 'Tommy wash his hands now' or 'Molly's turn'. But in this instance the use of the third person must belong to fiction rather than to what would have happened in practice. Without perhaps noticing how peculiar it all appears, the reader moves seamlessly between the familiar and the unfamiliar. But then an equally arresting interpretation asserts itself. For it could be the child, now grown up and looking back on this episode from his childhood, who is telling the reader 'I was baby tuckoo'. Or, more likely, it is the child informing the reader that he is baby tuckoo, a character who migrated from a fairy tale into the real world of story-telling and that of his family. All the time we recognise an artist in the making, that is, an artist who is or was always alive to the possibility of telling stories even if he is or was, at first, part of one. In its own way this is another form of the artfulness of Joyce's art, of living through the making of something.

As we have seen, of all the words in Joyce's title 'Artist' is perhaps the one that stands out and invites further consideration. In a way similar to how branding works, everything in the novel comes under the banner of 'The Artist', and our minds are seduced accordingly. With seduction in mind, I am making the assumption that 'artist' is a genuine term and not to be confused with a Dublin slang term for a person who is a 'character'. In conversation with John Elwood and with Joyce and 'epiphany' in mind, Gogarty quipped that an artist was 'a quaint fellow or a great cod: a pleasant and un-hypocritical poseur, one who sacrifices his own dignity for his friends' diversion'.[132] At a later stage we might want to lower our sights and accept Gogarty's description, but at first there is merit in taking a positive view that Stephen is an artist in the normal sense. Gogarty did not need to be so uncomplimentary, for the Irish word 'ealada'/'ealadain' is rendered by the celebrated lexicographer, Patrick Dinneen, as art or science; skill, learning; trade, profession or calling; pretence, shamming, artfulness, feigned politeness.[133] He might have added that there is also an art in feigning.

---

132 Oliver St John Gogarty, *As I Was Going Down Sackville Street* (London: Penguin, 1954) 299. Elwood and Gogarty were worried about Joyce rushing off to the toilets to take down notes or epiphanies on their conversation. Elwood is a model for Temple, the medical student, in *A Portrait*.

133 Patrick Dinneen, *Foclóir Gaedilge agus Béarla: An Irish-English Dictionary* (Dublin: M.H. Gill, 1904).

Perhaps not surprisingly, Stephen's first words are interpreted by some critics as offering an insight into the artistic temperament. He listens to the lines of a song:

> O, the wild rose blossoms
> On the little green place.

And even though he responds in a garbled fashion, changing in the process 'wild rose' to 'green wothe', what we witness is not so much childish nonsense as a creative move that transforms the world even as, in this instance, he gets things confused. The quoted lines are taken from 'Lilly Dale', an American ballad described by one commentator as 'a sentimental Victorian account of death'. [134] 'Now the wild rose blossoms o'er her little green grave' is how the original line reads, so we realise how the neutral concept 'place' is substituted by his father for the troubling word 'grave'. And, on reflection, it is clear that a song about death is not particularly suited to the entry of a young boy into life.

The sensation of being thrown into this novel never leaves us. If we knew more about the child, we might be reassured. But, as indicated, what we encounter can only be described as a form of estrangement. Quite naturally, we find ourselves seeking answers to more basic questions. Is this an artist in the making? Is this the boy who will grow up to be the young man and known as an artist? And what's particularly significant about a glimpse into childhood that many people experience? Or is it that we are dealing with types rather than an individual, 'the artist' rather than 'an artist'? As the French critic, Valéry Larbaud, once suggested, *A Portrait* is 'l'histoire de la jeunesse de l'artiste en général, c'est-à-dire de tout homme doué du tempérament artiste', or the story of the youth of the artist in general, that is to say of every man endowed with the artistic temperament.[135] If the emphasis is on language acquisition and development, what is especially artistic about any of this? Isn't this what we are all subject to? Where is the palette or the artist's studio or the crucible of the creative imagination? Indeed, there is no paintbrush mentioned in this novel, no discussion of any classical painting, and the only reference to a nude statue is when we learn from Lynch that he had once scrawled his name 'in pencil on the backside of the Venus of Praxiteles in the Museum' (*P* 205).

Unaware of our concerns, Stephen, who is a fitting subject for a researcher in psycholinguistics or child language acquisition, continues

---

134 Ruth Bauerle, *The James Joyce Songbook* (New York: Garland, 1982), 183.
135 Valéry Larbaud, *Gens de Dublin* (1926; Paris: Gallimard, 1974), 19.

with what is in effect an exercise in substitution when, instead of the green place, he stumbles upon a green rose. Or, rather, a green 'wothe'.[136] If we were familiar with Old Norse, which few of us are, 'wothe' might enter our thoughts as the word for danger, but this move, we would rightly conclude, must be wide of the mark – unless we felt it anticipates the threat from the eagles waiting to swoop down and pull out the boy's eyes.

Every detail and comment contributes to a feeling that we need something solid to stop us falling further. To prevent this from happening, we resort to all kinds of things, including how images can be taken for signs. Thus, for some readers the 'green rose' must be a reference to the green carnation that Wilde sported in his lapel, while for others it represents the rose of Irish nationalism. The sceptical reader, on the other hand, refuses to be drawn. That Stephen emerges as someone defining himself in artistic terms is perfectly plausible. However, the evidence for something less forthright also looks compelling. This is where the words in the title are worth returning to. Their privileged position alone should convince us that from his first moments, with the evidence of some slightly obscure scratch marks on a canvas, Stephen finds himself being defined in such terms. At first the boy is a passive creature, who, to invoke an image from the novel, is not unlike a bowl being filled with drops of water. In time, he will establish his own independence, free to discover his own psychology, personality, and artistic temperament.

Unlike the potentially bloody fate awaiting Carter's protagonist, Stephen's future is unknown, but it is not essentially 'unguessable'. As readers, we wait, but we don't wait to be surprised; the tension lies elsewhere. For this reason *A Portrait* offers a cautionary tale, and it might be better if at this stage we temporarily abandoned the word 'artist' and substituted 'writer'. In a note composed for the university section of *Stephen Hero*, Joyce contended that 'Art has the gift of tongues'.[137] Such a view was there from the start. At each phase in his development, the boy's fascination with words catches our attention. At first he alights on single

---

136 The Norton Critical Edition, which is edited by Hans Walter Gabler and Walter Hettche, uses the 1916 Huebsch edition of the novel. Instead of 'green', which appears in the 1918 Egoist Press edition, this edition has 'geen'. See *James Joyce, A Portrait of the Artist* (ed. John Paul Riquelme), (New York: W.W.Norton, 2007). Arguments can be advanced either way as to what Joyce intended.

137 Robert Scholes and Richard Kain (eds), The *Workshop of Daedalus: James Joyce and the Raw Materials for A Portrait of the Artist* (Evanston, Ill: Northwestern University Press, 1965), 70.

words such as 'suck', where sound and meaning are closely allied, or 'kiss', which causes him to blush when asked if his mother kisses him at night. 'Dieu', the French word for God, causes him a different kind of problem. Now something more conceptual enters his thoughts as he attempts to understand how God is perceived, or, rather, can be conceived, in different languages. His next question, the subject of much discussion in centuries past, might have been 'What language is spoken in heaven?'

Through not knowing as much as through knowing, through words which allude to a sensuous world he will later inhabit or words which already elicit embarrassment, the boy is caught between language and reality. He notices things but he cannot yet express his thoughts or feelings. He *sees* the tears of his father at the end of the Christmas Dinner scene, but he cannot yet absorb or articulate how he, the eldest son, dressed for the occasion in his Eton jacket, should respond – unless that is precisely what he is beginning to detect, a changing relationship with his father. Joyce doesn't delay at this point or tell us what the narrator thinks. Instead, almost immediately, he moves on, the asterisks inserted across the page impossible not to notice. However, we are in no doubt that something is taking place in the mind of the future artist or writer. A threshold in his development has been passed.

With every page we turn, we accompany Stephen on a journey, watching him mature as a writer/artist. He, on the other hand, studiously refuses to reciprocate, so he never turns to us and says 'This is what I was like at this age'. Our role is to watch and wait, always recognising that it is through language, inside the folds of language that is, that the boy will grow intellectually and emotionally and in every other way as a person. He is a subject-in-process, often observed observing the world around him, less often noticed taking a full part in that world. In the way it shows the growth of a mind, the novel cannot be faulted. In some respects we like Stephen because he isn't the soul of the party but one who, as an adolescent, disappears after the school play to be alone with his thoughts. Brooding is one of his characteristic traits. Victims in literature always have a better press than those who don't need our sympathy. And we admire him for his determination to seek freedom from the nets around him. It should come as no surprise to learn that Ralph Ellison, the great African American novelist and critic, identified with Stephen in his struggle for identity, for both understood the importance of rejecting 'all negative definitions imposed upon [them] by others'.[138]

---

138 Ralph Ellison, *The Collected Essays of Ralph Ellison* (ed. John F.Callahan with preface by Saul Bellow) (New York: Modern Library, 2003), 58.

IN THE CLASSROOM

In the early years of secondary school an English teacher sometimes invites pupils to explore different kinds of writing, some marked by exaggeration or deliberately excessive description. 'Imagine walking through a wood in autumn with the rays of sunshine penetrating the gathering darkness. The ground is wet and you are trying to keep your balance with the wet leaves all around. Describe what you see or feel and include examples of onomatopoeia and words that in themselves conjure up a scene.' Here is Stephen on the night mail train travelling with his father back to Cork to sell off the mortgages on his property there:

> He saw the darkening lands slipping away past him, the silent telegraphpoles passing his window swiftly every four seconds, the little glimmering stations, manned by a few silent sentries, flung by the mail behind her and twinkling for a moment in the darkness like fiery grains flung backwards by a runner. (*P* 87)

With its echo in terms of style of Pater, this is the writer/artist learning his trade. The language is rich, as is the imagery, and, in keeping with the artistic theme, it is visually alive. The rhythms are in sync with the train as it moves though the darkening lands. Things are 'slipping away', and we sense this also applies to Stephen and his father and how they are slipping away from each other. The insertion of a detail such as 'every four seconds' conjures up a boy's world and a boy's ability to isolate himself from the world around him and retreat into a shell. On the other hand, 'telegraphpoles', without a hyphen, draws attention to the author, James Joyce, who insisted on joining compound words, as happens throughout the corrected version of the novel.[139] One minute we are inside Stephen's head, the next vaguely aware of the author who created him, the other artist or the real artist that is. This is the person who prefaced this particular scene with 'Stephen was once again seated beside

---

139 For a select list of the errata to the first American edition of *A Portrait* as indicated by Joyce in 1917, see Peter Spielberg, 'James Joyce's Errata for American Editions of *A Portrait of the Artist*' in *Joyce's Portrait: Criticisms and Critiques* (ed. Thomas Connolly) (London: Peter Owen, 1964). Joyce preferred, for example, 'breadbasket' to 'bread basket', 'deathwound' to 'death wound', 'turfcoloured' to 'turf-coloured', 'customhouse' to 'Custom House', 'jews' to 'Jews', 'fellowstudents' to 'fellow-students', 'sixtyone' to 'sixty-one', 'Goodbye' to 'Good-bye'. In modern editions these have been corrected.

his father in the corner of a railway carriage at Kingsbridge' (86).[140]

If the 'darkening lands' sentence was set out as verse – and it is a long sentence waiting to be cut down to size - we would recognise at once its poetic qualities and how metre is used both to slow down and to quicken the pace:

> He saw the darkening lands slipping away past him,
> x / x / x x / / x x / / x
> the silent telegraphpoles
> x / x / x /   /
> passing his window swiftly every four seconds,
> / x   x /   x   / x / x x /   / x
> the little glimmering stations,
> x / x /   x x   / x
> manned by a few silent sentries,
> /   x x / / x / x
> flung by the mail behind her
> /   x x / x /   x
> and twinkling for a moment in the darkness
> x   /   x x x /   x x x /   x
> like fiery grains flung backwards by a runner.
> x   / x   /   /   /   x   x x / x

This can be read as either poetry or prose. It is reminiscent of the heightened prose the narrator deploys in capturing Gabriel Conroy's feelings at the end of 'The Dead'. As he gazes out of the window of his hotel room in Dublin, Gabriel follows in his mind the course of the snow falling all over Ireland, through the Irish Midlands and the Bog of Allen, across the 'mutinous Shannon waves', and finally to the churchyard in Galway where Gretta's former boyfriend is buried. Stephen, presumably with his back to the engine of the train, is also looking back, though without the drama that engulfs Gabriel, for he is the adolescent, at the start of a process, learning the rudiments of how to express himself in writing.

With the sentence set out in verse, we can also discern how

---

140 The insertion of the phrase 'once again' is worth thinking about, for we have had no mention before of a train journey with his father. Perhaps the two had indeed travelled back to Cork before, as happened to Joyce father and son. Perhaps we are supposed to infer that journeys back to Clongowes were normally undertaken by train. Or it could be that Joyce forgot to cut this phrase from material he had written for *Stephen Hero*.

the movement of the last line, with a series of three full stresses, is deliberately slowed down, allowing the reader to pause on the image of grains and the runner. At the same time, the vocabulary is clearly excessive as if the writer is trying too hard for effect. We might also fault the imagery, which is too much for the reader to take in. The reference to 'fiery grains' would not be out of place in an alchemist's handbook, and it has the potential to confuse readers. Unless, that is, Stephen has in mind his running coach, Mike Flynn, and how tobacco grains would drop to the ground when he was refilling his pouch. If this is the allusion, then it just manages to work, and it sets us thinking about tobacco grains, which, when lit, have a fiery character, like the coal being shovelled into the train's steam engine.

From a classroom perspective, excessive description, whether in the memory or imagination, might have been what the teacher was looking for, to awake in her or his pupils an awareness of the creative power of language to describe and evoke. And, if we were familiar with the classics, we might recognise the figure Daedalus, the bronze age craftsman on the island of Crete learning to extract metals from sulphur oxides. One 'flung' would be commented on by the English teacher, but the second example would be cut. Or the second 'flung' would be kept and the first one queried as to what exactly is being flung. Presumably, the boy on the night mail train imagines the stations are being flung backward as they recede into the distance, like the coals being flung into the fire. The gendered language is intriguing but not terribly convincing as part of a thought-out position. On the other hand, it looks as though Stephen, on the cusp of adolescence, is half-aware of the pervasiveness of a sexual world awaiting him. So, the use of 'her' and 'manned' might be relevant to a boy growing up and about to meet his father's one-time associates, one of whom will ask him to compare girls from Cork and Dublin in the beauty stakes. Equally, the runner kicking up the grain might be allowed by the teacher anxious not to suppress youthful excess.

The choice of 'sentries' in the passage would be silently noted by the teacher, and put to one side as being of potential interest. Later in the novel it reappears in a sentence marking Stephen's transition from school to university: 'he had passed beyond the challenge of the sentries who had stood as guardians of his boyhood' (*P* 165). On the trip to Cork with his father the sentries provide what we might assume is simply local colour, but now they have become a powerful metaphor in recording a major transition in his life. In recalling the first reference to sentries, the reader recognises again a developing narrative in which a boy grows up in the folds of the language he is using. With each passing station the mail is collected and eventually arrives at its destination. Growing up has a quality of immediacy. The here and now exerts pressure over all else, but at the same time something is being stored, so, as with the technique of storytelling, reality at times includes an anticipatory quality. Joyce's novel never stops sharing this insight with us.

An earlier train journey is described in Chapter 1, and it occurs in a dream or reverie Stephen has of going home from college. This can be read on its own or, once we get to the second passage, as anticipating the journey back to Cork with his father:

> The train was full of fellows: a long long chocolate train with cream facings. The guards went to and fro opening, closing, locking, unlocking the doors. They were men in dark blue and silver; they had silvery whistles and their keys made a quick music: click, click: click, click.
> And the train raced on over the flat lands and past the Hill of Allen. The telegraphpoles were passing, passing. The train went on and on. (*P* 20)

This is evocative of a younger Stephen, who alights on sound and colour. The guards are guards, not 'sentries'; they were men, he adds, who are dressed not so much in uniforms but in colours and, therefore, they remind us of how the world is classified by a very young boy. The sound of keys locking and unlocking doors also impresses him. In both accounts telegraph poles and the movement of the train are reported on, as is the passing landscape, interestingly rendered as 'lands'. In one description the boy sees 'flat lands'; in the other, we read of the 'darkening lands' and of something more threatening, therefore, or capable of a wider resonance in an unfolding narrative.

The repetition of 'click, click: click, click' anticipates the 'pick, peck, pock, puck' that Stephen hears on the school playing field at Clongowes watching a game of cricket. The sound of the cricket ball strikes a deeper chord than the sound of the train moving over the gaps in the track, for Joyce compares the sound to 'drops of water in a fountain slowly falling in the brimming water'. It's as if we can *hear* in these 'wonderful vocables' the passage of time not only for Stephen and for his life at Clongowes, but also, as previously suggested, for a whole period of history including the colonial history that once linked Ireland to the United Kingdom.[141] In this respect sounds resemble brush-strokes seen up-close on an artist's canvas.

By way of contrast, the dream sequence stays close to description, and this in its own way throws up another issue. For what constitutes the language of dreams? Not presumably as set out in full sentences. Leaving aside their latent aspect, at the surface level dreams are often so fast and anarchic as to leave us at times not knowing how they arose. There is something perverse about how they defy the ordered mind's ability to make sense of them. Speed is of their essence; lengthy description isn't. Hence the appropriateness of the word 'raced' in the dream passage. Trains frequently race along in fiction. When the mind races it needs to be slowed down as if out of control, but we have few resources to impede the course of our dreams. A waking dream, even one of some complexity, can take just minutes and yet can seem like hours. In dreams, colours when they appear do so as colours, as images that is, not words. When we read 'a long long chocolate train with cream facings', such a description can occur only in writing. So there is something curious about these first chapters of *A Portrait*, where dreams are juxtaposed with reality, for, when we look closely at the relevant passages, there is no contrast but only language in play.

By not informing the reader when a dream begins, Joyce disrupts the narrative convention, but it is a disruption which makes for an enjoyable reading experience and keeps us on our toes. When recounting the dream, however, Joyce obeys the convention, and what he depicts is a boy describing his dream in words and sentences that are appropriate to his age group. Freud famously declared that dreams are 'the royal road to the unconscious', but the passage in *A Portrait* offers little support – unless the telegraph poles are phallic symbols.[142] Without the symbols, it is simply a boy at boarding school wishing he was home. What we can observe, however, is, firstly, a graphic reminder of the window through which we filter external reality, and, secondly, how the psychology of Stephen is obliquely registered in the very act of watching the telegraph poles passing. For this is a reality that goes 'on and on' with him watching or without

---

141 I write more about this in a section entitled "Cricket in *A Portrait of the Artist* ' in *Light, Freedom and Song: A Cultural History of Modern Irish Writing* (London and New Haven: Yale University Press, 2005), 162-5.

142 Sigmund Freud, *Complete Psychological Works of Sigmund Freud, Vol 5* (trans. James Strachey). (1900; London: Vintage, 2001), 608.

him watching, and, what is more, it is 'insistent', as he notices on awaking from sleep in the carriage.

For a Catholic boy like Stephen away from home, repetition, especially in the shape of the rule book, always had a potentially sinister side. Later in the novel, during the retreat sermons, Stephen takes it personally when he learns of the 'ceaseless repetition' of Hell as described by St Thomas Aquinas: 'ever to be in hell, never to be in heaven' (*P* 132). With his debt to Aquinas on display throughout his remarkable modern 'summa', Bernard Lonergan, the Canadian philosopher and Jesuit, has some thoughtful and pertinent comments on duration in *Insight: A Study of Human Understanding* (1958): 'What a man experiences, he also can imagine... As he experiences duration, he also imagines duration.'[143] Those responsible for the retreat sermons that Stephen hears knew exactly how to dwell on the experience of duration. They would dwell not so much on time, which is redeemable in religious terms, but on duration.

Sitting in front of the Jesuit preacher for the retreat, Stephen is at the mercy of such thoughts. The word 'duration' appears twice in *A Portrait* and it is fitting that both occur in the retreat episode, once in connection with the fire of hell burning for ever, and once in reference to the equally threatening philosophical issue of 'limitless duration' (130). Now listen to a sentence on duration from Giovanni Pietro Pinamonti's *Hell Opened to Christians* (1845), the book that Joyce relied on for his account in *A Portrait*: 'The torment of one hour is a great pain, that of two must be twice as much; the torment of a hundred hours must be a hundred times as much, and so on, the pain still increasing in proportion of the time of its duration.'[144] And, to twist the knife even further, the seventeenth-century Italian Jesuit then adds 'that which never ends, can never be comprehended'. For the young Stephen, experiencing duration and then imagining duration must have been truly terrifying. In her study of the sermons, Elizabeth E.Boyd notices how Joyce translated a simple observation in Pinamonti ('consider') into the more insistent 'imagine': 'Imagine some foul and putrid corpse.... Imagine such a corpse....imagine this sickening stench.... Imagine all this' (120).[145]

---

143 Bernard J.F.Lonergan, *Insight: A Study of Human Understanding* (London: Darton, Longman,Todd, 1958), 143.

144 Giovanni Pietro Pinamonti, *Hell Opened to Christians; To Caution Them From Entering It* (Derby and London:T. Richardson and Son, for the Catholic Book Society, 1845), 89-90.

145 See her essay 'Joyce's Hell-Fire Sermons' in *Portraits of an Artist* (eds. W.E.Morris and C.A.Nault Jr) (New York: Odyssey Press, 1962), 261.

Fr James Cullen was probably the Jesuit priest who in November
1896 gave the sermons that had a profound impact on Joyce.
Courtesy of Fr Bruce Bradley S.J.

143

In dramatically switching between dreams and reality, Joyce emphasises the contrast between school and home but in a way that involves us, for we are not at first sure whether we are in the world of Stephen's imagination or at school or home. *A Portrait* captures how we internalise the world, so we, too, are carried along the same path as Stephen in his self-discovery. Writing is part of this process and Joyce takes care to describe where and what he writes, from the desk at school in Chapter 1 (which is violated by Fleming, writing on the opposite page), to the bed by a window in his room where he composes the villanelle, to the private diary at the close, where the absence of a location adds to a sense of dislocation.

Internalisation is more than a theme, therefore; it is also a strategy in how a narrative can be constructed. We accompany him going home for holidays and the journey by car and train and the family's welcome and his mother kissing him, but this is followed by noise in the dormitory and wash-room and then by the sickness that affects him. We attend to the flight in his imagination without realising it is indeed in his mind, and, like Icarus before him, we witness him falling back to earth and facing a return to the routine of school life, where he is ridiculed for kissing his mother. What propels Stephen on his artistic path is a certain unsettling in his consciousness. Yeats believed that it was 'Between extremities / Man runs his course', but in *A Portrait* it is between dreams and reality, between highs and lows, that the young Stephen runs his course.[146]

When reflecting on the passage about the train journey to Cork with his father, it is evident that Joyce is an artist quite capable of producing imperfect sentences. It might be considered improper for a 'great' writer to be involved in warping the language in this way. What English teacher would approve of such a move? And yet there is an art in producing sentences which are not quite appropriate or pertinent to the situation. Stephen's attempt at reconstructing the journey back to Cork is visually alive even if it is slightly overdone, but, as already suggested, he is an artist in the making and in the process of discovering how to use language. 'Eumaeus', an episode towards the end of *Ulysses*, is full of odd-looking or what we might describe as warped sentences or failures. However, many of these grammatically incorrect sentences are quite funny and delightful, as when Bloom inquires after Stephen's father:

---

146 From 'Vacillation' in *W.B. Yeats: Selected Poetry* (ed. Timothy Webb) (London: Penguin, 1991), 175.

> Where does he live at present? I gathered in the
> course of conversation that he had moved.
> – I believe he is in Dublin somewhere, Stephen
> answered unconcernedly. Why?
> – A gifted man, Mr Bloom said of Mr Dedalus senior,
> in more respects than one and a born raconteur
> if ever there was one. He takes great pride, quite
> legitimate, out of you. (*U* 16:256-262)

Readers of *A Portrait* will appreciate that the first question is a leading
one because the Dedalus family are in constant transit. And it is not
a question that would be 'gathered in conversation' for it is more like
gossip. When we hear that Stephen's father is gifted, it is accompanied
by the phrase 'in more respects than one', which raises doubts in
the mind of the reader. The last sentence confirms Bloom's lack of
confidence when addressing a young man who has a degree, writes
poetry, and with whom he wants to become acquainted. As for his
father taking pride out of Stephen, we would normally say a father
takes pride in his son not out of him. So perhaps Bloom has, somewhere
in his mind, the half-thought that Simon has a pecuniary interest in
his son. This might explain the insertion of 'quite legitimate', a phrase
which might recall at first 'quite' as a qualifier rather than an intensifier:
'quite difficult' as opposed to 'quite brilliant'. But the absence of –ly
after 'legitimate' takes us in a different direction inside Bloom's mind,
as if he was speaking to himself.

Other aspects of the father-son relationship can be mentioned.
Here is Bloom, the Odysseus figure, meeting his son, Telemachus, on
his return from his wanderings. Simon is the legitimate father but
Bloom, too, has fatherly feelings. Not surprisingly, Stephen's initial
response is consistent with the person we have already encountered in
A Portrait. This is the boy who watched his father in Cork falling yet
further in his estimation when drinking with his 'cronies', and who
now answers 'unconcernedly', with an adverb that manages to capture
a whole history in their relationship.

With all its faults, or because of its faulty phrasing and uncertain
language, 'Eumaeus' affords a brilliant and unfailingly humorous take
on the language we all speak. But it has its origins in the novel that
preceded it. The point is worth repeating: nearly every sentence in
A Portrait reveals something of interest for the reader to explore or
to discuss with others. At times we are not sure what it is that Joyce
intends, but we should resist the temptation not to delay, for, normally,

Joyce plays fair with the reader by offering clues to interpretation. Although he championed the impersonality or the invisibility of the artist hiding behind his creation, his work reveals something else, namely a belief in the idea of a contract with his reader. At the same time – though this is not often remarked upon – he offered tips on how to write. In spite of what is sometimes said, most recently by Banville, Joyce did not close off the future of fiction for later writers. Indeed, if he possesses the gift of tongues and can do anything with words, then so, too, can others. The boy looks out of the train window, notices the telegraph poles, and then looks back. It's good advice for the budding writer. Put on one side talk of Joyce's legacy and the weight of tradition. Keep looking back and a whole world opens up to the imagination.

If we found ourselves overwhelmed by the great writer idea, we might find comfort in discovering that Joyce was capable of writing badly. Compare, for example, the train passage below, a passage that appears in a manuscript of additional pages associated with *Stephen Hero*:

> From the Broadstone to Mullingar is a journey of some fifty miles across the midlands of Ireland. Mullingar, the chief town of Westmeath, is the midland capital and there is a great traffic of peasants and cattle between it and Dublin. This fifty-mile journey is made by the train in about two hours and you are therefore to conceive Stephen Daedalus packed in the corner of a third-class carriage and contributing the thin fumes of his cigarettes to the already reeking atmosphere. The carriage was inhabited by a company of peasants nearly every one of whom had a bundle tied in a spotted handkerchief. The carriage smelt strongly of peasants (an odour the debasing humanity of which Stephen remembered to have perceived in the little chapel of Clongowes on the morning of his first communion) and indeed so pungently that the youth could not decide whether he found the odour of sweat [unpleasant] offensive because the peasant sweat is monstrous or because it did not now proceed from his own body. (*SH* 237-8)

It is unclear if this additional page was ever intended to be incorporated into *Stephen Hero*. Joyce never destroyed it, and perhaps in his mind he intended to rework some of it for use elsewhere in his writing. The episode relates to a journey Stephen made to Mullingar in 1898 to visit his grandfather, 'Mr Fulham'. In *A Portrait* we are never quite sure of topography or the location of the 'lands' he passes. By contrast, in this passage, we seem to be reading a local guide to the area and learn that Mullingar is the chief town of Westmeath. What also stands out is a social eye lacking in discrimination and, as in the phrase 'a bundle tied in a spotted handkerchief', cliché-ridden. The so-called 'peasants' in the carriage would have been agricultural labourers or small tenant farmers or from the ranks of the rural poor. They would not have been peasants, who disappeared from the Irish countryside in the long ago. Some words struggle to sound right: the carriage is 'inhabited', the peasants form a 'company'.

Clearly, Joyce did not begin as a great writer but had to learn what is, arguably, his most important lesson: more means less and less means more. As the reduction of the long vowel in Daedalus to the short vowel in Dedalus might serve to illustrate, Joyce's motto after writing so many laboured passages in *Stephen Hero* must have been 'Keep cutting'. It paid off, for, as Pound declared on the publication of *Dubliners* in 1914: 'Mr Joyce's merit, I will not say his chief merit but his most engaging merit, is that he carefully avoids telling you a lot that you don't want to know.'[147]

WRITING POETRY

The villanelle Stephen composes in *A Portrait* is a reminder of another ambition Joyce entertained. Joyce began writing poems as a teenager, and he took care to show them to friends and, later, to Ireland's leading poet, Yeats. In his last years at Belvedere College, according to his brother, Stanislaus, Joyce began collecting his poems in an exercise book, which bore on the fly-leaf the word 'Moods'. (*MBK* 85) The volume contained fifty or sixty lyric poems, mostly short pieces, with some translations from Latin and French. According to the narrator in *Stephen Hero*, 'He sought in his verses to fix the most elusive of his moods and he put his lines together not word by word but letter by letter.' (*SH* 32) Moods helped to direct his writing; he had a ready-made subject matter waiting for the lyrical poet to explore. Fixing a mood was even more profitable, for it offered a way into writing that was immediate and grounded.

---

147 Ezra Pound, '"Dubliners" and Mr James Joyce' in *The Egoist* 15 July 1914, 267.

Arguably the most attractive photo of Yeats as a young man.
From *The Outlook* (New York) 2 January 1904.

Paradoxically, the more elusive the mood the more determined was the search for the right word or phrase. Herbert Gorman, his first biographer, offers in passing an intriguing observation, which perhaps owes something to Joyce himself. For he suggests that, in contrast with his early poems, prose required 'the full measure of discipline demanded by his aesthetic discipline'.[148] Walking the streets of Dublin or listening to the sounds of the world around him, Joyce could find the rhythm of a poem. He could also indulge the fantasy that 'This is what I feel; it must be a reflection of the times in which I live.'

In a short essay published in 1895 and called 'The Moods', Yeats sought to put a steer on the kind of literature he saw emerging: 'Literature differs from explanatory and scientific writing in being

---

148 Herbert Gorman, *James Joyce* (New York: Rinehart, 1948), 116.

wrought about a mood, or a community of moods, as the body is wrought about an invisible soul.'[149] Stephen would have agreed. Moods touched the soul and gave voice to a reality not available to the everyday world. In addition, moods were associated with something else: they were close to music. As Stanislaus recalls, the Joyce family, his mother at the piano, had an affection for 'the moody men' of romantic piano music such as Chopin, Mendelssohn, Liszt, Schumann, Schubert. (*MBK* 65-6) Moreover, moods signalled the separation of body and soul and allowed Stephen space to withdraw into himself and thereby take on the role of the artist, the figure he later defined as 'invisible, refined out of existence, indifferent, paring his fingernails'. Ironically, moods, which in their own way constituted a form of enchantment, were essential to Stephen's engagement with the world.

Music and moods dominate *Chamber Music* (1907), Joyce's first volume of verse. The Lover describes a woman playing the piano; he listens to sounds of 'soft sweet music'; imagines he is the 'visitant' singing by her gate; hears her singing 'a merry air'; imagines the winds of May 'dancing a ringaround in glee'; and concludes that 'love is unhappy when love is away'.[150] Poems on the sorrow of love by Yeats and Seumas O'Sullivan are also never far away. Running through *New Songs: A Lyric Selection*, edited by George Russell and published in 1904, there are images and sentiments which anticipate *Chamber Music*. Autumn winds sigh through the trees, the forest wind sets the withered leaves fluttering, O season of the withering of the leaves, God has made nothing fairer than the little flowers of earth, veils of twilight, soft dews fall round me. In the final stanza of O'Sullivan's 'The Sorrow of Love', sadness and the wind come together with the woman perhaps cruelly laughing at the lover:

> But she stands laughing lightly
> Who all my sorrow knows,
> Like the little wind that laughing
> Across the water blows.[151]

According to Yeats, in a letter dated 18 December 1902, Joyce's verse stood out from his contemporaries: 'Your technique in verse

---

149 W.B.Yeats, *Essays and Introductions* (New York: Collier Books, 1977), 195.
150 James Joyce, *Chamber Music* (1907; London: Jonathan Cape, 1945). Quotations are from the early selection of poems I-IX.
151 George Russell (ed.), *New Songs: A Lyric Selection* (Dublin: O'Donoghue; London: A.H.Bullen, 1904), 22.

is very much better than the technique of any young Dublin man I have met during my time.' The thought in one of the poems Joyce sent him was 'a little thin', but Yeats was impressed: 'The work which you have actually done is very remarkable for a man of your age who has lived away from vital intellectual centres.' (*MBK* 208-9)

With some reservations, Yeats, then, approved, but, as the last remark suggests, Joyce's poetry betrayed a certain provincial background. Such a comment would never be said about his prose, about which he never felt he needed anyone's approval. He persisted, however, with writing verse, and wider recognition eventually came when the final poem in *Chamber Music*, 'I Hear An Army', was included in an imagist anthology. In some respects the inclusion was a mismatch. Joyce was not an imagist, but Pound was anxious to recruit him to his cause. Indeed, Joyce's early verse was closer to late-nineteenth-century symbolism, and owed much to Yeats's own poetry, especially his early collections, *The Rose* (1893) and *The Wind Among the Reeds* (1899). In a recent essay on Joyce's use of silence, the Polish American translator and critic, Jolanta Wawrzycka, has convincingly underlined just how indebted he was to Yeats:

> It may appear that probing *Chamber Music* for silence is counterproductive, given that the poems resonate with titular music (playing of strings, harp, and piano), with sounds of nature, or with the clatter of the army of charioteers. However, the process of translating the poems into Polish revealed that many poems also convey measured silences of stylised pauses and near-stillness amidst the imagery of feebly stirring breezes, subdued muffled sighs, faint, sometimes distant music, and the air of quietude and repose.[152]

Joyce's early poetry recalls the enormous debt which he owed to others and which he shared with others such as Padraic Colum, Seamas O'Sullivan, Eva Gore-Booth, Ella Young, Alice Milligan, George Roberts, and Susan Mitchell. In his introduction to *New Songs*, Russell suggested the collection 'revealed a new mood in Ireland'. Stephen Dedalus is part of this new mood, the would-be

---

152 See her essay, '"Mute Chime and Mute Peal": Translating Silences in *Chamber Music*', in Jolanta Wawrzycka and Serenella Zanotti (eds.), *James Joyce's Silences* (London: Bloomsbury, 2018), 192.

poet in the making, as the villanelle suggests. *Ulysses* is a novel which is anchored in the year 1904, and in 'Scylla and Charydis', the Library episode, Stephen somewhat facetiously remarks, with Colum and others in mind, 'We are becoming important it seems' (*U* 9. 312-3).[153]

At some stage, then, the dreaming had to stop, and it is fitting that his best early verse came in two broadsides full of anger and bitterness and composed when he was either leaving Ireland or thinking of doing so. 'The Holy Office', a satire on the contemporary literary scene in Dublin, was written in August 1904 on the eve of his departure from Dublin with Nora Barnacle. 'Gas from a Burner', his most vitriolic poem, was composed in September 1912 on his way home to Trieste after leaving Ireland for what turned out to be his last time. In retrospect, were it not for the fiction which followed, his early verse would not merit so much attention. Heaney in a single sentence manages to sum up Joyce's early achievement in terms of music and mood and simultaneously to offer a judgement which is at once positive and negative: 'It is poetry as the handmaiden of music, as evocation, invitation to dream.'[154]

How, then, are we to respond to the 'Villanelle of the Temptress' Stephen composes in *A Portrait*? Does it belong to the sequence of poems some of which are collected in *Chamber Music*? What did Joyce think of the poem's quality? Do we rate it? Does Stephen? Perhaps we should remember the context, how it was composed in an impoverished bedroom with 'tattered wallpaper' on the inside of a cigarette packet, possibly after Stephen has awoken from a wet dream or after masturbating. He places the one remaining cigarette carefully on the window ledge and reflects on 'ardent ways' and the consumption of passion. (*P* 218-9) This is an image of the

---

153 The poems by Padraic Colum in the volume stand out, especially 'The Plougher. 'A Drover', and the opening poem 'A Portrait', which he later changed to 'A Poor Scholar of the Forties'. In the Library episode in *Ulysses*, Stephen praises Colum and in particular 'The Drover' and the last line of 'A Portrait ', which, apparently, also impressed Yeats. (*U* 9.303-5) The poem looks back to the 1840s and the Famine decade, and asks what was the point of teaching Latin and Greek to the rural poor? The reply ends somewhat enigmatically but forcefully: 'Years hence in rustic speech, a phrase / As in wild earth a Grecian vase.' The last line is quoted by Stephen seemingly with approval, for Joyce, with his eye in *Ulysses* always alert to Greek parallels, must have seen the quality in Colum's verse. See *U* 9:304-5.
154 Seamus Heaney, *Finders Keepers: Selected Prose 1971-2001* (London: Faber, 2002), 389.

impoverished artist not so much in a garret in Montmartre as in his family's rented house in an impoverished neighbourhood of Dublin trying desperately to counter his environment by an appeal to his lyrical impulse. The ironies are not lost on the reader.

We can begin with a passage in *Stephen Hero*, a passage which links the villanelle with the concept of an epiphany:

> He was passing through Eccles' St one evening, one misty evening, with all these thoughts dancing the dance of unrest in his brain when a trivial incident set him composing some ardent verses which he entitled a 'Vilanelle of the Temptress'. A young lady was standing on the steps of one of those brown brick houses which seem the very incarnation of Irish paralysis. A young gentleman was leaning on the rusty railings of the area. Stephen as he passed on his quest heard the following fragment of colloquy out of which he received an impression keen enough to afflict his sensitiveness very severely.
> The Young Lady - (drawling discreetly) ... O, yes ... I was ... at the ... cha ... pel ...
> The Young Gentleman - (inaudibly) ... I ... (again inaudibly) ... I ...
> The Young Lady - (softly) ... O ... but you're ... ve ... ry ... wick ... ed ...
> This triviality made him think of collecting many such moments together in a book of epiphanies. By an epiphany he meant a sudden spiritual manifestation, whether in the vulgarity of speech or of gesture or in a memorable phase of the mind itself. He believed that it was for the man of letters to record these epiphanies with extreme care, seeing that they themselves are the most delicate and evanescent of moments. He told Cranly that the clock of the Ballast Office was capable of an epiphany. (*SH* 210-11)

The title of the villanelle and the choice of the adjective 'ardent' suggests Joyce was in the process of composing a version of the poem that appears in *A Portrait*.[155] This would make sense when we consider how Stephen had 'written verses for her again after ten years' (*P* 222). The 'her' presumably refers to Emma Clery, who features by name throughout *Stephen Hero* and as E---C--- for much of *A Portrait*. She is modelled in part on Mary Sheehy, the woman who was the inspiration for two poems published in *Chamber Music*, 'What counsel has the hooded moon' and 'Lightly come and lightly go'. While at Belvedere Joyce regularly spent Sunday evenings at the Sheehy family home singing songs and playing charades. However, his relationship with Mary, who was two years younger than he was, is not that easy to determine, and perhaps neither Stephen nor Stanislaus are reliable guides to Joyce's feelings in these matters. Equally, we cannot help hearing the advice Richard receives in Meredith's Victorian novel how women are 'our ordeal' and how when you encounter them 'you are thoroughly on trial'.[156]

Stanislaus believed he was never in love with her, and, as far as he knew, they never met except at the Sheehy home or on other rare occasions such as an excursion. (*MBK*, 150) However, he also adds: 'Mary Sheehy was the only girl who had ever aroused any emotional interest in him' (*MBK*, 151). Even if Stanislaus's observations are not as accurate as he thought they were, they can still contribute to our understanding of the villanelle in *A Portrait*. But we need to recall something else, for, according to his brother, Joyce believed that 'a poet must always write about a past or future emotion, never about a present one' (*MBK* 148).

The reference to ten years increases the complexity. If we assume an outside date of 1902 for the villanelle episode in *A Portrait*, this would take us back to 1892 when Joyce would have been around 10 and Mary 8 or 9. We would imagine any recourse to that particular chronology must be wrong, but perhaps it is not. In the novel we learn that, before he entered Belvedere College, Stephen attempted to write a poem to E- C- (see page 70). His age would have been

---

155 The leading textual critic, Hans Walter Gabler, has suggested that the villanelle was perhaps composed after 1911, but he also enters a caveat that it could have belonged to the manuscript which was rescued from the fire in that year. See 'The Genesis of *A Portrait of the Artist*' in *Critical Essays on James Joyce's A Portrait of the Artist* (eds. Philip Brady and James F. Carens) (New York: G.K. Hall, 1998), 95-6. I would need something more substantial to alter my view as expressed here.

156 George Meredith, *The Ordeal of Richard Feverel* (1859; London: Chapman and Hall, 1889), 159.

around 11, an age when a boy might well have amorous feelings stirring inside him. And after all he wrote a poem to Parnell when he was 9. For some readers it would make more sense if Joyce is recalling the Sunday evenings at the home of the Sheehy family, for this would mean around 1896-8, when Joyce would have been around 14 or so and Mary on the verge of adolescence or as the backward-looking Stephen imagines 'before the strange humiliation of her nature had first come upon her' (*P* 222). What, of course, Stephen/Joyce means is not strange humiliation but familiar denigration, for there is nothing humiliating about menstruation. Ten years later would then suggest 1906-8, when he would have been writing *A Portrait*.

At times with Joyce clarification sometimes clouds matters, and, equally, it is often unclear what purpose is being served, unless it belongs in part to the revenge motif in Joyce's career as a writer, to his victory lap therefore.[157] Paradoxically, the remark seems to throw us off the scent that the villanelle was written years before. In this way the poem is seen as being constructed by the artist for the novel in which it appears. If Joyce had simply inserted the complete poem, it might appear as 'lifted' from elsewhere and the integration of the novel undermined. If the villanelle represents the high point in the novel, confirming Stephen's role as an artist, we need, then, to insert a certain qualification, for Joyce composed the villanelle perhaps some years before he wrote the novel, indeed perhaps years before he had even conceived of writing a novel.

The villanelle sequence occupies a separate section of nearly 2,400 words, so, clearly, we are dealing with more than simply a nineteen-line poem. The poem needs to be seen therefore in this wider context, and seeing the two together ensures a certain ambiguity in our response. Thus, the priest, who is a rival for Emma's affection, resurfaces in this section, and he is accompanied by Stephen's graphic image of the 'virgin womb of the imagination' and how, like a sperm-laden epiphany, the 'instant of imagination…flashed forth' (*P* 217). Stephen might fail to notice the sexually charged imagery here or the links between the female Muse, the Virgin Mary, and Emma

---

157 Ten years clearly meant something to Joyce. Hence the dates 1904 and 1914 at the end of *A Portrait*. *Ulysses* is set in 1904 but was begun ten years later in 1914. Mulligan, who is in part modeled on Oliver St John Gogarty, pours scorn on Stephen's ambition as a writer in the 'Wandering Rocks' episode of *Ulysses*: 'He is going to write something in ten years'. 'Seems a long way off,' replies Haines. (*U* 10:1089-91). Joyce delighted in getting his own back against former friends and associates.

Clery, but the attentive reader does not. Throughout these pages we notice a constant crisscrossing between the sacred and secular, between the physical and the metaphorical, between male and female, and between guilt and innocence. Equally, we might discern another extraordinary claim: whereas the priest was the person to whom she would unveil her nakedness in the confessional, Stephen was the 'priest of eternal imagination' transmuting 'the daily bread of experience into the radiant body of everlasting life' (*P* 222).

Some of the most important ingredients in Stephen's aesthetic theory are given to us in this section of the villanelle. If the poem itself lacks energy, the theory, clothed in prejudice against the 'priested peasant' (*P* 221), does not. In an insightful essay on the villanelle, Robert Adams Day observes that 'Stephen the youthful poet systematically violates every rule and requirement of Stephen the precocious critic'.[158] Day continues by suggesting that, while the villanelle is not meant to be taken seriously, Stephen's aesthetic principles are. But, to my mind, embedding the poem inside the fiction leads to another insight not dependent on contrasting them. It is true that Joyce's prose technique differs radically from Stephen's villanelle, but perhaps we shouldn't ignore the surrounding fictional context, for this can add something to our interpretation.

A villanelle is a traditional verse form of nineteen lines divided into six stanzas, with the first and third lines of the first stanza repeating alternately in the following stanzas. The last two lines of the final stanza, which forms a quatrain, rhyme.

> Are you not weary of ardent ways,
> Lure of the fallen seraphim?
> Tell no more of enchanted days.
>
> Your eyes have set man's heart ablaze
> And you have had your will of him.
> Are you not weary of ardent ways?
>
> Above the flame the smoke of praise
> Goes up from ocean rim to rim.
> Tell no more of enchanted days.

---

158 Robert Adams Day, 'The Villanelle Perplex: Reading Joyce', *James Joyce Quarterly* 25.1 (1987), reprinted in *Critical Essays on James Joyce's A Portrait of the Artist* (eds. Philip Brady and James F.Carens) (New York: G.K.Hall, 1998), 63.

> Our broken cries and mournful lays
> Rise in one eucharistic hymn.
> Are you not weary of ardent ways?
>
> While sacrificing hands upraise
> The chalice flowing to the brim.
> Tell no more of enchanted days.
>
> And still you hold our longing gaze
> With languorous look and lavish limb!
> Are you not weary of ardent ways?
> Tell no more of enchanted days. (*P* 223-4)

Repetition dominates the villanelle as a form and Stephen's is no exception. Thirteen lines end with the same rhyme in 'ways' and 'days', and the remaining six lines end the same, beginning with 'seraphim' and ending in 'limb'. The rhythm is less regular but the overall effect is like an invocation and slightly soporific. By contrast, the rage against death in Dylan Thomas's 'Do Not Go Gentle Into That Good Night', perhaps the best-known modern villanelle, shows what an insistent rhyme scheme can achieve. Stephen's effort seems slightly under par.

In Franco Mormando's recent biography of Gian Lorenzo Bernini, we learn that the sculptor's patron, Cardinal Barberini, had 'an unusually ardent devotion' to Saint Sebastian, which resulted in Bernini's first commission from the Cardinal.[159] Stephen's use of 'ardent' positions the temptress on a pedestal, another step removed from the suppliant. Unlike the seventeenth-century Roman Cardinal, she is the ardent one, or, rather, she is the one who produces 'ardour' in the one who is tempted. The poem belongs to the mood of *Chamber Music* with the lover addressing his beloved with a mixture of emotions and sexual frustration. With her 'languorous look and lavish limb' she has been the source of attraction to the male gaze, but then comes disappointment for the lover, who, perhaps accusingly, responds by asking if she isn't weary of 'ardent ways'.

What we make of 'languorous look and lavish limb' or of the exclamation mark is unclear. In Skeat's *Etymological Dictionary*, languor has nothing languorous about it; it simply means dullness.

---

159 Franco Mormando, *Bernini: His Life and his Rome* (Chicago and London: University of Chicago Press, 2013), 41.

In Alfred Lord Tennyson's poem, 'Eleanore', the poet muses on the 'languors of thy love-deep eyes'; so the word is also associated with romantic yearning.[160] When Stephen recalls passing from 'ecstasy to languor' (P 223), the meaning here is closer to lassitude than to yearning. But then immediately following this we encounter the 'look of languor' in the eyes of the 'temptress', where lassitude gives way to the woman as sexual object and sexually attractive. The liquid look and the lavish limb will remind some readers of a sensuous Pre-Raphaelite painting, but for others they reveal a young man's attempt at not so much reflecting experience but discovering it in the process of writing. From languor to languorous, from noun to adjective, the male gaze is at work.

The villanelle is less about the sorrow of love and more about a judgement on 'enchanted ways'. 'Tell no more of enchanted days.' The days of enchantment and the ways of enchantment are now over. The mood of the poem is expressed through a lack of intensity with only passing regrets remaining. We might have anticipated as much when, at the end of a previous section given to a noisy discussion with his contemporaries, Lynch whispers to Stephen 'Your beloved is here.' (P 215) The line can serve to recall Dante's *Vita Nuova*, and at the same time it conjures up a characteristic way Joyce has in using a predecessor for his own purposes. In Dante's Chapter II we read 'Now your bliss has appeared', where the remark stands out from its surrounding prose by its simplicity and directness. It is followed in the next chapter by an equally startling remark, 'I am your master'.[161]

Throughout *Vita Nuova* Dante's love for Beatrice is both a constant and an eruptive force. On the one hand, everything that happens leads back to Beatrice, and, on the other hand, we see a poet at work, outlining the course of their relationship in explanatory prose and heightened verse. The relationship is, therefore, in the process of being memorialised and celebrated in writing. The writing of the villanelle marks one of the end-points in Stephen's relationship with Emma. As noted above, Joyce believed a poet must always write about a past or future emotion, 'never about a present one'. Stephen's mood in *A Portrait* is sombre, with the new life, the 'vita nuova' with

---

160 Alfred Tennyson, *Poems Volume 1* (London: Edward Moxon, 1842), 98.
161 Dante Alighieri, *Vita Nuova* (trans. Mark Musa) (London: Oxford University Press, 2008), 4-6. Mary Reynolds finds in Lynch's remark an echo of Chapter III. See *Joyce and Dante: The Shaping Imagination* (1981; Princeton, NJ: Princeton University Press, 2014), 196.

his 'beloved', draining away. As we rehearse his various contacts in the novel with her, we realise Stephen has entered a new phase, where writing a fixed form of verse such as a villanelle has taken over from dreamy emotion. With each repetitive phrase and line, the past is being consigned to the past, and Stephen moves closer to the scene of farewell.

If we keep the contrast with Dante in mind, we realise that Stephen is the artist largely unaware that he is 'The Artist' in the title of the novel. He is also unaware of his namesake, Daedalus, and of the classical myth underlying his story of escape. 'What kind of a name is that?' (*P* 9) taunts 'Nasty' Roche. And for half-a-moment we imagine the characters will step out of the fiction and give us the truth, which would constitute a rare moment in the novel. When an original name is identified, as with 'Dante', we soon recognise our mistake, for she has little in common with the author of the *Vita Nuova* or the *Divina Commedia*. So, when we ask if Stephen is the author of his story, we have to admit he is not. And yet all the way through this chapter there has been a suggestion that he is the author of his own fiction.[162] At one level Joyce is the only-begetter, and we never forget that he is the author of all he surveys. The portrait he delineates for us is a portrait of a young man called Stephen Dedalus. Joyce stays close to his development as an artist because the new departure for fiction insists on immediacy, on consciousness, and on the art of defamiliarisation.

After spending five-and-a-half years writing about her, Flaubert believed that he was Emma Bovary, but we are certain, or we are more certain today than we ever have been, that Stephen Dedalus is not Joyce, and that Joyce is not Stephen. But, for those with an interest in intrigue, perhaps there is a third position, a position somewhere between the two. We might recall a comment made by Mary Sheehy's brother, Eugene, about his university friend, Joyce, which suggests a common trait underlying the person and the artist: 'In charades in our house on Sunday nights he was the star turn. His wit and gift for improvisation came into ready play. He was also a clever mimic

---

162 For an introductory survey into the problem of autobiography, written over sixty years ago, see Maurice Beebe, 'Joyce and Stephen Dedalus: The Problem of Autobiography' in Marvin Magalaner (ed.), *A James Joyce Miscellany* (second series) (Carbondale, Ill: Southern Illinois University Press, 1959).

and his impassive poker face helped his impersonations.'[163] The voices we hear in Joyce's fiction are evidence of an impersonator's art, but they also suggest something else, namely the artist who threw off one mask to reveal not so much himself as another artist. Or, as Robert Scholes once enigmatically remarked, 'James Joyce was always in search of the artist James Joyce'.[164]

---

163 Eugene Sheehy, *May It Please the Court* (Dublin: C.J.Fallon, 1951), reprinted in *The Joyce We Knew: Memoirs of Joyce* (ed. Ulick O'Connor) (Dingle, Kerry: Brandon, 2004), 28. Cornelius Weygandt, a contemporary critic, reminds us of the proximity between 'impersonality' and 'impersonation'. George Moore, he suggests, 'has in greatest measure...this greatest gift of the Gael, the gift of dramatic impersonation of all manner of men in all their changing moods.' In part this is the reason Weygandt calls him 'Ireland's greatest novelist'. Cornelius Weygandt, *Irish Plays and Playwrights* (London: Constable; New York: Houghton Miflin, 1913), 100-1. When he wrote this comment, Joyce was yet to make an appearance.

164 Robert Scholes, *In Search of James Joyce* (Urbana and Chicago: University of Illinois Press, 1992), 131. Scholes then quotes the opening to Joyce's narrative essay 'A Portrait of the Artist'.

Memorial Arch, Stephen's Green, Dublin.

With its general air of movement, complete with brightly coloured clothes and conspicuous umbrellas to shade the sun, this Edwardian postcard of the main entrance to Stephen's Green evokes a comfortable world that Joyce enjoyed only temporarily. However, that is not the whole story, for when he crosses Stephen's Green in the closing pages of *A Portrait*, Stephen tells himself that it is 'my Green'. It was through his writing that Joyce came to possess his city and country..

The National Library
what do you think of our police?
Published by Hely's Limited, Dame Street, Dublin
Dublin

The National Library was very important to Joyce and his fellow students, who would come down here after class, passing on the way the Dublin Metropolitan Police in their distinctive uniform. In conversation with the Dean of Studies, Stephen's soul 'frets in the shadow of his language'. The note on this Edwardian postcard, sent in November 1903, perhaps confirms why Stephen feels his country is occupied by the English foreigner..

CHAPTER 6:
WORKING WITH WORDS

EPIPHANY

In *Stephen Hero*, as we saw in the last chapter, Stephen Daedalus provides a handy definition of an 'epiphany'. In Skeat's *Etymological Dictionary* the word is defined as 'Twelfth Day' and 'manifestation' or to 'shew forth'. In the *Concise* version of the *Dictionary*, Skeat adds 'SEE phantom', while in the full version he inserts 'SEE fancy'. 'Phantom' is explained by 'vision', 'spectre' 'cause to shine'; 'fancy' by 'making visible (hence imagination)'. All of this hinterland of meaning informs Joyce's take on epiphany. His use of 'spiritual' recalls the Feast of the Epiphany, twelve days after Christmas, when the three kings from the east, bearing gifts, arrive to pay homage to the new-born king. In many traditions, where water as a symbol is foregrounded, the feast also commemorates the baptism of Jesus, but this meaning lies outside the word as understood by Skeat and Joyce. In the original meaning, we can discern how 'manifestation' is an act of reciprocity whereby the infant Jesus is shown or made visible to the world and deserving of a gift in return. Joyce, through his epiphanies, aligns himself not only with the spiritual over the vulgar but also with the power of the imagination to make visible.

Joyce had been working on the idea of an epiphany from his late teens and early twenties. As already indicated, the epiphanies, around 70 plus in total, were composed for the most part in the years between 1900 and 1903. They were short pieces of prose, some narrative, others dramatic, some ironic, others banal, some pious, others cold or emotionless. The variety of moods and attitudes complements the varied nature of the topics. These include material from his dreams or his 'subconscious', as Stanislaus called them, as well as observations of conversations heard in people's houses, especially the Sheehy family in Belvedere Place, or beggars he encountered in the street in Mullingar, or the funeral of his mother in August 1903, or prostitutes in Paris.

At the beginning of *The Complete Dublin Diary of Stanislaus Joyce* (1971), there is a revealing passage, written in 1903 by his solicitous younger brother, which is full of positive insights into Joyce before his career as a writer began:

> His intellect is precise and subtle, but not comprehensive. He is no student.... His literary talent seems to be very great indeed, both in prose and in verse.... His 'epiphanies' – his prose pieces (which I almost prefer to his lyrics) and his dialogues – are again subtle. He has put himself into these with singular courage, singular memory, and scientific minuteness; he has proved himself capable of taking very great pains to create a very little thing of prose or verse. The keen observation and satanic irony of his character are precisely, but not fully, expressed.[165]

The passage is worth considering in detail, but here we must concentrate on Joyce as a prose writer and specifically on his 'epiphanies'. As already noted, *Chamber Music* included a poem which was later anthologised in *Des Imagistes* (1914). Joyce wasn't an imagist as such, but his writing, in particular his prose writing, does have connections with imagism. Stanislaus is right to hesitate over whether he preferred his brother's prose over his lyrics, for, as we observed with the 'fiery grains' passage in the last chapter, Joyce's prose frequently reminds us of poetry. Joyce's epiphanies recall the programme of the imagists as outlined by F.S. Flint and Pound in 1912-3. Two of the famous three rules are: 'Direct treatment of the "thing" whether subjective or objective.' And 'To use absolutely no word that does not contribute to the presentation.'[166] The new poetry endorsed something that also influenced Joyce as

---

165 *The Complete Dublin Diary of Stanislaus Joyce* (ed. George H.Healy) (1971; Dublin: Anna Livia Press, 1994), 2.
166 Ezra Pound, 'A Few Don'ts by an Imagiste' in *Poetry* March 1913. For a useful survey of imagism, which includes Pound's essay, see Peter Jones (ed.), *Imagist Poetry* (1972; London: Penguin, 2001).

Studio photo of Stanislaus Joyce taken in Trieste in 1905.

a writer of fiction, notably the insistence on the concrete image as opposed to a general authorial comment: 'Go in fear of abstractions.' In time we realise that Joyce went beyond the imagists and rewrote the relationship between the concrete and the abstract. But at first it is clear that the world he creates, as with the Christmas Dinner scene or the classroom scene where he is punished by the Prefect of Studies, has much in common with imagist ideas and their programme for writers. And nothing could be more direct than the opening of *A Portrait*.

Joyce's epiphanies are like a quarry; they store material for later use, even if in their candour, paradoxically, they can also serve to hide things. When an author begins his career writing economically, it stimulates the imagination to focus on the task in hand, and focus is a pivotal word here. We might recall at this point the words of Des Esseintes in Huysmans's *Against Nature*, a novel written two decades before:

> Of all literary forms, the prose poem was the one which Des Esseintes preferred. In the hands of an alchemist or genius, it should, he believed, contain within its small compass, like beef essence, the power of a novel, while eliminating its tedious analyses and superfluous descriptions.[167]

Joyce was also a courageous writer, prepared to tackle things many of us would avoid or pass over as too painful or embarrassing or private, and writing epiphanies helped him develop sooner than might have been the case otherwise. His brother's 'singular courage' in confronting the world made an impact on Stanislaus. Joyce's contemporaries often commented on his shyness, but, when he took up his pen, he exhibited another quality. In writing, brevity helped, but so too did courage. It was a powerful combination, and perhaps issued from the same source. When he read Meredith's novel *The Ordeal of Richard Feverel*, perhaps the words that stood out for him were 'hero' and 'ordeal'.

There is such an economy about Joyce's prose that it has the look of something that has been processed through a sifting machine, where anything that doesn't contribute is removed and where what's left has a quality to fix or hold our attention. In his comments above, Stanislaus conveys a shrewd insight into the earliest stages of Joyce's career as a writer. Joyce's application impressed Stanislaus, as did his concern not to write at length and to focus on 'a very little thing'. The use of the

---

167 *Against Nature*, 162.

word 'thing' keeps recurring at this time in general discussions about poetry and in poetry itself, as happens in William Carlos Williams's injunction in his poem, *Paterson*: 'Say it - no ideas but in things'.[168] If Joyce's early verse has a dreamy quality and is given to exploring moods, his prose conveys precision, where images frequently have an almost tangible quality.

To advance an idea or concept, or to make it sound highly intelligent and original, the young Joyce raided the vocabulary of the classics and the history of the language, encouraging some later critics to spend a considerable time deciphering the hidden meaning of epiphanies in his early work. Underlying an epiphany there is no doubt a spiritual layer, and we know that Joyce was not averse to making use of his religious inheritance. Such an inheritance included the occult and influential occult figures such as Yeats and Russell. In this regard the reference to *ignotas...artes* or unknown arts in the epigraph to *A Portrait* might contain an allusion to the occult.[169] Stephen tells us he remembered every word of Yeats's occult story, *The Tables of the Law*, which appeared in print in 1897. (*SH* 177) But I think we should not overdo the hidden meaning of an epiphany and, instead, give some thought to how it functions in a text, especially in regard to consciousness, conscience, and the role of the artist.

The mundane world surrounding Joyce's concept of epiphany is also worth stressing, therefore. The 'vulgarity of speech and gesture' conveys something of Joyce's descent into that region inhabited by sinners and ordinary mortals. It was there that his concept was played out among his contemporaries. In *As I Was Going Down Sackville Street* (1937), his one-time companion, Gogarty, provides a lively sketch of how the youthful Joyce would take notes on company and turn them into 'epiphanies':

> [Lady Gregory] had no room for playboys except on the stage.... So Ulysses had to strike out for himself. Dublin's Dante had to find a way out of his own Inferno. But he had lost the key. James Augustine

---

168 See William Carlos Williams, *Paterson* (rev. edition) (ed. Christopher MacGowan) (1946; New York: New Directions, 1995), 6. A cognate discussion on things is also on display among scientists at this time. See for example the chapter 'On the Nature of Things' in Arthur Eddington *Space, Time and Gravitation: An Outline of the General Relativity Theory* (London: Cambridge University Press, 1920). Joyce, too, is involved in redefining our idea of things.
169 For further discussion of the epigraph see my *Reading Joyce*, 158-9.

Joyce slipped politely from the snug with an 'Excuse me!'

'Whist! He's gone to put it all down!' 'Put what down?'

'Put *us* down. A chiel's among us takin' notes. And, faith, he'll print it.'...

I was trying to recall what spark had been struck or what 'folk phrase' Joyce had culled from Ellwood or me that sent him out to make his secret record.

Secrecy of any kind corrupts sincere relations. I don't mind being reported, but to be an unwilling contributor to one of his 'Epiphanies' is irritating.

Probably Fr Darlington had taught him, as an aside in his Latin class - for Joyce knew no Greek - that 'Epiphany' meant 'a showing forth'. So he recorded under 'Epiphany' any showing forth of the mind by which he considered one gave oneself away.

Which of us had endowed him with an 'Epiphany' and sent him to the lavatory to take it down?[170]

With the benefit of hindsight, and knowing how his place in history was being recorded, Gogarty's comments are deliberately provocative, and were perhaps fully deserved. When John Eglinton (aka W.K.Magee) recalled the artist as a young man in 'The Beginnings of Joyce', an essay published in 1932, what struck him was Joyce's determination to succeed, for at the time 'no one took him at his own valuation'.[171]

Unlike the artist sketching his subject in a public space, the writer with his notebook disappearing from company to record what he has just heard or witnessed must have been an unwarranted interruption to the flow of conversation or an evening's drinking. But this was Joyce

---

170 Oliver St John Gogarty, *As I Was Going Down Sackville Street* (1937; Harmondsworth: Penguin, 1954), 298-99. Lady Gregory, Synge, and Yeats were the leading figures in the establishment of the Abbey Theatre in 1904. The reference to 'playboys' is to Synge's *Playboy of the Western World* (1907). Fr Darlington, who is the model for the Dean of Studies in *A Portrait*, also taught Joyce at University College Dublin. John Ellwood was one of Gogarty's friends when they were medical students in Dublin. 'A chiel's among us takin' notes' carries the implication 'So best be careful with your p's and q's.' A snug was traditionally a small, quiet room in a pub.

171 John Eglinton, 'The Beginnings of Joyce', *Life and Letters* 8:47, December 1932, 404.

the apprentice learning his trade in public. He was not confined to an artist's garret but in the full gaze of his mocking contemporaries, who would in turn provide him with some of the best material for his art. As his career developed, Joyce relied on notes, and he would take care to check off items in his notebooks as he proceeded. But, as is apparent in his critical portrait of Malachi 'Buck' Mulligan, the first character we encounter in *Ulysses* and who is modeled in part on the arch-mocker Gogarty, few got the better of him,

APOLOGISE

While the word 'epiphany' is not used in *A Portrait,* there are several occasions when Joyce reworks some of the epiphanies he wrote between 1900 and 1903. The memory of one of his earliest epiphanies dates from 1891 and refers to an episode in the house in Martello Terrace in Bray where the family lived from 1887 to 1891:

> Mr Vance- *(comes in with a stick)* … O, you know, he'll
> have to apologise, Mrs Joyce.
> Mrs Joyce- O yes … Do you hear that, Jim?
> Mr Vance- Or else - if he doesn't - the eagles'll come
> and pull out his eyes.
> Mrs Joyce- O, but I'm sure he will apologise.
> Joyce- *(under the table, to himself)*
> Pull out his eyes,
> Apologise.
> Apologise,
> Pull out his eyes.
> Apologise,
> Pull out his eyes,
> Pull out his eyes,
> Apologise.[172]

Compare this with how the scene is reproduced at the beginning of *A Portrait*:

> The Vances lived in number seven. They had a
> different father
> and mother. They were Eileen's father and mother.
> When they were grown up he was going to marry
> Eileen. He hid under the table. His mother said:

---

172   See *The Workshop of Daedalus,* 11.

—O, Stephen will apologise.

Dante said:

—O, if not, the eagles will come and pull out his
eyes.

> *Pull out his eyes,*
> *Apologise,*
> *Apologise,*
> *Pull out his eyes.*

> *Apologise,*
> *Pull out his eyes,*
> *Pull out his eyes,*
> *Apologise.* (P 8)

The word 'apologise' is repeated six times in the epiphany and five times
in the novel. The epiphany includes names for the boy and the family;
in the novel the boy is called 'Stephen'. The name of Vance, who in
real life owned a chemist shop on Main Street, Bray, and who was the
father of Eileen, is retained in both accounts. In the epiphany Mr Vance
occupies the intimidating role; in *A Portrait* this is undertaken by Dante.
The dramatic entry of Mr Vance brandishing a stick and threatening the
boy is followed by the equally disturbing way the adults unite against
the child. We assume Mr Vance is angry because of some misdemeanour
by the boy. In neither account is the misdemeanour revealed, but in the
novel, with the mention of Eileen Vance, it appears as if it has something
to do with prying eyes and of a sexual nature. In both accounts the boy
hides under the table and his mother calls on him to apologise, which
suggests it is more than a case of bullying.

In the epiphany the lines of verse are to my mind uttered by the
boy, whereas in the novel it looks as though the boy is listening to the
lines, which are italicised, uttered by the adults, perhaps in unison. So the
novel fictionalises the epiphany and draws us into the drama of Stephen's
childhood. This is a key scene in Joyce's early career as a novelist, for in
it we can observe how he used material he had composed some time
before and for another purpose. By drafting into his fiction such material
Joyce reveals a characteristic method of working that accompanied him
throughout his career. Nothing was lost and everything had the potential
to find another life elsewhere in his fiction. Although the earlier version
may be closer to what actually happened, it is no more authentic than
its transformation, so to fictionalise is not to make up something but
to reveal an imaginative truth in a larger frame that includes narrative,

theme, and discourse. In this epiphany, Joyce removes the dramatic entrance of Mr Vance, and rewrites the incident from inside the orbit of the boy's consciousness. At the same time, he draws attention to the motif of transgression and its links with eyes. *A Portrait* is not therefore an apology for his life in how that word is used in traditional accounts, such as the *Apologia Pro Vita Sua* by Newman, but it is striking that punishment is one of the first things we encounter in Joyce's portrait of the country of his birth, and we cannot overlook that it was one of the first epiphanies he composed.

Intriguingly, the phrase in the epiphany 'to himself' should make the scene more personal, but in fact it is the reverse, because Stephen is a victim and not in control of his thoughts. This is a clever move on Joyce's part, because the age of the boy in the epiphany would have to be older for him to have recourse to such a conscious means of self-defence, and this is more so if he parodies the lines by the adults. Assuming there is a gap in ages between the two boys, Stephen's response as a five-year-old boy appears more natural. In the epiphany the boy might be slightly older, say 8, and such a discrepancy might explain how the two passages diverge. A larger generalisation offers itself, for at times *A Portrait* resembles an artist's canvas, where elements from the past are inserted and where they retain the look of being inserted, with the lines of the original showing. The process by which Joyce polished his material was not, therefore, always successful.

When we return to epiphany as defined in terms of 'a sudden spiritual manifestation, whether in the vulgarity of speech or of gesture or in a memorable phase of the mind itself', we realise this is easier to apply to the epiphany itself and *Dubliners* than it is to *A Portrait*. On the other hand we might be persuaded by the argument made by the editors of *The Workshop of Daedalus* on the scene we have been discussing: 'Changed only slightly for [*A Portrait*], this episode is used to present a dramatic foreshadowing of Stephen's future, as he finds a refuge from authority in art and makes a poem out of his predicament.'[173] Such a conclusion is possible, but it is not one I would want to pursue, and the changes between the two versions are more than 'slight'. The comment recalls a period of criticism when, in their attempt to defend the novel against formlessness, critics made much of narrative cohesion and the importance of art as a bulwark against society. Today, we are more ready to notice all the surface lines and scratch marks on the canvas.

---

173 *The Workshop of Daedalus*, 11.

SMUGGING

—Do you know why those fellows scut? I will tell
you but you must not let on you know.
—Tell us, Athy. Go on. You might if you know.
He paused for a moment and then said mysteriously:
—They were caught with Simon Moonan and
Tusker Boyle in the square one night.
The fellows looked at him and asked:
—Caught?
—What doing?
Athy said:
—Smugging.
All the fellows were silent: and Athy said:
—And that's why.
Stephen looked at the faces of the fellows but they
were all looking across the playground. He wanted to
ask somebody about it. What did that mean about the
smugging in the square? Why did the five fellows out
of the higher line run away for that? (*P* 41)

In recent years, 'smugging' has excited critics and annotators alike.
What exactly were the boys doing that it could result in them being
expelled from College? In the standard or recommended edition of
A Portrait (1968), Chester Anderson, from a conversation he had with
John Ryan, a former student at Clongowes, suggests that 'smugging'
was 'Clongowes slang for a mild form of homosexual petting'.[174] In
Joyce Annotated (1982), Don Gifford quotes an obsolete definition
from Joseph Wright's *The English Dialect Dictionary* (1898-1905) 'to toy
amorously in secret', and then proposes that the context in *A Portrait*
'means the practice of schoolboy homosexuality'.[175] Gifford uses the
same gloss for the word when it appears in the phrase 'hugging and
smugging' in *Ulysses*.[176]

---

174 *A Portrait of the Artist: Text, Criticism and Notes* (ed. Chester Anderson)
(New York: Viking, 1968), 497.
175 Don Gifford, *Joyce Annotated: Notes for Dubliners and A Portrait of the Artist*
(second edition) (Berkeley, CA: University of California Press, 1982), 151.
176 Don Gifford with Robert J. Seidman (second edition), *Ulysses Annotated:
Notes for James Joyce's Ulysses* (Berkeley, CA: University of California Press,
1989), 340. Line 12.807.

In *The English Dialect Dictionary*, the example given for this definition is a Scottish song which includes the lines 'An' while we hug an' kiss an' smug / I'll haud thee firm by ilka lug / An ca' thee ay my Davy'.[177] The illustration is taken from Ebenezer Picken's poem 'Dainty Davy', which is not about a homosexual encounter but rather about a humorous take on love between a woman and a man. The notes accompanying the Scottish dialect words reveal that the meaning of 'Dainty' is not so much effeminate as 'fine, agreeable, good-humoured'.[178] Wright's claim that this is 'to toy amorously in secret' can only be supported if we invoke the definition found in Picken's *A Dictionary of the Scottish Language* (1818), where to smug is to 'kiss as if smuggling or concealing it'.[179]

One meaning of several for 'smug' in the OED is 'steal, filch, or run away with', so the idea of concealment accompanies some uses of the word. According to the OED the origin of the word is dubious, which is not the case with 'smuggle'. So we might agree that the connection between 'smugging' and 'smuggling' is not that easy to determine. However, if we were persuaded that there is a link, we might conclude that the Clongowes boys were, say, kissing, doing so together as a group, and concerned they were not spotted by their teachers. If such a conclusion is warranted, we might also agree that we could probably deduce as much without recourse to the history of the Scottish language or the OED. What is more certain is that in the context of 'shawls' in the poorer district of Bride Street in Dublin, 'hugging and smugging' in the 'Cyclops' episode of *Ulysses* looks closer to heterosexual than to homosexual behaviour.

Jeri Johnson in her Oxford World's Classics edition follows Gifford, and is more definitive: 'here clearly "homosexual amorous toying"'.[180] The note in the Penguin edition edited by Seamus Deane is similar, proposing 'amorous homosexual behaviour'.[181] In the notes to an

---

177 *The English Dialect Dictionary* vol 5 (ed. Joseph Wright) (Oxford: Henry Frowde, 1905), 562. 'I'll haud thee firm by ilka lug' or 'I'll hold thee firm by each ear'.

178 Ebenezer Picken, *Miscellaneous Poems, Songs etc* vol. 1 (Edinburgh: James Clarke, 1818), 176. Davy is comely, charming, as well as dainty.

179 Ebenezer Picken, *A Dictionary of the Scottish Language* (Edinburgh: James Sawers, 1818), 192.

180 *A Portrait of the Artist as a Young Man* (ed. Jeri Johnson) (Oxford: Oxford University Press, 2000), 234.

181 *A Portrait of the Artist as a Young Man* (ed. Seamus Deane) (London: Penguin, 1992), 288.

attractive edition published by the Alma press, Marc A.Mamigonian and John Turner similarly rely on Gifford and, without amplification, cite *The English Dialect Dictionary*.[182] J.S.Atherton in his 1964 edition of the novel introduces a more explicit note by suggesting the boys were masturbating, an assumption that has become more widespread. Atherton also informs us that Stephen is 'too young to understand the word'.[183] John Paul Riqueleme is reluctant to commit: 'Probably homosexual contact but possibly masturbation', citing Katherine Mullin.[184] Mullin herself argues that 'Both the secrecy and the group nature of "smugging" in *A Portrait* indicate to me that masturbation is most probably meant.'[185]

Translators, too, have their own take on the word, but, unlike annotators, they do not have the luxury of being indecisive. The French translation of the novel by Ludmila Savitsky, which was overseen by Joyce, indicates they were kissing, or smooching or, more colloquially, necking: 'Ils se bécotaient'.[186] In a more recent translation by Jacques Aubert they were 'touchaient', adding in his note that 'Ce terme d'argot à valeur sexuelle reste assez vague' (This slang word of a sexual nature is somewhat unclear).[187] In Italian the boys were 'A toccarsi', feeling themselves or touching.[188]'Fummeln' appears in a recent German edition by Friedhelm Rathjen, which translates as fumbling or making out.[189] In Spanish they were canoodling or smothering with kisses: 'Besuqueándose'.[190] And in Dutch, according

---

182 *A Portrait of the Artist as a Young Man* (eds. Marc A.Mamigonian and John Turner) (Richmond, Surrey: Alma, 2012), 229.

183 *A Portrait of the Artist as a Young Man* (ed. J.S.Atherton) (London: Heinemann, 1964), 241.

184 *A Portrait of the Artist as a Young Man* (ed. John Paul Riquelme) (text edited by Hans Walter Gabler and Walter Hettche) (New York: Nortton, 2007), 37.

185 Katherine Mullin, *James Joyce, Sexuality and Social Purity* (Cambridge: Cambridge University Press, 2003), 93.

186 *Dedalus: Portrait de L'Artiste Jeune Par Lui-Même* (trans. Ludmila Savitsky) (Paris: Gallimard, 1943), 50.

187 *Portrait de L' Artiste en Jeune Homme* (trans. Jacques Aubert) (Paris: Gallimard, 1992), 89 and 398.

188 *Un ritratto dell'artista da giovane* (trans. Franca Cavagnoli) (Milan: Giangiacomo Feltrinelli, 2016), 43.

189 *Porträt des Künstlers als junger Mann: Roman* (trans. Friedhelm Rathjen) (afterword Marcel Beyer) (Zurich: Manesse Verlag, 2012), 50.

190 *Retrato del Artista Adolescente* (trans. Damaso Alonso) (Barcelona: RBA, 1995), 35.

to Erik Bindervoet and Robbert-Jan Henkes, they were 'Rotzooien', or messing around.[191]

Quite clearly, the word 'smugging' has invited a range of interpretations from the clear to the vague. Atherton indicates it was masturbation. Mullin is almost certain about what they were doing and provides an explanation. It is certainly possible that the boys could have been involved in an exercise of joint-masturbation or even masturbating or feeling each other. Joyce could not have been too explicit in the period when he was writing. Many readers, however, might recoil from an interpretation that is too explicit. Joyce, after all, was an expert in innuendo. To my mind, 'smugging' reflects a deliberately vague moment when Stephen, because of his age, is positioned at the border between inclusion in a group of older boys and exclusion from it. Atherton's additional point, that Stephen would have been excluded from the group, is surely right and has implications.

The word 'smugging', then, does not mean masturbating; it means 'smugging', that is, some form of behaviour which is known to older boys at Clongowes and which signals their membership of a club. Kissing, which is how it is glossed by Hugh Leonard in his 1962 play, *Stephen D.*, has much to recommend it.[192] Indeed, the boys kissing would be an echo of Stephen's confusion when asked if he kissed his mother. Equally, reading the novel with Stephen in mind means being aware of the difference between language and experience. If Joyce had provided the meaning for the word, and made it explicit, we would be reading a different novel from the one we have. Some readers will decide 'smugging' is masturbating, but others will enjoy speculating about the range of possible meanings. The Dutch translation is right therefore to keep the word general in application: fooling around or messing around. However, Stephen would have understood precisely what such a term meant.

UNCLE CHARLES

Every morning, therefore, uncle Charles repaired
to his outhouse but not before he had greased and

---

191 *Zelfportret van de kunstenaar als jonge man* (trans. Erik Bindervoet and Robbert-Jan Henkes) (Amsterdam: Athenaeum-Polak & Van Gennep, 2014), 48.
192 Hugh Leonard, *Stephen D.* (London and New York: Evans Brothers, 1964), 9.

brushed scrupulously his back hair and brushed and
put on his tall hat. (*P* 60)

The story of Joyce's life and writing comes complete with ironies.
As one of the high priests of modernism, his name is synonymous
with the shock of the new and the air of rebellion, the Irish writer
who sought in the words of his protagonist Stephen Dedalus to
forge in the 'smithy of my soul the uncreated conscience of my race'
(*P* 253). On the other hand, *Ulysses* tells a different story in that it
seeks to convey a world given to routine and repetition and, for
some, boredom. The novel is set on one day in June 1904 when the
Gold Cup at Ascot races is taking place and when a sultry game of
cricket is being played in the grounds of Trinity College, Dublin.
No author has done verisimilitude quite like this. Even the rate of
flow of the river is so precise that the same insignificant piece of
paper, a throwaway, tossed into the river, is seen in transit by different
characters at different times of the day and thereby given significance
(and linked to a horse named 'Throwaway' running in the Gold
Cup on that day). So realistic is Joyce's world that we even forget its
fictional quality.

With throwaway in mind, if we were intent on suggesting an
alternative title for *Ulysses*, we could do worse than choose *Life and
Habit* (1878), Samuel Butler's late-Victorian, post-Darwinian study
of consciousness. Put on one side Shakespeare's *Hamlet* or Homer's
Greek epic under which it shelters, and invoke a study informed by
science, psychology and the social sciences. Butler's inquiry into the
patterns of unconscious behaviour is full of arresting insights. Thus,
in an intriguing chapter on 'Conscious and Unconscious Knowers',
Butler, with the minimum of fuss, declares: 'Certain it is that we
know best what we are least conscious of knowing.' In his novel, *The
Way of All Flesh*, he notices that '[a] child of ordinary powers learns
to walk at a year or two old without knowing much about it.'[193]
What Butler seeks to do is not so much to explain how this might
be the case but to raise questions about the nature of knowledge
and consciousness. Or consider a comment on the self through
time, which, without the adverb at the end, could be deployed to
summarise the changes Stephen Dedalus undergoes in *A Portrait*:
'Personality is the creature of time and space, changing, as time

---

193 Samuel, Butler, *The Way of All Flesh* (1903; London: Penguin, 2013), 385.

changes, imperceptibly.'[194] Such sentences strike us so forcefully in part because they are unaccompanied by any qualification. Butler, then, affords a corrective to the conventional supposition that Joyce's fiction is all about lighting out for the new territory and not also, as Uncle Charles serves to illustrate, about the discovery of sameness and the familiar.

Everyday behaviour is mostly about habit and routine. Often it is unconscious, and, even when it's conscious, habit dies hard. 'Every morning,' then, Uncle Charles 'repaired to his outhouse' to enjoy a 'morning smoke' in what I like to imagine is the outside toilet, taking care at the same time to 'brush scrupulously his black hair' and, like a good Victorian gentleman, 'put on his tall hat'. (*P* 60) Joyce relishes describing Uncle Charles's customary behaviour, anchoring the sentence with an observation that exists between what Uncle Charles did and how in stilted prose he might describe what he did. Joyce has fun with the character and the moment, something many readers might miss. It is not, for example, the family outhouse but 'his outhouse', as if he has a monopoly on it, which is something we remember when he tells Stephen that American apples are 'good for your bowels' (*P* 63).

Uncle Charles could have said to his friends, 'Every morning I go and sit in the outhouse and enjoy a smoke.' Instead, as if he was familiar with Elizabethan prose or a character in an old-fashioned Victorian novel and perhaps trying to impress, he 'repaired' to the outhouse.[195] Of course, he wouldn't need to put any of this into words, because, as Butler might well claim, Uncle Charles is a creature of habit and, thus, an 'unconscious knower' therefore. But what is such a detail doing

---

194 Samuel Butler, *Life and Habit* (ed. R.A. Streatfeild) (London: Jonathan Cape, 1910), 20, 98. In his library in Trieste Joyce had five books by Butler including his novels *The Way of All Flesh* and *Erewhon*, as well as *The Authoress of the Odyssey*, and *The Humour of Homer*.

195 The French translation has 'se rendait à son hangar', he went to the shed (or warehouse). But this is not what Uncle Charles did. He neither went nor took himself off, though the latter is a close approximation. Instead, he repaired. 'Shed' is a possible translation because 'outhouse' could be a workshop space, but that would miss out on the humour associated with washrooms and stilted prose. In the French translation by Jacques Aubert, Uncle Charles goes to the 'appentis', a word signalling an extension or lean-to at the side of a house. See *Portrait de L' Artiste en Jeune Homme* (trans. Jacques Aubert) (Paris: Gallimard, 1992), 111. If we knew the layout of the house where the Dedalus family were then living, things would be clearer. In *Ulysses* Bloom goes to the 'jakes', which is a more familiar term than Uncle Charles might use.

in a book about an artist's development, for there is no indication Stephen will follow in his uncle's footsteps or adjourn of a morning to the outhouse with a tall hat on his head. The style, as Hugh Kenner famously insisted, intrigues us, but so also should the detail.[196]

As another example of routine from *A Portrait*, we might notice how, on the inside of his desk at his boarding school, Stephen crosses off the days until term ends and he can return home to his family. Time is duration, habit is deadening, and in this instance both are felt by the boy as working against him. A day-pupil does not suffer like this, for every day s/he has a home to go to. The environment at a boarding school, with its insistence on silence and obedience, is immersive and can be tough and unforgiving with time becoming the enemy. The suffering is offset temporarily in Stephen's case by the relative comfort of the sick bay and, as we have seen, the sympathy of Michael, the Jesuit brother in charge. Not surprisingly Stephen's thoughts turn to home, and he writes a letter, bypassing the college authorities, politely requesting his parents to come and fetch him. Home, then, is a place free of the excesses of the rule-book, and it is where time can be enjoyed or redeemed without constantly thinking about it.

The infirmary resembles a half-way house between school and home, where the normal college rules do not apply. Stephen's stay in the infirmary is a reminder of life that is away from the ordinary. The routine of school life continues without Stephen, but through it all, in the rough and tumble of school life away from home, his consciousness is being formed. We wonder why Joyce doesn't insert a scene where Stephen reflects on the routine of home life continuing without him while he is away at boarding school, for this, too, is something many boarders experience. At the end of the novel, his mother 'prays' that he may learn in his own life 'away from home and friends what the heart is and what it feels' (*P* 252). This is the direction of the novel, a novel about the artist learning through experience not so much what the heart is but what constitutes his subject matter. That subject matter is in part about the nature of consciousness in the face of adversity, something I explore more fully in Chapter 1 of *The Joyce Country*. The

---

196 For more on the 'Uncle Charles Principle', a principle now well-established in Joyce studies, see Hugh Kenner, *Joyce's Voices* (Berkeley, CA and London: University of California Press, 1978), 18. Kenner stresses the peculiar nature of the narrative idiom used by Joyce at the beginning of Chapter 2 and how the reader needs to appreciate that 'the narrative idiom need not be the narrator's'.

ending should be about the destiny that awaits Stephen beyond the shores of Ireland, but, instead, it rebounds on us as readers. Thus the momentum of the novel carries us forward, but then, with the diary entries and Stephen's determination to cut all his ties with friends and family, something stalls, and we are left with simply his determination to set down a marker. Any hope for a third-person narrator to make a re-entry and tell us how the story ends turns out to be in vain.

When Stephen does return from Paris at the beginning of *Ulysses*, he is still the dispossessed son in struggle, but he has lost energy and purpose, and, with the entrance of Bloom, he is no longer at the centre of things. In the light of *Dubliners* and *Ulysses*, *A Portrait* gives the appearance of a novel at odds with the author's future direction, for what Stephen the character is attempting to discover is, quite simply, a life outside of habit and routine. In the words of Pater what he sought was: 'To burn always with the hard gem-like flame, to maintain, this ecstasy, is success in life. Failure is to form habits; for habit is relative to a stereotyped world.'[197] In the process of writing the novel, Joyce began on a different path, which found expression in the figure of Leopold Bloom, who was himself, like Uncle Charles, a creature of routine.[198]

In the novel we have, the theme that stands out is loss and struggle, and, in particular, the struggle by Stephen to formulate and understand his own development as an artist. This is one of the reasons the passage about Uncle Charles at the beginning of Chapter 2 looks odd. But there is another reason. Gabler suggests that the passage was originally intended as part of the Christmas Dinner scene, where Uncle Charles's calming influence would help to counter the intensity of the political debate and accompanying sense of claustrophobia. That his role is summed up for the reader by his daily routine of repairing to the outhouse is a reminder of two things. Firstly, that the novel survives its occasional piecemeal construction without too many questions being asked. And, secondly, creatures of habit would not only come to dominate Joyce's imagination, but, at least for the reading experience, such people would also serve to qualify what Butler had suggested that 'we remember best what we have done least often'.[199]

---

197 Walter Pater, *Studies in the History of the Renaissance* (1873; London: Oxford University Press, 2010), 120.

198 When he was working in Rome, Joyce referred to the idea and title of *Ulysses* in letters of 30 September and 13 November 1906 respectively. For further discussion, see Giorgio Melchiori's essay in *Joyce in Rome: The Genesis of Ulysses* (ed. Giorgio Melchiori) (Rome: Bulzoni, 1984).

199 Butler, 155.

ROPE ENDS

> Two great yellow caravans had halted one morning
> before the door and men had come tramping into the
> house to dismantle it. The furniture had been hustled
> out through the front garden, which was strewn with
> wisps of straw and rope ends and into the huge vans
> at the gate. (*P* 65)

Joyce constantly keeps us on our toes as readers. Near the beginning
of Chapter 2 there is a scene involving the removal caravan. Stephen's
time at Clongowes is coming to an end as a consequence of the
family's declining fortunes. A period of unrest and intensity ensues
for Stephen as he starts to recognise things are also changing inside
him. His sexuality is entering his consciousness, at first in spiritual
terms and occupying somewhere on the periphery of his full
consciousness or apprehension. In his reading, he is drawn to the
alluring figure of Mercedes from Alexandre Dumas's novel *The Count
of Monte Cristo* (1846). Rather grandly, he wants to 'meet in the real
world the unsubstantial image which his soul so constantly beheld'
(*P* 65). He imagines being 'transfigured', a strongly charged word the
reader perhaps associates with the transfiguration of Christ himself
when his divine nature and prophetic character were revealed to his
chosen apostles. A sudden shift then occurs, for this is followed almost
immediately by a row of asterisks and the transition to the next section,
which begins in deadbeat fashion with removal men tramping into the
house and 'dismantling' it.

Only one letter separates pathos, with its appeal to suffering and
the emotions, from the sinking or depth of bathos. Citing Alexander
Pope's *The Dunciad* (1728), Skeat defines bathos as 'ludicrously applied
to a descent from the elevated to the mean in poetry or oratory'.
Pathos is defined as 'emotion, deep feeling' with associated words such
as 'suffering' and 'yearning'.[200] At times reading Joyce there is a sense
in which he plays on the close proximity between the two. Although
Skeat deploys 'ridiculous' in his definition of the term, bathos is as
much to do with the unintentional collapse of an elevated expression.
So, even as the ridiculous or the maudlin comes into view in this
passage, we recognise how the contrasting highs and lows serve a wider

---

200 Walter W. Skeat, *An Etymological Dictionary of the English Language* (Oxford:
Clarendon Press, 1882). 54 and 426. Pope's short essay, *Peri Bathous, Or the Art
of Sinking in Poetry*, which was first published in 1728, expands on these terms.

purpose. This is Stephen's world, a world which exists in a conflict zone waiting to be understood in the present or resolved at some time in the future. Bathos, then, or depth as it was once defined, is more than a rhetorical term for Joyce but constitutes part of a larger framework, connected with the general theme of falling in his work.

From early in his career, Joyce possessed a writer's instinct, so that, from the vantage point of the twentieth century, he could discern how bathos was not confined to history and musty textbooks on critical or rhetorical terms, but was, indeed, particularly suited to conveying the psychology of a boy growing up in a family financially on the decline and forced to keep moving. More broadly, bathos was a term especially relevant to conveying the years of adolescence, which, for many, is a period in life given to emotional extremes. Sympathetic readers even allow for Stephen's identity with Christ and the possibility of Cranly being positioned as a John the Baptist figure, for *A Portrait* is a story where the sacred and the secular meet, where heightened emotions and certain forms of ecstasy are followed almost immediately by the reality of ugliness and even, as here, with dispossession, with 'rope ends' that is. We respond to pathos by identifying with the character, but with bathos we discover more complex responses involving the practice of writing, the use of counterpointing, and the construction of narrative, where emotion is not so much repressed or prevented as held at bay in a kind of stasis. Among the many drivers in the novel there is one marked 'stasis' or 'stillness', the opposite that is of 'unrest' or 'restless', words which are each mentioned on ten separate occasions.

The extra details he provides in the removal scene, such as 'wisps of straw' and 'rope ends', are designed to be read as more than just local colour or additional pieces of information. The family's goods are loaded onto wagons perhaps used to transport agricultural or farm stuff and tied down with ropes. Almost the same phrase, 'wisp of hay', occurs in E.M. Forster's novel *Howards End* (1910), which serves to illustrate not so much their similarities but rather their differences as novelists. Forster's novel, set within a nineteenth-century classical tradition, is informed by a network of imagery to do with continuity and nature as a living force, vividly conveyed by its epigraph 'Only connect'. Images and details in *A Portrait,* on the other hand, delay us, seemingly, at first, for their own possibly obscure, stony, purposes. But, in a move frequently made by the reader of Joyce, we discern something else or something else going on. For the images seem to run parallel to Stephen's thoughts rather than to express them, idly waiting, like an imagist poem, for integration or incorporation. Bathos, then, adds depth to the surface, capable at times of transfiguring it.

OFT IN THE STILLY NIGHT

> The voice of his youngest brother from the farther side of the fireplace began to sing the air *Oft in the Stilly Night*. (*P* 163)

A Portrait includes many scenes of dispossession. In Chapter 4 Stephen returns home to learn that the family were on the move again, with his father, as one of the siblings mutters, gone to look at a house: 'Goneboro toboro lookboro atboro aboro houseboro.' (*P* 163) In the face of the routine nature of dispossession, the rhythmic language of a child is as appropriate as anyone else's in the family. In real life, with the removal van, often in the 'stilly night' hurriedly arranged to escape the rent demands of a landlord, went all the family possessions including a small collection of books, family portraits and religious objects, and, probably from at least one address, prints of Meredith and Walt Whitman belonging to Joyce's brother Stanislaus.[201] And as if Joyce, the suppressed lyricist, wanted to drain the removal scene of too much sentimentalism, or of anyone ever confusing his novel with a memoir, he continues by adding another detail, how from the other corner of the room the youngest child starts singing Thomas Moore's moving song about the light of other days, a song which is then taken up by his other siblings:

> Oft, in the stilly night,
> Ere slumber's chain has bound me,
> Fond memory brings the light
> Of other days around me.[202]

In terms of writing, the risks here are considerable, but Joyce manages to avoid them. The reader's emotions are engaged but not overwhelmed. We might be tempted to follow the path marked out by Moore with its beautiful evocation of a still night, slumber, fond memories, and

---

201 For this information see Stanislaus Joyce, *The Complete Dublin Diary of Stanislaus Joyce* (ed. George H. Healey) (Dublin: Anna Livia Press, 1994), 79.

202 Printed in the first number of *A Selection of Irish Melodies, with Symphonies and Accompaniments by Sir John Stevenson, Mus. Doc., and Characteristic Words by Thomas* (London: J. Power; & Dublin: W. Power 1818), 51.

Moore's song 'Oft in the Stilly Night' was a favourite with audiences throughout the nineteenth century. Taken from the third edition of Alfred Moffat, *The Minstrelsy of Ireland* (1905).

the powerful if conventional phrase about the light of other days. But then we realise the song functions not just as background but as the articulation of a distressing domestic scene and set down without irony. Joyce's immersion in writing epiphanies had paid off. If the song was omitted, the scene would merit no more, but no less than, a pitying glance. As it is, the impression conveyed is of a writer who has no intention of abandoning the culture's past in favour of the present. Instead, unlike his more selective contemporary T.S.Eliot, he wants to bring everything along from the past including his most recent century. Joyce possessed a modernist sensibility which, if not quite at home with its Victorian and Romantic inheritance, was more than ready to use that past for his own creative purposes. Even Moore, who is sometimes wrongly dismissed as a sentimental lyricist, gains a new lease of life in his hands.

SOUL

In *A Portrait* 'soul' is mentioned on 172 occasions, plus 31 'souls' for good measure. No play of Shakespeare comes close to this figure. *Macbeth*, a play steeped in the old Catholic faith, contains 73 references, the most of any Shakespeare play, followed by *Richard III* (54), *Othello* (37), *Hamlet* (34) and *Richard II* (34). For contemporary audiences of Shakespeare's plays the word 'soul' triggered a whole series of emotions, some of which, as in *Macbeth*, focussed on the seriousness of mortal sin and the risk of eternal damnation. In a play about a non-Christian Moor, Shakespeare distinguishes between spirit and soul, the soul being eternal. At the very moment Othello is about to murder Desdemona he stops to tell her:

> I would not kill thy unprepared spirit;
> No; heaven forfend! I would not kill thy soul.[203]

Life is a preparation for a good death, and a good death needs the properly contrite state of mind. Desdemona's spirit can save her soul. During the retreat sermons in Chapter 3 of Joyce's novel, we hear the word 'soul' on 75 occasions, an indication of what is at stake for the character of Stephen. The priest in the confessional tells Stephen that 'It kills the body and it kills the soul' (144), and he has in mind the sin of masturbation. Richard Wilson argues persuasively that Shakespeare was a recusant in Protestant England, occupying 'dual residence'. If

---

203 *Othello* 5.2.30-32.

true, the playwright would have understood precisely some of the fears Stephen faced four centuries later.[204]

Whether at school or in his family or in conversations in the streets of Dublin, Joyce on a daily basis must have heard the word 'soul' and given some thought to the religion that lay behind it. As we saw above, Stephen is intent on forging in the 'smithy of my soul the uncreated conscience of my race' (*P* 253); he wants to 'meet in the real world the unsubstantial image which his soul so constantly beheld' (*P* 65); at the beginning of Joyce's Chapter 3, we are told that a 'cold lucid indifference reigned in his soul' (*P* 103); in conversation with the Dean of Studies his 'soul frets in the shadow of his language' (*P* 189). A writer outside the influence of the Church might use a different vocabulary for 'soul' such as 'being' or 'spirit' or 'heart' or 'mind' or 'feeling' or a personal pronoun. But Joyce keeps returning to the vocabulary of his childhood and youth.

The question then prompts itself: what does Joyce mean by 'soul'? Renan believed that the nation is 'une âme, un principe spirituel', a soul, a spiritual principle, which is based on memories from the past and consent in the present.[205] With a slight twist, this can be compared with Joyce's own view of the soul as a spiritual entity formed of a past and a present. According to Stephen, the soul is born, not at the moment of conception, which would be consistent with the Church's traditional teaching, but slowly. Presumably, the nets that are thrown over the soul would not be felt by the infant but by the self-conscious subject. The reference to 'man' seems to confirm that Joyce is thinking of the person beyond infancy, of past and present. At the same time, the birth of the soul is more mysterious than the birth of the body. But here we need to enter a distinction. The impression created by Joyce is that the soul is close to consciousness or to what the Canadian Jesuit philosopher, Lonergan, discusses extensively in *Insight* (1958) as

---

204 Further discussion of Shakespeare's invisibility can be found in Richard Wilson, *Secret Shakespeare: Studies in Theatre, Religion and Resistance* (Manchester: Manchester University Press, 2004), 22.

205 Ernest Renan, *Qu'est-ce qu'une nation?* (ed. Shlomo Sand) (Paris : Flammarion, 2011), 74. For Renan, the nation *is* a soul, not *has* a soul. It is constituted by its past communal efforts and sacrifices, so 'is' is the appropriate word. A century later, Ernest Gellner asks a different question involving the body: 'Do Nations Have Navels ?' See *Nationalism* (London: Phoenix, 1997), 90–101. For the 1890s Walter Scott edition of *Poetry of the Celtic Races*, William Hutchison translates 'une âme' as 'a living soul'.

'insight' or 'intelligibility'.[206] In today's climate, the term is not gender-neutral, for it seems not to include the soul of a woman.

Regardless of our objections, Joyce's drift remains: the soul is not a steady state but is something that is changeable. And we might well feel that the soul cannot be identified with consciousness, for we can be conscious of what our mind is telling us, just as we can be conscious of sinning or transgressing. So the soul, not unlike the nation through time, must exist independent of how the subject might change and develop. We need to enter another qualification, for Stephen is intent on forcing the soul into an active role, but in many respects the soul is a spiritual principle, largely passive but also, not unlike conscience, lying in wait. Not for nothing did Renan include in his theory of memory the fertile idea of forgetfulness in the construction of nationhood. We face problems, then, in attempting to identify what Joyce and to some extent what Renan meant by the soul.

If we were to invoke Aquinas, one of Joyce's influences, we would discover he had his own take on the soul. In a passage commenting on St Paul's Letter to the Corinthians, which concerns the belief in the resurrection of Christ after death, Aquinas makes the assertion that 'my soul is not me'.[207] This is what I suggest above, and it sounds eminently sensible. Deprived of a body at death the soul will exist imperfectly, but, with the resurrection of the body, the soul will find the union it

---

206 Bernard Lonergan, *Insight: A Study of Human Understanding* (London: Darton Longman and Todd, 1958), *passim*. Lonergan's erudite study, which has been compared to a modern 'summa' of neo-scholastic philosophy, takes its cue from Aquinas. It strikes a particularly modern note by taking seriously the rise of modern science. His stress is on what can be known about human understanding without invoking the divine. It is in keeping that there is no reference to 'soul' in the Index. His comments on consciousness include a discussion of what happens when we think.

207 Thomas Aquinas, *Selected Philosophical Writings* (ed. Timothy McDermott) (London: Oxford University Press, 2008), 192. In Chapter XXXVIII of *Vita Nuova* Dante distinguishes between 'cuore' 'appetito' (the heart or desire) and 'anima' 'ragione' (the soul or reason). See Dante Alighieri, *Vita Nuova* (trans Mark Musa) (London: Oxford University Press, 2008), 76. For the original, see *La Vita Nuova* (Torino-Roma: Roux e Viarengo, 1902), 151. This was the edition Joyce had in his library in Trieste. The first line of the Church's ancient canticle '*Magnificat*' contains the Latin word 'anima', the word normally used for 'soul' in the Church. *Magnificat anima mea Dominum*, my soul doth magnify the Lord. Soul here means something closer to spirit or the 'heart's deep core' to adopt a phrase by Yeats in his poem 'The Lake Isle of Innisfree'. Joyce would have been familiar with all these examples.

had in life. The soul is, therefore, only part of the whole human being. Joyce seems to imply something else, that the soul is the true self or is that which has the potential to become the true self. In this sense the soul is closer to 'being in process', in Lonergan's terms, than to the idea of a permanent state.[208] Stephen is born with a soul awaiting development. With his growth in individuality we can observe a soul in the making. From today's perspective, we might be reminded of an existentialist position where existence defines essence. However, because Joyce uses 'soul' in so many different contexts, he cannot be tied to the existentialist label.

Stephen or Joyce believed the soul could be killed. Hence the power exerted by the priest giving the retreat sermons. The death of the soul also finds expression in Ibsen's *When We Dead Awaken* (1900), a play that Joyce commented on favourably in *Fortnightly Review*. Early in the play, Professor Arnold Rubek, a sculptor, tells Irene, his model: 'And the superstition took hold of me that if I touched you, if I desired you with my senses, my soul would be profaned.'[209] Later in the play, Irene turns on Rubek and accuses him directly: 'You have killed my soul - so you model yourself in remorse' (113). At one point, Irene uses a word that injects another dimension into our discussion, the word 'soulless': 'I gave you my young living soul. And that gift left me empty within – soulless' (65). The indifference that Stephen succumbs to at the beginning of Chapter 3 could also be described as his 'soulless' moment. But the most relevant passage for our purposes here is when Joyce comments on Rubek possessing Irene's soul. Rubek's 'transgression' is made worse because 'he has withheld from its rightful throne the child of her soul', namely the statue he has made of her from what she calls 'living clay'. (*CW* 57)

Arguably, when Joyce began writing *A Portrait,* the idea of the soul was a constant and unconscious accompaniment. If pressed for a summary, we might well submit that the novel is about the soul of Stephen awakening to its task. At times the soul is portrayed as the person's inner core, the innermost being, 'the life in life' (*CW* 50), the phrase Joyce uses in connection with the characters in Ibsen's play. According to one of his friends in Paris in the inter-war years, Louis Gillet, 'The only freedom worthy of a man had nothing to do with the

---

208 Bernard Lonergan, *Insight: A Study of Human Understanding,* 625. This phrase occurs in a discussion on existentialism and ethics.
209 Henrik Ibsen, *When We Dead Awaken* (trans. William Archer) (London: William Heinemann, 1900), 36.

political state – it was the freedom of soul that he was jealous.'[210] So the soul is there to be protected from the wiles of the world and is like an inner holy shrine.

In November 1902 when he was leaving Dublin for Paris to study medicine, Joyce wrote to Lady Gregory, seeking help with his fees. At the end of the letter he distinguishes between faith and the soul:

> All things are inconstant except the faith in the soul, which changes all things and fills their inconstancy with light. And though I seem to have been driven out of my country here as a misbeliever I have found no man yet with a faith like mine. (*Letters* I, 53)

There is an echo here of chapter 11 of St Paul's Letter to the Hebrews, which contains a list of what a strong faith can achieve, and how, in the words of the King James Bible, 'faith is the substance of things hoped for, the evidence of things not seen'. By faith Noah prepared an ark; by faith Abraham sojourned in the land of promise; by faith Abraham offered up Isaac, and so on. That much is clear when we isolate what Joyce is saying about faith. He has a strong faith, strong like Abraham sojourning as in a strange country or in Joyce's case even as he is driven out of his country. Equally, Joyce's description of the soul as a constant shining light on the changing world around him is in keeping with traditional views expressed above.

The problem lies in the phrase 'faith in the soul', for in a different context this could sound like God inserting faith into the soul at birth, which is not what Joyce intends. I assume the phrase has a necessary degree of ambiguity so that for 'faith' read 'determination' and for 'soul' read 'shrine' or 'life in life'. According to Chrissie van Mierlo, 'There is…no clear line of connection between the vaguely spiritual vocabulary…and a conventional religious faith.'[211] Characteristically, Joyce is defining his secular self in religious terms or perhaps his religious self in secular terms, and on this occasion he is doing so for the benefit of a possible benefactress with fairly conventional religious views. If we continue with such a line of interpretation, the insertion of 'misbeliever' is also part of this 'cross-over' and presumably designed to cloud matters further. Thus, initially, Joyce holds back from

---

210   Louis Gillet, *Claybook for James Joyce* (trans. Georges Markow-Totevy) (London and New York: Aberlard-Schuman), 1958. 98.

211   Chrissie van Mierlo, *James Joyce and Catholicism: The Apostate's Wake* (London: Bloomsbury Academic, 2017), 2.

declaring himself an 'unbeliever' only to continue by claiming he has a remarkably strong faith, not, we might add, in God but in himself.

In this light, references to 'soul' in *A Portrait* are more straightforward and seem less calculating. Stephen's sinning, especially against the body, harms the soul, and he learns at one point in Chapter 3 to accept that there is a 'dark peace' between body and soul (*P* 103). Confession restores his soul to full health, but temptation remains. At the same time, with echoes of Pater, the soul is in progress, on a journey, 'going forth,' as we learn in Chapter 3, 'to experience' (*P* 103). Joyce wasn't but he might have been distracted by Wilde's claim in *The Picture of Dorian Gray* that 'Nothing can cure the soul but the senses'.[212] Yeats stressed the tension between the self and soul (or self and anti-self), but Joyce is too involved in the turmoil and struggle to step back. So Stephen is subject to ecstasy and abasement. As we accompany him on his journey from childhood to manhood, we are reminded of Shakespeare's 'dual residence', only in Joyce's case he is both inside and outside the faith of his fathers.

'Joyce remained always under the emotional influence of the faith he abandoned.'[213] This is Sullivan's assessment, and, to my mind, it is one that commands assent. Indeed, the beard Joyce grew in later life to conceal 'a slight curve of scar on his chin, left there by a mongrel dog nearly as big as he when he was only five' was like that of a 'thoughtful but unsorrowing Christ' (48). His physical appearance and dress sense meant almost as much to Joyce as the defences he erected to prevent anyone prying too closely into his soul. In 1923, when the artist, Patrick Tuohy, who had arrived at Joyce's flat in Paris to paint his portrait, began to philosophise about capturing the soul in painting, Joyce made his own position abundantly clear: 'Never mind my soul. Just be sure you have my tie right.' (*JJ* 566) For Tuohy it must have been a sudden revelation executed by the one-time master of epiphanies. When Joyce died in Zurich in January 1941, his wife, Nora, was approached by a Catholic priest to allow a religious service, but she, too, was equally adamant in her own Joycean way: 'I couldn't do that to him' (*JJ* 742). Wherever his soul is today, one thing is certain; it is not in the Fluntern Cemetery where his body is buried.

---

212 *The Picture of Dorian Gray*, 22.
213 Kevin Sullivan, *Joyce Among the Jesuits*, 58.

SELECT BIBLIOGRAPHY

Adams, Robert M., *Surface and Symbol: The Consistency of James Joyce's Ulysses* (New York: Oxford University Press, 1962).

Alighieri, Dante, *Vita Nuova* (trans. Mark Musa) (London: Oxford University Press, 2008).

Aquinas, Thomas, *Selected Philosophical Writings* (ed. Timothy McDermott) (London: Oxford University Press, 2008).

Aubert, Jacques and Maria Jolas, *Joyce and Paris 1902...1920 – 1940...1975* (Paris: Éditions du CNRS, 1979).

Ayrton, Michael, *The Testament of Daedalus* (1962; London: Robin Clark, 1991).

— *The Maze Maker: A Novel* (1967; Chicago: University of Chicago Press, 2015).

Banville, John, *Time Pieces: A Dublin Memoir* (photographs by Paul Joyce) (Dublin: Hachette Books, 2016).

Baudelaire, Charles, *The Flowers of Evil* (trans. James McGowan) (intro. Jonathan Culler) (London: Oxford University Press, 1998).

— *Baudelaire As A Literary Critic* (trans. Lois Boe Hyslop and Francis E. Hyslop) (University Park, PA: Pennsylvania State University Press, 1964).

Bauerle, Ruth, *The James Joyce Songbook* (New York: Garland, 1982).

Beckett, Samuel, *Watt* (Paris: The Olympia Press, 1953).

Beckett, Samuel *et al., Our Exagmination Round His Factification for Incamination of Work in Progress* (1929; New York: New Directions, 1972).

Beerbohm, Max, *Observations* (London: William Heinemann, 1925).

Benstock, Bernard, 'Review of Thornton Weldon's *The Anti-Modernism of Joyce's A Portrait of the Artist as a Young Man*' in *English Literature in Transition 1880-1920* 38:2, 1995.

Bettelheim, Bruno, *The Uses of Enchantment: The Meaning and Importance of Fairy Tales* (New York: Random House, Vintage Books, 1977).

Brady, Philip and James F.Carens (eds.), *Critical Essays on James Joyce's A Portrait of the Artist* (New York: G.K.Hall, 1998).

Budgen, Frank, *James Joyce and the Making of 'Ulysses' and Other Writings* (1934; Oxford and New York: Oxford University Press, 1972).

Butler, Samuel, *The Way of All Flesh* (1903; London: Penguin, 2013).

— *Life and Habit* (ed. R.A.Streatfeild) (1878; London: Jonathan Cape, 1910).

Byrne, John Francis, *Silent Years: An Autobiography with Memoirs of James Joyce and Our Ireland* (New York: Farrar Straus and Young, 1953).

Campbell, Richard F. S.J., 'Clongowes Forty Years Ago' in *The Clongownian*, June 1924.

Carter, Angela, *The Bloody Chamber and Other Stories* (London: Gollancz, 1979).

Clarke, Austin, *Twice Round the Black Church* (London: Routledge and Kegan Paul, 1962).

Cohn, Dorrit, *Transparent Minds: Narrative Modes for Presenting Consciousness in Fiction* (Princeton, NJ: Princeton University Press, 1978).

Connolly, Thomas (ed.), *Joyce's Portrait: Criticisms and Critiques* (London: Peter Owen, 1964).

Culler, Jonathan, *Flaubert: The Uses of Uncertainty* (London: Elek, 1974).

Curran, Constantine, *James Joyce Remembered* (London: Oxford University Press, 1968).

Davis, Thomas, *Literary and Historical Essays* (Dublin, 1846).

Day, Robert Adams, 'The Villanelle Perplex: Reading Joyce', *James Joyce Quarterly* 25.1, 1987, reprinted in *Critical Essays on James Joyce's A Portrait of the Artist* (eds. Philip Brady and James F. Carens) (New York: G.K. Hall, 1998).

Dinneen, Patrick, *Foclóir Gaedilge agus Béarla: An Irish-English Dictionary* (Dublin: M.H. Gill, 1904).

Dylan, Bob, *Chronicles* Vol. 1 (London: Simon and Schuster, 2004).

Eliot, T.S., *The Waste Land and Other Poems* (London: Faber, 2002).

Eglinton, John, 'The Beginnings of Joyce', *Life and Letters* 8:47, December 1932.

— *A Memoir of AE, George William Russell* (London: Macmillan, 1937).

Ellis. Edwin and William Butler Yeats (eds.), *The Works of William Blake: Poetic, Symbolic and Critical* Vol. 1 (London: Bernard Quaritch, 1893).

Ellison, Ralph, *Invisible Man* (1952; London: Penguin, 1986).

— *The Collected Essays of Ralph Ellison* (ed. John F. Callahan) (New York: Modern Library, 2003).

Ellmann, Richard, *The Identity of Yeats* (New York: Oxford University Press, 1954).

— *The Consciousness of Joyce* (London: Faber, 1977).

—— *James Joyce* (revised edition) (Oxford and New York: Oxford University Press, 1982).

Ford, Ford Madox, *The Good Soldier* (second edition) (ed. Martin Stannard) (New York: Norton Critical Edition, 2012).

Freud, Sigmund, *The Psychopathology of Everyday Life* (trans. Anthea Bell) (1901; London: Penguin, 2002).

—— *Complete Psychological Works of Sigmund Freud, Vol 5* (trans. James Strachey) (1900; London:Vintage, 2001).

—— *The Standard Edition of the Complete Psychological Work of Sigmund Freud, Volume XIX (1923-26) The Ego and the Id and Other Works* (eds. James Strachey, Anna Freud, et al) (London: Hogarth Press, 1978).

Gabler, Hans Walter, 'The Genesis of *A Portrait of the Artist* ' in *Critical Essays on James Joyce's A Portrait of the Artist* (eds. Philip Brady and James F.Carens) (New York: G.K.Hall, 1998).

Gautier, Théophile, *Mademoiselle de Maupin* (trans. Helen Constantine) (intro. Patricia Duncker) (1835; London: Penguin, 2005).

Gheerbrant, Bernard, *James Joyce, Sa Vie, Son Oeuvre, Son Rayonnement* (Paris: La Hune, 1949).

Gifford, Don, *Joyce Annotated: Notes for Dubliners and A Portrait of the Artist* (second edition) (Berkeley, CA: University of California Press, 1982).

Gillet, Louis, *Claybook for James Joyce* (trans. Georges Markow-Totevy) (London and New York: Aberlard-Schuman), 1958.

Gissing, George, *New Grub Street* (London: Smith, Elder, 1891).

Gogarty, Oliver St John, *I Follow Saint Patrick* (London: Rich and Cowan, 1938).

—— *As I Was Going Down Sackville Street* (1937; Harmondsworth: Penguin, 1954).

Gorman, Herbert S., *James Joyce: His First Forty Years* (London: Geoffrey Bles, 1926).

—— *James Joyce: A Definitive Biography* (London: John Lane The Bodley Head, 1941).

—— *James Joyce* (London: Rinehart, 1948).

Greene, Roland *et al.* (eds.), *Princeton Encyclopedia of Poetry and Poetics* (fourth edition) (Princeton and Oxford: Princeton University Press, 2012).

Hancock, Leslie, *Word Index to James Joyce's Portrait of the Artist* (Carbondale, IL: Southern Illinois Press, 1967).

Hardy, Thomas, *Jude the Obscure* (1895; London: Oxford University Press, 2008).

Hauser, Arnold, *The Social History of Art: Naturalism, Expressionism and the Film Age* Vol. 4 (1951; London: Routledge and Kegan Paul, 1977).

Heaney, Seamus, *Station Island* (London: Faber, 1984).

— *Finders Keepers: Selected Prose 1971-2001* (London: Faber, 2002).

Huysmans, Joris-Karl, *Against Nature (A rebours)* (trans. Margaret Mauldon) (intro. Nicholas White) (London: Oxford University Press, 2009).

Ibsen, Henrik, *Prose Dramas Vol. 2: Ghosts, An Enemy of the People, The Wild Duck* (ed. William Archer) (London: Walter Scott, 1890).

— *When We Dead Awaken* (trans. William Archer) (London: Heinemann, 1900).

Igoe, Vivien, *James Joyce's Dublin Houses and Nora Barnacle's Galway* (Dublin: Lilliput, 2007).

Jackson, Holbrook, *The Eighteen Nineties: A Review of Art and Ideas at the Close of the Nineteenth Century* (1913; reprinted London: Grant Richards, 1922; Brighton: Edward Everett Root, 2017, intro. Christophe Campos).

James, Henry, *The Portrait of a Lady* 3 vols. (London: Macmillan, 1881).

— *The Spoils of Poynton* (intro. David Lodge) (1897; London: Penguin, 1987).

Jones, Peter (ed.), *Imagist Poetry* (1972; London: Penguin, 2001).

Joyce, James, *Chamber Music* (1907; London: Jonathan Cape, 1945).

— *The Critical Writings of James Joyce* (eds. Ellsworth Mason and Richard Ellmann) (1959; New York: Viking, 1966).

— *'Dubliners': Text, Criticism, and Notes*, (eds. Robert Scholes and A. Walton Litz) (New York: Viking, 1979).

— *Gens de Dublin* (trans. Valéry Larbaud) (1926; Paris: Gallimard, 1974).

— *Finnegans Wake* (1939; London: Faber and Faber, 1964).

— *Letters of James Joyce* (ed. Stuart Gilbert) (London: Faber and Faber, 1957).

— *Letters of James Joyce Vol II* (ed. Richard Ellmann) (New York: Viking, 1966).

— *Selected Letters of James Joyce* (ed. Richard Ellmann) (New York: Viking Press, 1975).

— *Pomes Penyeach* (London: Faber and Faber, 1933).

— *A Portrait of the Artist as a Young Man* (New York: Benjamin Huebsch, 1916).

— *A Portrait of the Artist as a Young Man* (London: Egoist Press, 1917).

— *A Portrait of the Artist as a Young Man* (intro. Sean O'Faolain) (New York: Signet Books, 1954).

— *A Portrait of the Artist as a Young Man* (ed. J.S.Atherton) (London: Heinemann, 1964).

— *'A Portrait of the Artist as a Young Man': Text, Criticism, and Notes* (ed. Chester Anderson) (New York: Viking, 1968).

— *A Portrait of the Artist as a Young Man* (ed. Seamus Deane) (London: Penguin, 1992).

— *A Portrait of the Artist as a Young Man* (ed. Jeri Johnson) (Oxford: Oxford University Press, 2000).

— *A Portrait of the Artist as a Young Man* (ed. John Paul Riquelme) (text edited by Hans Walter Gabler and Walter Hettche) (New York: Norton, 2007).

— *A Portrait of the Artist as a Young Man* (eds. Marc A.Mamigonian and John Turner) (Richmond: Alma, 2012).

— *Dedalus: Portrait de L'Artiste Jeune Par Lui-Même* (trans. Ludmila Savitzky) (1924; Paris: Gallimard, 1943).

— *Portrait de L' Artiste en Jeune Homme* (trans. Jacques Aubert) (Paris: Gallimard, 1992).

— *Retrato del Artista Adolescente* (trans. Damaso Alonso) (Barcelona: RBA, 1995).

— *Porträt des Künstlers als junger Mann: Roman* (trans. Friedhelm Rathjen) (afterword Marcel Beyer) (Zurich: Manesse Verlag, 2012).

— *Zelfportret van de kunstenaar als jonge man* (trans. Erik Bindervoet and Robbert-Jan Henkes) (Amsterdam: Athenaeum-Polak & Van Gennep, 2014).

— *Stephen Hero* (London: Faber and Faber, 1944).

— *Stephen Daedalus* (trans. Georg Goyert) (Frankfurt and Hamburg: Surhkamp, 1965).

— *Ulysses* (Paris: Shakespeare and Company, 1922).

— *Ulysses: The Corrected Text* (ed. Hans Walter Gabler with Wolfhard Steppe and Claus Melchior) (London: The Bodley Head, 1986).

Joyce, Stanislaus, *My Brother's Keeper* (ed. Richard Ellmann) (London: Faber and Faber, 1958).

— *The Dublin Diary of Stanislaus Joyce* (ed. George Harris Healy) (London: Faber and Faber, 1962).

— *The Complete Dublin Diary of Stanislaus Joyce* (ed. George H.Healy) (1971; Dublin: Anna Livia Press, 1994).

Kenner, Hugh, *Dublin's Joyce* (London: Chatto and Windus, 1955).

— 'The Cubist Portrait' in Thomas Staley and Bernard Benstock (eds.), *Approaches to Joyce's 'Portrait': Ten Essays* (Pittsburg PA: University of Pittsburg, 1976).

— *Joyce's Voices* (Berkeley, CA and London: University of California Press, 1978).

Kettle, Thomas, *The Day's Burden: Literary and Political and Miscellaneous Essays* (Dublin: Maunsel, 1918).

Kiely, David M., *John Millington Synge: A Biography* (Dublin: Gill and Macmillan, 1993).

Lawrence, D.H., *Sons and Lovers* (1913; London: Penguin, 2006).

— *The Rainbow* (1915; London: Penguin, 2007).

— *Women in Love* (1920; Harmondsworth: Penguin, 1982).

Leonard, Hugh, *Stephen D.: A Play in Two Acts* (London and New York: Evans Brothers, 1964).

Lonergan, Bernard, *Insight: A Study of Human Understanding* (London: Darton, Longman, Todd, 1958).

Magalaner, Marvin (ed.), *A James Joyce Miscellany* (second series) (Carbondale, Ill: Southern Illinois University Press, 1959).

Melchiori, Giorgio (ed.), *Joyce in Rome: The Genesis of Ulysses* (Rome: Bulzoni, 1984).

Meredith, George, *The Ordeal of Richard Feverel* (1859; London: Chapman and Hall, 1889).

Mierlo, Chrissie van, *James Joyce and Catholicism: The Apostate's Wake* (London: Bloomsbury Academic, 2017).

Moore, George, *Confessions of a Young Man* (London: Swan Sonnenschein, Lowrey, 1888)

— *Esther Waters* (London: Walter Scott, 1894).

— *The Untilled Field* (London: T.Fisher Unwin, 1903).

— *The Lake* (London: William Heinemann, 1905).

— *Memoirs of My Dead Life* (1906; London: William Heinemann, 1925).

— *Hail and Farewell: Ave, Salve, Vale* (1911-4; Gerrards Cross: Colin Smythe, 1976).

Moore, Thomas, *A Selection of Irish Melodies, with Symphonies and Accompaniments by Sir John Stevenson, Mus. Doc., and Characteristic Words by Thomas* (London: J. Power; & Dublin: W. Power 1818).

Mormando, Franco, *Bernini: His Life and his Rome* (Chicago and London: University of Chicago Press, 2013).

Morris, W.E. and C.A. Nault Jr. (eds.), *Portraits of an Artist* (New York: Odyssey Press, 1962).

Mullin, Katherine, *James Joyce, Sexuality and Social Purity* (Cambridge: Cambridge University Press, 2003).

Newman, John Henry, *Apologia Pro Vita Sua* (London: Longman, Green *et al.*, 1864).

Norburn, Roger, *A James Joyce Chronology* (Basingstoke: Palgrave Macmillan, 2004).

O'Faolain, Julia, *Three Lovers* (1970; New York: Coward, McCann and Geoghegan, 1971).

O'Leary, John, *Recollections of Fenians and Fenianism* Vol 2 (London: Downey, 1896).

O'Rourke, Fran, 'Joyce's Early Aesthetic' in *Journal of Modern Literature* 34:2, Winter 2011.

Pater, Walter, *Studies in the History of the Renaissance* (1873; London: Oxford University Press, 2010).

— *Marius the Epicurean: His Sensations and Ideas* (1885; London: Penguin, 1985).

Picken, Ebenezer, *Miscellaneous Poems, Songs etc* Vol.1 (Edinburgh: James Clarke, 1818).

— *A Dictionary of the Scottish Language* (Edinburgh: James Sawers, 1818).

Pierce, David, *James Joyce's Ireland* (London and New Haven: Yale University Press, 1992).

— *Yeats's Worlds: Ireland, England and the Poetic Imagination* (London and New Haven: Yale University Press, 1995).

— (ed.), *Irish Writing in the Twentieth Century: A Reader* (Cork: Cork University Press, 2001).

— *Light, Freedom and Song: A Cultural History of Modern Irish Writing* (London and New Haven: Yale University Press, 2005).

— *Reading Joyce* (Harlow: Pearson Longman, 2007).

— *The Joyce Country: Literary Scholarship and Irish Culture* (Brighton: Edward Everett Root, 2018).

Pinamonti, Giovanni Pietro, *Hell Opened to Christians; To Caution Them From Entering It* (Derby and London: T. Richardson and Son, for the Catholic Book Society, 1845).

Pound, Ezra, 'A Few Don'ts by an Imagiste' in *Poetry* March 1913.

— '"Dubliners" and Mr James Joyce' in *The Egoist* 15 July 1914.

— *Pound/Joyce: The Letters of Ezra Pound to James Joyce* (New: New Directions, 1984).

Pound, Ezra, Hilda Doolittle, and Richard Aldington (eds.), *Des Imagistes* (London: Poetry Bookshop, 1914).

Potts, Willard (ed.), *Portraits of the Artist in Exile: Recollections of James Joyce by Europeans* (Seattle and London: University of Washington Press, 1977).

Renan, Ernest, *Souvenirs d'enfance et de jeunesse* (Paris: Calmann-Lévy, 1883).

— *Recollections of My Youth* (trans. C.B.Pitman) (revised by Madam Renan) (London: Chapman and Hall, 1892).

— *The Poetry of the Celtic Races and Other Essays* (London and New York: Walter Scott, n.d).

— *Qu'est-ce qu'une nation?* (ed. Shlomo Sand) (Paris: Flammarion, 2011).

Reynolds, Mary, *Joyce and Dante: The Shaping Imagination* (1981; Princeton, NJ: Princeton University Press, 2014).

Robinson, Lennox, *The Lost Leader* (1918; Belfast: H.R.Carter, 1954).

— *The Whiteheaded Boy* (New York and London: Samuel French, 1921).

Russell, George (ed.), *New Songs: A Lyric Selection* (Dublin; O'Donoghue; London: A.H.Bullen, 1904).

Scholes, Robert, *In Search of James Joyce* (Urbana and Chicago: University of Illinois Press, 1992).

Scholes, Robert and Richard Kain (eds.), The *Workshop of Daedalus: James Joyce and the Raw Materials for A Portrait of the Artist* (Evanston, Ill: Northwestern University Press, 1965).

Sheehy, Eugene, *May It Please the Court* (Dublin: C.J.Fallon, 1951).

Viktor Shlovsky, 'Art as Technique' in *Russian Formalist Criticism: Four Essays* (second edition) (trans. and intro. Lee T.Lemon and Marion J.Reis) (Lincoln and London: University of Nebraska, 2012).

Skeat, Walter W., *An Etymological Dictionary of the English Language* (Oxford: Clarendon Press, 1882).

Spark, Muriel, *The Girls of Slender Means* (London: Macmillan, 1963).

Sullivan, Kevin, *Joyce Among the Jesuits* (New York: Columbia University Press, 1958).

Swinburne, Algernon, *William Blake: A Critical Essay* (London: John Camden Hotten, 1868).

Symons, Arthur, *The Symbolist Movement in Literature* (intro. Richard Ellmann) (1899; New York: E.P.Dutton, 1958).

Synge, John Millington, *The Autobiography of J.M.Synge* (ed. Alan Price) (Dublin: Dolmen Press and London: Oxford University Press, 1965).

Tennyson, Alfred, *Poems Volume 1* (London: Edward Moxon, 1842).

Valente, Joseph, 'Will to Artistry in *A Portrait of the Artist as a Young Man*' in the *James Joyce Quarterly* 50(1-2), September 2012.

Villiers de l'Isle Adam, *Axël* (Paris: Maison Quantin, 1890).

Wawrzycka, Jolanta and Serenella Zanotti (eds.), *James Joyce's Silences* (London: Bloomsbury, 2018).

Weygandt, Cornelius, *Irish Plays and Playwrights* (London: Constable; New York: Houghton Miflin, 1913).

Wilde, Oscar, *The Picture of Dorian Gray* (1891; Richmond, Surrey: Alma Classics, 2017).

— *Ballad of Reading Gaol by C.C.3* (London: Leonard Smithers & Co, 1898).

— *The Letters of Oscar Wilde* (ed. Rupert Hart-Davis) (London: Rupert Hart-Davis, 1962).

— *The Annotated Oscar Wilde* (ed. H.Montgomery Hyde) (New York: Clarkson N.Potter, 1982).

Williams, William Carlos, *Paterson* (rev. edition) (ed. Christopher MacGowan) (1946; New York: New Directions, 1995).

Wilson, Richard, *Secret Shakespeare: Studies in Theatre, Religion and Resistance* (Manchester: Manchester University Press, 2004).

Wollaeger, Mark A. (ed.), *James Joyce's A Portrait of the Artist: A Casebook* (New York: Oxford University Press, 2003).

Woolf, Virginia, *To the Lighthouse* (1927; Oxford: World's Classics, 1999).

— *The Common Reader: Second Series* (1932; London: Hogarth Press, 1986).

— *A Writer's Diary* (ed. Leonard Woolf) (1953; San Diego, New York, and London: Harcourt, 1983).

— *Moments of Being: Autobiographical Writings* (ed. Jeanne Schulkind) (London: Pimlico, 2002).

Wright, Joseph (ed.), *The English Dialect Dictionary* vol 5 (Oxford: Henry Frowde, 1905).

Yeats, J.B., *Letters to His Son W.B. Yeats and Others 1869-1922* (ed. Joseph Hone) (preface Oliver Elton) (London: Faber and Faber, 1944).

Yeats, William Butler, *The Wanderings of Oisin* (London: Kegan, Paul, Trench, 1889).

— *The Celtic Twilight: Men and Women, Dhouls and Faeries* (1893) in *Mythologies* (London: Macmillan, 1959).

— *The Countess Kathleen and Various Legends* (London: T. Fisher Unwin, 1892).

— *The Tables of the Law: The Adoration of the Magi* (privately printed 1897) in *Mythologies* (London: Macmillan, 1959).

— *Reveries Over Childhood and Youth* (London: Macmillan, 1916).

— *The Winding Stair and Other Poems* (London: Macmillan, 1933).

— *The Letters of W.B. Yeats* (ed. Allan Wade) (London: Rupert Hart-Davis, 1954).

— *Mythologies* (London: Macmillan, 1959).

— *Essays and Introductions* (London: Macmillan, 1961).

— *Autobiographies* (London: Macmillan, 1977).

— *Selected Poetry* (ed. Timothy Webb) (London: Penguin, 1991.

Young, Filson, *Memory Harbour: Essays Chiefly in Description* (London: Grant Richards, 1909).

Zweig, Stefan, *The World of Yesterday: Memoir of a European* (trans. Anthea Bell) (1943; Lincoln and London: University of Nebraska Press, 2011).

INDEX